Runnin' Redbirds

Runnin' Redbirds

*The World Champion 1982
St. Louis Cardinals*

Eric Vickrey

McFarland & Company, Inc., Publishers
Jefferson, North Carolina

LIBRARY OF CONGRESS CATALOGUING-IN-PUBLICATION DATA

Names: Vickrey, Eric, 1979– author.
Title: Runnin' redbirds : the World Champion 1982 St. Louis Cardinals / Eric Vickrey.
Description: Jefferson, North Carolina : McFarland & Company, Inc., Publishers, 2024 | Includes bibliographical references and index.
Identifiers: LCCN 2023048918 | ISBN 9781476693644 (paperback : acid free paper) ∞
 ISBN 9781476651392 (ebook)
Subjects: LCSH: St. Louis Cardinals (Baseball team)—History. | World Series (Baseball) (1982) | BISAC: SPORTS & RECREATION / Baseball / History
Classification: LCC GV875.S3 V53 2023 | DDC 796.357/640977866—dc23/eng/20231102
LC record available at https://lccn.loc.gov/2023048918

BRITISH LIBRARY CATALOGUING DATA ARE AVAILABLE

ISBN (print) 978-1-4766-9364-4
ISBN (ebook) 978-1-4766-5139-2

© 2024 Eric Vickrey. All rights reserved

No part of this book may be reproduced or transmitted in any form or by any means, electronic or mechanical, including photocopying or recording, or by any information storage and retrieval system, without permission in writing from the publisher.

Front cover: Darrell Porter and Bruce Sutter embrace following the final out of Game 7 of the 1982 World Series (National Baseball Hall of Fame Library, Cooperstown, New York)

Printed in the United States of America

McFarland & Company, Inc., Publishers
 Box 611, Jefferson, North Carolina 28640
 www.mcfarlandpub.com

To Gina, my fellow baseball fan and partner in life.
And to Mary, whom we miss every day

Acknowledgments

I would have not had the audacity to pursue this project without the experience I gained writing with the Society for American Baseball Research. Thank you to Rory Costello, Gregory Wolf, and scores of other editors and fact-checkers with the BioProject team who pushed me to become a better writer. I owe gratitude to the sportswriters who documented the 1982 season, in particular the late Rick Hummel, whose game stories and thorough coverage were a pleasure to read. John Horne and Rachel Wells from the National Baseball Hall of Fame provided photos and postseason files, respectively. Thank you to Jonathan Hall and Jerry Pirtle for looking at early drafts of the book and providing encouraging feedback. I greatly appreciate former players John D'Acquisto, Warren Cromartie, Barry Foote, Dane Iorg, Jeff Keener, Randy McGilberry, George Medich, Mike Ramsey, Roe Skidmore, Greg Terlecky, and Stefan Wever for providing memories through phone interviews or email. Gratitude to my parents, Barb and Mike Edler, for their constant support, and for taking me to my first game. Lastly, I thank my wife Gina for her never-ending patience and encouragement during the year I spent researching and this book.

Table of Contents

Acknowledgments	vi
Preface	1
Introduction	4
1. A Decade of Mediocrity	7
2. 1980—St. Louis Welcomes the White Rat	14
3. 1981—The Bearded Prophet and a Split Season	32
4. Spring Training—The Wizard Arrives	54
5. April—A Dozen Straight W's	61
6. May—The Injury Bug Bites and McGee Debuts	82
7. June—Stuper Is Super and Sutter Struggles	100
8. July—Pitching Carries the Cards	117
9. August—Brummer Steals a Game	129
10. September—Andújar Shines, Cardinals Clinch	144
11. League Championship Series	159
12. Game One—Brewers Pounce	169
13. Game Two—Sutton Versus Stuper, Part One	175
14. Game Three—The Humble Hero	179
15. Game Four—Seventh-Inning Debacle	185
16. Game Five—Cards Pushed to the Brink	189
17. Game Six—Sutton Versus Stuper, Part Two	192
18. Game Seven—For All the Marbles	196

Table of Contents

Epilogue 203
Chapter Notes 209
Bibliography 221
Index 223

Preface

While waiting in the drive-thru line of the long-since defunct Mexican fast-food restaurant Zantigo, I sat in the passenger seat of my mom's brown Chevy Camaro and opened up a pack of 1986 Topps baseball cards. The Topps design that year was simple: a black banner at the top with the team name in bold capital letters corresponding to the team's colors, a white border, and the player's name at the bottom. The back featured a red background with the player's statistics in black font. To my six-year-old eyes they were like a stack of Rembrandts. As I thumbed through the rectangular pieces of cardboard, I came across Willie McGee, the center fielder for my hometown team—the St. Louis Cardinals. In McGee's photo, he is wearing a red hat with the STL logo, a red spring training jersey, and is staring off in the distance with a pained expression on his face. "Oh, he's really fast," said my mom when I showed her my newfound treasure. She knew little about baseball, but she was aware that Willie could run like the wind.

Later that summer, I attended my first Cardinals game at Busch Memorial Stadium, a cylindrical mass of concrete in the middle of downtown St. Louis. The date was August 10, 1986, a hot and sunny Sunday afternoon. Thankfully, the arches of the upper deck provided shade for our nosebleed seats. The fourth-place Cardinals hosted the last-place Pittsburgh Pirates in a matchup that would have no bearing on the National League pennant race. Though the game was meaningless in the grand scheme of the 1986 season, to me it may as well have been Game Seven of the World Series.

My memorable day proved to be equally special for the Cardinals' starting pitcher, Bob Forsch. In the bottom of the fifth inning, he came to bat with the bases loaded and redirected a Mike Bielecki pitch over the blue outfield wall for a grand slam. It was the only granny of Forsch's 16-year big-league career, and it would be nearly nine years before another pitcher would replicate the feat. It was an early lesson that on any given day at the ballpark, you are likely to see something unusual. In that same game, the Cardinals' fleet-footed left fielder—Vince Coleman—stole four bases, giving him 82 on the season. Even though everyone in the ballpark knew he was going to steal when he got on base, he was usually successful. His speed was breathtaking. The Cardinals beat the Pirates that day, and I was hooked.

For the next few years, no trip to the gas station or grocery store was complete without a couple of wax packs. The cards featuring members of my favorite team were carefully placed in plastic sleeves. Most of the Cardinal games at that time were not televised, so I listened to the broadcasts on KMOX, the mighty AM radio station that blasted the voices of Jack Buck and Mike Shannon across the Midwest and beyond. A shelf in my bedroom was adorned with plastic Starting Lineup figurines that vaguely resembled the men they were intended to portray. I could recite the statistics and jersey numbers of every Cardinal, and every now and then I got to meet one of them. Backup outfielder John Morris once visited my youth league summer camp. I met Frank DiPino at a local department store and Milt Thompson at Hardee's. Once, I heard that Hal Lanier—then the manager of the Astros—would be visiting one of my neighbors. Undeterred by the fact that it was Thanksgiving Day and we were showing up unannounced, a friend and I rode our bicycles over and rang the doorbell of the house that supposedly contained a real-life major leaguer. Indeed, Mr. Lanier appeared wearing his bathrobe and graciously gave us a few minutes of his time. One of my biggest thrills as a kid was meeting Ozzie Smith at Johnny Londoff Chevrolet. I waited in line for hours to have the Wizard sign his Topps card.

My own baseball career stalled in high school. It turned out neither scouts nor Division I recruiters were interested in an awkward 6-foot-2, 140-pound southpaw with a 75-mph fastball. I graduated from college, married my best friend (a fellow Cardinal fan), and continued to follow the team from afar. I watched on television when they won the 2006 World Series—two decades after I had attended my first game. I vowed to be there in person if, and when, they made it back to the Fall Classic. When they did only five years later, I was there to witness the unimaginable thrill of Game Six, thanks to David Freese, followed by the exaltation of a Game Seven clincher.

I took a career path in the medical field, but I got to experience life as sportswriter for one day in 2001 when my good friend Jonathan, then a reporter at the *Edwardsville Intelligencer*, procured for me an extra media credential for a game between the Cardinals and Brewers. I watched the action from the press box and wrote up an article that appeared in the next day's paper.

Preface

I was content with my 15 minutes as a writer, but then came 2020. Like most people at the start of the pandemic, I was looking for something to pass time while stuck inside our 600-square-foot condominium. I came across a writing opportunity with the Society for American Baseball Research's BioProject, an undertaking to produce biographies for every player who has worn a major-league uniform. I signed up to write a bio on Cal Browning, an obscure Cardinals pitcher whom I discovered while doing a deep-dive on baseball-reference.com, the invaluable online baseball encyclopedia.* I enjoyed the writing process and followed up with several more bios, including a few members of the 1982 Cardinals. Through this process, I had the opportunity to interview Whitey Herzog, whose baseball brilliance and razor-sharp memory were uncanny. My work on the SABR BioProject and conversation with Herzog were the genesis of this book.

The research for this project led me down many roads. I scoured game stories in the *St. Louis Post-Dispatch* and *Belleville News-Democrat*, searched newspapers covering opposing teams, dug through online editions of *The Sporting News*, and browsed files provided by the National Baseball Hall of Fame library. Herzog's memoir *White Rat* was particularly insightful, and books by Forsch, Jim Kaat, Ozzie Smith, and Darrell Porter all supplied useful anecdotes. Several members of the team provided memories to Rob Rains and Alvin Reid in their 2002 publication *Whitey's Boys*. Podcast interviews conducted in more recent years also proved to be enlightening. Along the way, I gathered additional perspectives and firsthand accounts from several major leaguers with experience playing for, with, and against the 1982 Cardinals. I hope readers enjoy this look back at a memorable era in our national pastime.

---

*Browning pitched a single game for the Cardinals in 1960 but was once considered a prospect on par with Bob Gibson.

Introduction

All championship seasons are special in their own way, but the manner in which the 1982 St. Louis Cardinals won is unique in the game's history. The Redbirds hit a mere 67 home runs—the fewest in the major leagues. Since 1930, no team has won a pennant with less reliance on the long ball. The 1965 Los Angeles Dodgers, who swatted only 78 home runs, are the only other National League team to claim a pennant despite hitting the fewest homers. Their success was largely due to the pitching of Sandy Koufax and Don Drysdale, who combined for 49 wins—more than half of the Dodgers' total.

Because Busch Stadium's dimensions were so expansive, it took a prodigious blast to hit a ball over its outfield wall. Whitey Herzog, who wielded the unusual dual authority of general manager *and* field manager, recognized the challenges of his home ballpark and tailored the roster to fit it. A baseball lifer with an encyclopedic knowledge of the game, Herzog knew that Busch's artificial turf provided more opportunities for infield hits on ground balls, and its vast outfield expanses required fielders to cover large swaths of ground. He acquired players with elite speed, including Willie McGee, Ozzie, and another Smith—Lonnie—who were instrumental to the team's success, contributing to a league-best 200 stolen bases. The Cards lacked a hitting star in the ilk of Dale Murphy, Reggie Jackson, or Dave Winfield, and its pitching rotation had no Steve Carltons or Nolan Ryans, but they could run laps around the rest of the league. Their speed put pressure on defenses, thereby forcing errors and frustrating opposing pitchers by turning routine ground balls into base hits. On defense, they did the exact opposite. Ozzie Smith, arguably the greatest defensive shortstop ever to play the game, took countless hits and runs away from the opposition with acrobatic plays that defied the laws of physics.

Though not the most talent-laden pitching staff in the league, the Cardinals' collection of arms flashed periods of brilliance. The group included the hard-throwing and eccentric Joaquín Andújar, crafty veterans Bob

Forsch and Jim Kaat, and rookies who stepped up in pivotal moments. The most important hurler on the team, however, was Bruce Sutter, a closer who rode his signature pitch—the split-fingered fastball—all the way to Cooperstown. Down the stretch, the unheralded staff keyed an historic run—two or fewer earned runs allowed in 11 straight contests—that cemented St. Louis's position atop the NL East division.

The Redbirds' pitching and defense kept the other team off the scoreboard at a league best clip—a stingy 3.76 runs per game. In the World Series, their run prevention skills were put to the test against the Milwaukee Brewers, an offensive juggernaut that led the majors with 216 home runs and 5.47 runs per game. Nicknamed Harvey's Wallbangers after their manager, Harvey Kuenn, the Brewers' lineup featured the likes of Paul Molitor, Robin Yount, Cecil Cooper, Gorman Thomas, and Ted Simmons. Ironically, it was a trade engineered by Herzog less than two years earlier that had propelled Milwaukee to the American League pennant.

In the end, Whiteyball won out, resulting in the Cardinals' ninth World Series championship. The 162-game marathon included contributions from all 33 players who donned the "birds on the bat" over the course of the season. From a third-string catcher winning a game in the unlikeliest of ways—to a limelight-averse rookie breaking out on the game's grandest stage—to a rookie outpitching a future Hall of Famer to stave off elimination, each player contributed in some way to the team's 99 wins—92 in the regular season and seven in the playoffs. This is the story of the 1982 season, a championship, and the ensemble cast of characters who made it happen.

1

A Decade of Mediocrity

Decades before Whitey, Willie, Bruce, and Ozzie became household names in St. Louis, the Cardinals established themselves as the class of the National League, winning nine pennants and six World Series titles between 1926 and 1946. Their success in the first half of the 20th century was largely because of a robust minor-league system invented and built by Branch Rickey—an executive who later helped integrate baseball by signing Jackie Robinson under the employ of the Brooklyn Dodgers. On Rickey's watch, the Cardinals' farm system churned out a seemingly never-ending supply of exceptional ballplayers, from Pepper Martin, Dizzy Dean, and Joe Medwick of the Gashouse Gang era to stars like Stan Musial, Enos Slaughter, Terry Moore, and Marty Marion in the 1940s. While other teams' rosters were depleted by World War II, Rickey's novel system of developing talent helped fill the void when the Cardinals lost players to the war effort, allowing St. Louis to capture three straight NL pennants during the World War II years.

By the late 1940s, Rickey had jumped to the Dodgers, and owner Sam Breadon sold the Cardinals to St. Louis attorney Fred Saigh. In 1953, Saigh was forced to sell the team after he was convicted of tax evasion and sentenced to 15 months in prison. He had interest from groups who wanted to relocate the franchise, but Anheuser-Busch—the St. Louis-based brewery—stepped in and bought the club for $3.75 million.[1] The deal was engineered by A-B president August Anheuser "Gussie" Busch Jr., whose grandfather founded the beer empire. Compared to the $134 million Busch spent on expanding brewery operations in the preceding three years, the purchase price of the Cardinals barely put a dent in the company budget.[2] Busch's decision to buy the team was not purely out of civic duty. He recognized that the investment could help sell more beer. The Cardinals and Anheuser-Busch quickly became synonymous. Busch bought Sportsman's Park from the Cardinals' previous landlord—the Browns of the American League—and poured millions into refurbishing the old ballpark. He wanted to rename it Budweiser Stadium, but Commissioner Ford Frick did not want the name commercializing a company product. Busch circumvented Frick's rule by rebranding the stadium after the family surname and then producing a new line of beer called Busch.

The flamboyant and gregarious Busch took to the celebrity status associated with owning a major-league team. However, he discovered that the business of baseball was different than the beer industry. Acquiring talented players from other teams proved to be a challenge, mistakes were scrutinized by media and the public, and his own input to the front office and field manager often went ignored. The Cardinals failed to win the pennant during the 1950s, and as a result Busch discarded a series of front office executives and managers like empty bottles of Budweiser.

By 1964, franchise icon Stan Musial had retired, but the Cardinals had accumulated a talented core of position players that included Ken Boyer, Bill White, Tim McCarver, Dick Groat, Julian Javier, and Curt Flood. The lineup was further buoyed by an infamous midseason trade for Lou Brock, acquired from the Chicago Cubs as part of a six-player deal that sent Ernie Broglio, Bobby Shantz, and Doug Clemens to the Windy City. The speedy Brock had been a below average hitter with the Cubs but caught fire with St. Louis, hitting .348 with 12 home runs and 33 steals in 103 games—the first glimpses of what would become a storied Hall of Fame career. On the pitching side, Bob Gibson was developing into a full-fledged ace. Despite all of this talent, the Cards' pennant hopes appeared slim as the season wound down. On August 23, they were in fourth place, 11 games behind the league-leading Philadelphia Phillies. The tables turned in September, however. The Cardinals surged while the Phillies collapsed, resulting in the Cards' first pennant under Busch's ownership. St. Louis then defeated the mighty New York Yankees in the World Series—the franchise's first title in 18 years. Subsequently, Busch wrote a $3 million check to construct a new downtown ballpark—Busch Memorial Stadium, also known as Busch II—that opened in 1966 as part of an urban renewal project.[3] The Redbirds enjoyed two more World Series appearances in the decade, beating the Boston Red Sox in 1967 and losing to the Detroit Tigers in 1968.

Cardinals general manager Bing Devine traded for Reds slugger Vada Pinson and then acquired Joe Torre from the Braves in exchange for Orlando Cepeda before the start of the 1969 season. Besides the dominant arm of Gibson, the Redbirds' pitching staff included Steve Carlton, who was blossoming into one of the game's elite young pitchers. Not only were the reigning NL champions bursting with talent, but the road to the playoffs got easier in the decade's final year. With the addition of expansion franchises in Montreal and San Diego, Major League Baseball transitioned to a division format. Instead of competing with nine other teams for a World Series birth, the Cardinals had to fend off only five division rivals and were heavy favorites to win the first-ever NL East crown. The season did not go as planned, however. St. Louis got off to a disappointing start and by July 4 were seven games under .500. The team's fortunes turned in the second half, but they had dug themselves too deep of a hole to catch the 100-win Miracle Mets.

Before the 1970 campaign, Devine traded Curt Flood to the Phillies for slugger Dick Allen. Flood refused to report to Philadelphia and requested the right to become a free agent. He told Commissioner Bowie Kuhn in a letter, "I do feel that I am a piece of property to be bought and sold irrespective of my wishes. I believe that any system which produces that result violates my basic rights as a citizen and is inconsistent with the laws of the United States and of several States."[4] Flood sued Major League Baseball over its reserve clause, which bound players to their teams for life or until the team decided otherwise. He ultimately lost the case in the Supreme Court, but the suit laid the foundation for the removal of baseball's antitrust exemption and the establishment of free agency in 1976 through collective bargaining. In place of Flood, the Cardinals sent Willie Montañez and first-round draft pick Jim Browning to the Phillies.

Torre and Allen each produced all-star seasons for the 1970 Cardinals, combining to hit 55 home runs and drive in 201 runs. Gibson was in customary form, winning 23 games and the Cy Young Award. Despite these excellent individual seasons, the Cardinals finished 10 games below .500. Allen, who was slowed by a hamstring injury during the season's final two months, lasted only one season in St. Louis. Devine sought to improve the team's defense and shipped him to the Los Angeles Dodgers for light-hitting infielder Ted Sizemore and backup catcher Bob Stinson. The Cards would sorely miss Allen's offensive production.

More roster churn left the 1971 Cards with just a handful of holdovers from the pennant-winning clubs of the 1960s, including Gibson, Brock, Javier, Carlton, and Dal Maxvill. Torre won the batting title with a .363 average and Carlton reached the 20-win mark for the first time in his career. These achievements helped the Redbirds win 90 games, but the Pirates finished seven games ahead to win the division. Heading into the 1972 season, Carlton asked for a raise. "The Cardinals always said, 'we can't pay the money the you want because you never won 20.' That was always their argument," recalled Carlton. Having reached that plateau, he requested a bump in his salary to $66,000, but Busch refused to budge off his offer of $60,000. "We got stuck on those two numbers," said Carlton. "So, opening day of spring training, Bing Devine calls me up and said, 'Lefty, we traded you to the Phillies.' I couldn't believe it."[5] Carlton, whose mental preparation contributed to his success, had envisioned himself winning 25 games the next year and having a long career in the Gateway City. He called Devine back a half hour later and said he would agree to accept the Cardinals' offer, but it was too late. Devine had already agreed to deal the southpaw to Philadelphia for pitcher Rick Wise.

Though Wise posted a pair of 16-win seasons for St. Louis, the trade would prove to be one of the more regrettable transactions in Cardinals history. In sending Carlton to the last-place Phillies, Devine had hoped to bury the young hurler on an irrelevant team. Though Carlton alone could not pull Philadelphia out of the NL East cellar in 1972, he authored one of the greatest seasons by any pitcher in the live-ball era (defined as post–1920). In 346⅓ innings, he struck out 310 batters, recorded a 1.97 ERA, and ran away with the NL Cy Young Award. Carlton's 27 wins accounted for nearly 46 percent of the Phillies' total victory count of 59. He was just getting started. Lefty went on to torment his former team for years to come, racking up 241 wins in 15 seasons with the Phillies and eventually leading the franchise to prominence in the latter half of the decade.

The emergence of budding star Ted Simmons at catcher was not enough to keep the 1972 Redbirds from sliding down in the standings to fourth place with a record of 75–81. A year later, the Cardinals rebounded from an abysmal 5–20 start to ultimately finish at .500. The NL East lacked a standout club, and the unexceptional Redbirds narrowly missed the playoffs, finishing a game and a half behind the Mets.

To bolster the lineup, Devine traded Wise and Bernie Carbo to Boston for outfielder Reggie Smith before the 1974 season. The Cardinals benefited from an infusion of talent from its minor-league chain in the form of starting pitcher Bob Forsch, first baseman Keith Hernandez, and outfielder Bake McBride, who won the NL Rookie of the Year Award with a .309 average and 30 stolen bases. Brock kept fans on the edges of their seats with a single-season record 118 stolen bases. The Cards appeared on the upswing, winning 86 games and remaining in the pennant race until the bitter end. The 88-win Pirates clinched on the season's final day as the Cardinals, snowed out in Montreal, watched helplessly.

In 1975, four regulars hit .300 or better—led by Simmons' .332 mark—but the Cardinals drew fewer walks than any other team and as a result were seventh in the NL in scoring. Young hurlers Forsch and Lynn McGlothen each racked up 15 wins and Al Hrabosky posted a stellar 13-3 record and 1.66 ERA out of the bullpen. Still, the club was middle of the pack, finishing with a third-place 82–80 record as Gibson threw the final pitches of his storied career.

The Redbirds went from mediocre to lousy the following season. Hector Cruz, the only Cardinal to reach double digits in home runs, accounted for 13 of the team's league-lowest 63 round-trippers. Playing in the spacious dimensions of Busch Stadium certainly played a part in the low total, but even on the road the Cards were outhomered 51–36. The pitching rotation got a boost from 23-year-old John Denny, who led the NL with a 2.52 ERA in 30 starts, but the 3.88 runs per game scored by the offense left little room for error. St. Louis lost 90 games for the first time since 1916, resulting in the dismissal of longtime manager Red Schoendienst.

The Cardinals returned to respectability in 1977 under new skipper Vern Rapp, a no-nonsense disciplinarian who banished high stirrups and facial hair. By then, Simmons was an established all-star catcher, Hernandez was rounding into an excellent all-around first baseman, and Ken Reitz hit 17 homers while playing superb defense at the hot corner. The Cards also welcomed the emergence of 21-year-old shortstop Garry Templeton, a quickly-rising star. However, the team still lacked offensive production from its outfielders. Brock, the only remaining cog from the last pennant winner, was 38 and winding down his career. Forsch established himself as a reliable front-end starter with a 20-win season, but behind him were a group of middling performers. St. Louis finished in third, a distant 18 games back of Carlton's Phillies and 13 behind the second-place Pirates.

With most of the Cardinals' key contributors returning for the 1978 season, there was reason for optimism, as evidenced by *The Sporting News* picking St. Louis to win the NL East. However, the Redbirds got off to a rocky start, on and off the field. Besides losing 11 of their first 16, Rapp had run-ins with two of the team's star players—Simmons and Templeton. Dick Kaegel of the *St. Louis Post-Dispatch* wrote that Rapp "knows the game, but he doesn't seem to know people, or how to handle them."[6] The final straw came on a road trip to Montreal when Rapp admonished Simmons, calling him "a loser."[7] After the comments were made public by broadcaster Jack Buck, Rapp's dismissal was swift. Third-base coach Jack Krol served as interim manager until Busch and Devine hired Ken Boyer, the team's former star third baseman who was managing the Cards' Triple-A team in Rochester, New York. Boyer, in contrast to Rapp, was considered a player's manager. The change did not translate to an improvement on the field, however. Two weeks after Boyer's hiring, the club lost 11 straight, the franchise's longest skid in 62 years. In hopes that adding some veteran leadership would improve his flailing team, Devine obtained outfielder George Hendrick from the Padres in exchange for pitcher Eric Rasmussen. Still, the losses continued to mount.

On June 23, 1978, Busch issued a statement blasting his team. "Management does not pay salaries to supposedly quality players for constant mental errors, for a loose and carefree attitude," bristled the beer baron. "My patience is getting very thin. Our fans are justifiably getting discouraged."[8] Indeed, many fans stayed away from the ballpark. The Cardinals averaged a home attendance of only 15,780.

By August 4, the Cardinals had fallen to 28 games under .500. Brock hit only .221 and lost his starting job. Hernandez's batting average had dipped to .255. Young pitchers Pete Falcone and John Urrea failed to find their footing, posting a combined record of 6–16 with ERAs above five. "Our guys were good, but none of them had been on a winner," said Reitz in retrospect. "We lacked the knowledge of how to win."[9] The shoddy play of the New York Mets was the only thing that kept the 93-loss Cardinals out of last place. The Cards' substandard showing compelled Busch to fire Devine, who was replaced with St. Louis native John Claiborne. Ironically, it was Devine who had given Claiborne his first job in baseball with the Mets 13 years earlier. Claiborne subsequently had served as farm director for the Oakland Athletics and assistant general manager with the Red Sox. He had also been employed with the Cardinals as an administrative assistant in the scouting and player development department in the early 1970s.

One of Claiborne's first goals in advance of the 1979 season was to acquire a left-handed starting pitcher. He settled on Bob Sykes, a 25-year-old southpaw who had compiled a mediocre 11–13 record in two seasons with the Tigers. Claiborne's attempts to lure in free agent pitchers Tommy John, Mike Marshall, and Jim Slaton were unsuccessful. Free agent Pete Rose also turned down the Cardinals' offer and instead signed with the Phillies. The Redbirds inked deals with outfielder Bernie Carbo and journeyman reliever Darold Knowles, both of whom would be released before the end of their contracts due to underperformance. Other than changes at the periphery of the roster, the team largely returned intact in 1979—including Brock, who was 100 hits away from 3,000 for his career. The 40-year-old outfielder dedicated himself to a strict weight training program during the winter and showed up to spring training poised to reclaim his starting role and reach the milestone. Indeed, he produced a campaign that defied his age, hitting .362 in May and June and .304 for the season. On August 13, Brock hit a line drive off Cubs pitcher Dennis Lamp for his 3000th hit. Making his major-league debut in the same game was a second baseman named Tom Herr.

Like Brock, Keith Hernandez rebounded with an excellent 1979 season, winning the batting title with a .344 average and sharing co-MVP honors with Pirates slugger Willie Stargell. Ken Oberkfell—a scrappy young infielder from nearby Highland, Illinois, whom the Cardinals signed as an undrafted amateur out of Southwestern Illinois College in Belleville—supplanted Mike Tyson as the starting second baseman and hit .301. Templeton and Hendrick also each hit .300 or better and Simmons belted a career-high 26 homers. Silvio Martínez and John Fulgham, a pair of 23-year-old righties, combined to win 25 games. All told, the Cardinals won 17 more than the previous season but still fell 12 games short of the division-winning Pirates. The 1970s, viewed by some as "The Lost Decade" of Cardinals baseball, ended without a postseason appearance. Brock, the last vestige of the organization's bygone glory days, hung up his cleats at the end of the season. The 1980s would usher in MTV, leg warmers, scrunchies, Hip-Hop, the Walkman, trickle-down economics, the war on drugs, and a new era for the St. Louis Cardinals.

2

1980

St. Louis Welcomes the White Rat

With most of the same lackluster roster returning in 1980, there was little reason to believe the Cardinals' 11-year playoff drought would end anytime soon. To fill the void left by Lou Brock's retirement, John Claiborne dealt pitcher John Denny and outfielder Jerry Mumphrey to Cleveland for 34-year-old outfielder Bobby Bonds. At the time, Bonds was the only player in major-league history with at least 300 home runs and 400 stolen bases, but he was on the downside of his career. The trade of Denny left only two established arms—Pete Vuckovich and Bob Forsch—in the starting rotation. Bob Sykes, coming off an injury-plagued season, and the promising but inexperienced tandem of John Fulgham and Silvio Martínez comprised the rest of the group. Fireballer Mark Littell and journeyman Don Hood were the only Redbird relievers with a proven track record. The front office had a chance to shore up the bullpen by acquiring all-star closer Bruce Sutter from the Cubs, but Claiborne reportedly rebuffed the Chicago club's insistence on a package of Leon Durham, Tom Herr, and Terry Kennedy.[1]

The Cardinals faced the defending-champion Pirates in eight of the first 11 games to start the 1980 docket. Vuckovich tossed an Opening Day three-hitter to defeat the Bucs and Bert Blyleven in a brisk one hour and 51 minutes. From there, the Cardinals' season precipitously went off the rails. The Cards muddled through April with an 8–10 record and then posted a disastrous 8–18 mark in May. The expectation that Bonds' right-handed bat would balance out a lefty-heavy lineup was thwarted by an early-season hit-by-pitch, which resulted in persistent pain and inflammation that zapped the slugger's power.

By the end of May, Ken Boyer's Cards led the league in batting average, but the pitching was not up to par. Forsch and Vuckovich were posting numbers similar to the backs of their respective baseball cards, but

2. 1980—St. Louis Welcomes the White Rat

the balance of the staff was woeful. Sykes had lost four of five decisions and owned an unsightly 10.13 ERA. Littell, pitching with bone chips in his elbow that would require surgery in June, had blown three of five save opportunities and had a 9.28 ERA. Jim Kaat, a ripe 41 years old, was purchased from the Yankees to solidify the bullpen but proceeded to compile a 7.27 ERA in his first 13 outings with St. Louis. It was fair to wonder how much gas the old southpaw had left in the tank. The Cardinals' dismal start was unacceptable in the eyes of Gussie Busch, who visited the clubhouse on May 31 and declared changes were coming. The Cardinals—last place in the NL East with an 18–30 record—traveled from New York to Montreal for a four-game series with Expos on June 6. Meanwhile, Busch and Claiborne devised a plan.

Dorrel Norman Elvert Herzog was born on November 9, 1931, in the small town of New Athens (pronounced AY-thens), Illinois, 35 miles southeast of St. Louis on the Kaskaskia River. His mother meant to name him Darrell, but the name was misspelled on his birth certificate, so Dorrel it was. He acquired the nickname "Relly" as a child and was the second of three boys born to Edgar and Lietta (Fanke) Herzog, who—like many in town—were of German descent. Though farming and coal mining were the primary industries in the region, Edgar made a living at the thriving Mound City Brewing Company and later the Illinois Highway Department. Lietta was employed at a local shoe factory. Traits such as tidiness, punctuality, and a strong work ethic were instilled in Relly at an early age.

Herzog learned the value of a dollar growing up in a working-class household. Mornings and evenings were spent delivering newspapers, though he would always take time to sneak a peek at the major-league box scores and baseball stories. As he got older, Herzog worked for a funeral home, where he would dig graves, then change clothes and drive the hearse. He also worked at the Mound City Brewery as the cleanup man in the brewhouse. "The only time I ever hit cleanup," he later quipped.[2] One perk of the job was that he could drink beer while doing his work. As was the case in many German families, Herzog grew up having a glass or two of beer at meals. In his first year of pro ball, his manager—Vern Hoscheit—took him out for dinner and was flabbergasted when the 17-year-old ordered a beer. The skipper put an end to that habit on the spot.

Without much else to do in New Athens, Herzog and his buddies played a lot of baseball—sometimes five or six full nine-inning games a day—on a local farm field they converted to a ball diamond. Herzog was a standout ballplayer by the time he got to New Athens High School, where he also starred at basketball. Though only 5-foot-8 and 130 pounds, he captained the cagers and was recruited by Illinois and St. Louis University. It was on the baseball diamond, however, where Relly found his passion, and his schoolwork took a backseat to the game he loved. "I didn't pay much attention to the books," Herzog once said. "As long as I stayed eligible and got passing grades, I wasn't worried about going to college."[3]

Most of Herzog's peers rooted for the Cardinals, but his favorite team growing up was the Yankees.[4] Still, he followed the Redbirds and listened to their games on the radio every night. "The thing that stuck in my mind was the gung-ho way that they played—full speed, fundamentally sound, taking the extra base, running hard all of the time," Herzog later wrote. "I grew up thinking that is the way baseball ought to be played."[5]

On occasion, Herzog would skip school and hitchhike to Belleville, where he would catch a St. Louis–bound bus to watch the Cardinals or Browns play at Sportsman's Park. He would sneak in early for batting practice to snag a few balls. He typically managed to sell a few and brought the rest back to use on the sandlots. Fortunately for Herzog, his principal was a baseball fan. "[He] would never tell my mother," Herzog reflected. "He'd call me up to the office, and we'd end up talking about the ballgame."[6]

Herzog—a left-handed first baseman, outfielder, and pitcher—helped lead his high school nine to the state baseball championship in his junior season of 1948. New Athens lost to Granite City, a defeat that he would harken back to 34 years later when he won a championship on a much larger stage.

Herzog was 5-foot-9 and 150 pounds when he graduated, too small in the eyes of the Cardinals scout who evaluated him. Jack Fournier, a talent evaluator with the Browns, offered him a contract as a pitcher, but Herzog believed his path in professional baseball was as an outfielder. A day after his high school graduation, he was invited to a Yankees tryout camp in Branson, Missouri. When scout Lou Maguolo suggested that he could be the heir apparent to Joe DiMaggio, Herzog was sold. Little did he know, Yankee scouts were saying the same thing to another youngster from Commerce, Oklahoma, named Mickey Mantle. Herzog signed for a $1,500 bonus and $150 a month.[7] Though their careers took different trajectories, Herzog would later enjoy bragging that his signing bonus topped Mantle's.

Herzog's first stop in the minor leagues was with a Class-D outfit in McAlester, Oklahoma, where a local sportscaster bestowed the nickname "Whitey" for his bleach-blonde hair. A few years later, he would also gain the nickname "White Rat" for his resemblance to Bob Kuzava—a Yankees hurler whose similar-colored locks had earned him the same moniker.

Herzog spent four years rising the ranks of the Yankees' minor-league system before being drafted into the United States Army during the Korean conflict. He served with the Corps of Engineers for two years at

Fort Leonard Wood, Missouri, where he played ball for the base squad. It was during this time that he married his high school sweetheart, Mary Lou Sinn.

Herzog returned to the Yankees' farm system in 1955 and spent a rookie camp learning under Casey Stengel, whom Whitey would later call his biggest influence as a manager. Herzog was assigned to the Triple-A Denver Bears, where the he hit .289, knocked 21 home runs, and posted a .412 on-base percentage as a starting center fielder. Following that successful season, he was added to the Yankees' big-league roster. He would never put on the pinstripes in a regular season game, however. Just before the start of the 1956 season, Stengel called Herzog up to his hotel suite. "Well, Herzog," said Stengel, "you're a pretty good ballplayer, but you're not as good as the feller I got."[8] Stengel informed Herzog that he had been traded to the Washington Senators. The "feller" Stengel was referring to—Mantle—won the Triple Crown that year.

Herzog made his major-league debut 16 days later against the team that had just traded him away and recorded his first career hit off Don Larsen. He had a decent rookie season, hitting .245 with four home runs in 117 games for the second-division Senators. His average plummeted to .167 as a part-time player in 1957, and as a result he spent the majority of the summer playing with the Triple-A Miami Marlins.

In 1958, Herzog was waived by Washington and picked up by the Kansas City Athletics—another franchise that was typically closer to the cellar than first place. He accepted his role on the team as a platoon player. "I came to the realization that I was never going to be a star in the big leagues, but I might still have a pretty good career if I hustled, kept my nose clean, and did the things that I did best as well as I could," Herzog later wrote.[9] To that end, he showed up to spring training in 1959 with a left-hander's catcher mitt, making himself more indispensable as the team's emergency backstop. He hit .293 that season and then .266 in 1960 despite dealing with a calcified hematoma in his leg that required surgery. He and Mary Lou settled in Kansas City with their three children. Whitey worked construction jobs during offseasons and built a house in nearby Independence, Missouri, laying bricks with the help of close friend and teammate Roger Maris. Herzog also spent winters as a well-respected high school and college basketball referee.

In 1961, the White Rat was traded to the Baltimore Orioles, where he hit .280 across two seasons before being dealt to the Detroit Tigers. With Al Kaline, Norm Cash, and Billy Bruton in the outfield and Rocky Colavito manning first base, the lineup was a tough one for Herzog to crack. Barring injury to one of the regulars, he was unlikely to see much playing time. To make the situation more daunting, he developed an inner ear problem during spring training that caused bouts of dizziness and affected his balance and reaction time. After hitting only .151 in 53 at-bats during the 1963 season, the 31-year-old decided his playing career was over.

The A's offered Herzog a scouting gig, but he could make more money in construction and enjoyed the work, so he took a job as a superintendent with a Kansas City builder. He oversaw a team of more than 30 laborers on a concrete crew and quickly realized that all but a handful were lazy. The hardest workers got the worst tasks because the others could not be trusted to get the job done. When he found out he could not fire anyone because they were protected by a labor union, he quit on the spot, then immediately drove to Municipal Stadium. Still wearing his construction clothes, he asked for the scouting job. Herzog displayed a keen eye for talent, signing seven eventual big leaguers during his first year on the job. He would have signed an eighth—future Hall of Famer Don Sutton—but notoriously frugal A's owner Charlie Finley would not budge on his offer, which was $6,000 less than Sutton wanted.[10]

Herzog was hired by the A's in 1965 to coach their "bonus babies," young players whose contracts required that their teams keep them on the big-league roster or risk losing them in the draft. The group included Sal Bando, Joe Rudi, Catfish Hunter, and Blue Moon Odom—a collection of players who would help form the nucleus of three World Series champion teams following the Athletics' relocation to Oakland. After Finley invited Mary Lou on a road trip and then charged her for the cost of the flight, an irate Herzog quit after one year on the job.

The New York Mets' brass, George Weiss and Bing Devine—the latter of whom had come to the Big Apple after being fired from his general manager position by Gussie Busch in 1964—called and offered Herzog employment as a third-base coach. Whitey took the job for the 1966 season, but after a year at the post he was homesick and prepared to return to the A's. Then, Devine offered him a job as a special assistant, a flexible role allowed for periodic trips to see the family. His duties involved scouting and helping with trade talks. He eventually took over as director of player development, guiding a system that contributed to the Mets' surprise championship in 1969. He remained in that position through 1972, along the way passing up overtures to manage the A's and Indians.

Herzog finally gave in to his desire to manage a big-league club in 1973, taking over the reins of the Texas Rangers in their second year of existence after owner Bob Short moved the franchise from Washington, D.C, where they were known as the Senators. The Rangers were coming off a 54–100 season under manager Ted Williams, who recommended Herzog for the job. "And I always tell him I'll never forgive him for it," Herzog later said. "I'd never seen such a motley assortment of has-beens and

2. 1980—St. Louis Welcomes the White Rat

never-wases."[11] The Rangers lacked fundamentals and pitching, a combination that resulted in many more losses than victories. Nevertheless, Herzog was confident that with a good organizational plan he could have turned the team into a winner within a few years. He would not get that chance. The Rangers were 47–91 when Short summarily canned Herzog and replaced him with Billy Martin, who had just been let go by the Tigers.*

Herzog coached third base for the California Angels in 1974 and served as the team's interim manager for four games between the firing of Bobby Winkles and hiring of Dick Williams. Whitey and his family enjoyed the sunshine of Southern California, and he was content enough there to sign a three-year contract to remain on as a coach. However, when the Kansas City Royals fired Jack McKeon mid-way through the 1975 season, Herzog was offered a job he could not refuse. It was a dream scenario—the chance to manage a major-league team a few miles from his home.

Herzog inherited a Royals roster that included a mix of up-and-coming prospects—Frank White, Dennis Leonard, and George Brett—and established regulars like John Mayberry, Amos Otis, and Hal McRae. The new skipper had the personnel to institute an aggressive running game that took advantage of Royals Stadium's sizable dimensions. Like Busch Stadium, it was one of the major league's more pitcher-friendly ballparks. The Royals were 50–46 when Herzog took over and surged to 41–25 the rest of the way, finishing in second place behind the A's. "When Whitey came in, all of the sudden there was a credibility there," recalled Royals pitcher Paul Splittorff. "He was so popular, so honest, so believable. He was a great fit."[12]

In the clubhouse, Herzog cultivated an atmosphere of earned respect and camaraderie. "Whitey treated men like men regardless of age or status," remembered Randy McGilberry, who pitched in parts of two seasons for Herzog's Royals. "I found the entire team to be the same." McGilberry recalled how Herzog could get his point across without chastising his players. In one spring training contest, Darrell Porter—the Royals' catcher—called for a changeup, a pitch McGilberry had never thrown. "Lee May

---

*The Rangers' ineptitude earned them the number one overall pick in the 1973 draft—left-handed flamethrower David Clyde. Short had no patience or discipline, however, and added Clyde directly to the big-league roster. Herzog agreed to start Clyde a couple of times and then farm him out for seasoning, but the teenage phenom proved to be a huge draw for the financially-strapped Rangers. Short blocked the young southpaw's demotion in favor of the short-term gain from gate receipts, a decision that proved detrimental. Short sold the Rangers in 1974. Martin's mismanagement of Clyde further hampered the youngster's development. Clyde finished his career with 18 wins in parts of five seasons, and the Rangers would not make the playoffs until 1996.

scalded it like three thousand feet," said McGilberry. "Whitey came out to the mound and said, 'Hey kid, what was that pitch?' I said, 'a changeup.' He smiled and said, 'can it,' and walked back to the dugout."[13]

From 1976 to 1978, the Royals averaged over 200 stolen bases per year while capturing three consecutive AL West division titles, each time losing to the Yankees in the League Championship Series. The 1977 club—what Herzog later called the best team he ever managed—won 102 games and at one point reeled off 24 victories in 25 games.[14] Unlike the Yankees, however, the Royals lacked a top-flight stopper in the bullpen and blew several late-inning leads in the ALCS during Herzog's tenure.* The skipper would prioritize getting his own elite closer in his next managerial post.

By 1979, Herzog had developed a rocky relationship with Royals owner Ewing Kauffman despite the team's success and robust attendance figures, which surpassed two million fans per year. Herzog had been critical of Kauffman and GM Joe Burke for not acquiring talent he felt was needed to win, specifically pointing to the fact that the Royals could have signed Goose Gossage in 1978. Several controversial decisions had led to rifts within the organization. Herzog fired well-liked hitting coach Charlie Lau and then demanded that Mayberry be traded after he showed up to Game Four of the 1978 ALCS in rough physical shape following a night of carousing. When the Royals dropped to second place in the AL West in 1979, Kauffman had the excuse he needed to fire Herzog.

While unemployed from baseball, the White Rat made more money doing Miller Lite commercials and promoting the beverage at golf tournaments than he had managing. Of course, he also did some fishing—one of his favorite hobbies. With three AL pennants on his résumé, Herzog knew it would not be long before another team came calling and was in a position to be selective about his next gig. Based on his experience with the Mets, Rangers, and Royals, he sought a post where he would have support from ownership down to player development.[15] When has was not hitting the links or casting a lure, Herzog would occasionally receive calls from Cardinals GM John Claiborne seeking an opinion on a player. Claiborne—a former colleague with the Mets—at one point had extended Herzog a consultant job, but he preferred to hold out for a managerial post.

On June 7, 1980, Herzog was at a golf tournament in the Lake of the Ozarks when he received a call from Lou Susman—Gussie Busch's attorney. The Cardinals owner wanted to see Herzog right away in St. Louis. Herzog knew that meant a job offer was coming and insisted that Ken be notified. "I don't want to be taking the man's job before he even knows

---

*The Yankees had 1977 Cy Young Award winner Sparky Lyle closing games in 1977 and then acquired Goose Gossage, who served as the stopper in 1978–79.

about it," said Herzog to Susman, who assured him that Claiborne was being dispatched to Montreal to notify Boyer of his dismissal.[16]

The next day, Herzog met with Susman and Busch at Grant's Farm, the sprawling Busch family estate. Susman did most of the talking and tendered a one-year contract. Herzog pointed out that managing on a series of one-year contracts, as he had done in Kansas City, put the manager in a less secure position than his players, who were often signed to longer deals. Thus, Herzog asked for a three-year pact. Busch spoke up: "You're right. I'll give you a three-year contract."[17] And with that, a new era was born for Herzog and the St. Louis Cardinals.

Whitey Herzog rebuilt the Cardinals as general manager and earned the respect of his players as field manager through a keen baseball sense, dogged preparation, and excellent communication (National Baseball Hall of Fame and Museum, Cooperstown, NY).

As Herzog negotiated his contract, the Cardinals were in the midst of a doubleheader in Montreal. The Redbirds were in a free fall, losers in 20 of their last 25. Claiborne had intended to fire Boyer before the first game of the twin bill, but a delayed flight in Chicago prevented him from making it to Olympic Stadium until the first game had already concluded. In the same office where Vern Rapp had been fired two years before, Boyer was writing out the lineup card for the second game when Claiborne walked in and broke the news.* Boyer was gobsmacked. "Guys were busting their butts," he lamented to reporters. "I don't think there was anything I could do."[18]

The firing of the well-liked skipper elicited strong responses in the clubhouse that ranged from anger to disappointment. The players directed

---

*Third base coach Jack Krol managed the second game of the doubleheader, a 9–4 loss that dropped the Cardinals' record to 18–34.

blame for the team's poor record at themselves. "The worst team I've been on since I've been in the major leagues," said Keith Hernandez. "The worst. We are bad. The manager is as only as good as his horses, and we don't have the horses. I'm going to miss Ken Boyer. Period."[19]

"There's lack of professionalism among certain players as far as guys running groundballs out, 100 percent all-out effort," said Tom Herr.[20]

"Unfortunately, there are not 25 people on this team that are as intense as Kenny Boyer," assessed John Fulgham. "Therein lies the problem. Anybody who has seen us play knows that."[21]

Herzog met his new team in Atlanta on June 9 but getting there was a challenge. He missed his flight after being told the wrong time and then his taxi driver took him to the city of Marietta instead of the Marriott Hotel. Once he made it to Fulton County Stadium, Herzog gave his last-place team a brief pregame speech in which he laid out some basic ground rules: no music in the clubhouse after losses, headphones must be used on team flights and buses, and those who didn't hustle would be fined. He also announced that there would be no curfew on road trips, and players were allowed to consume alcohol in the hotel bar—reversing an edict installed by Boyer. The team immediately noticed a more relaxed vibe. "It's amazing what one guy can do," said Ken Reitz. "He put new air in the atmosphere."[22] That night, George Hendrick's 10th-inning three-run homer off Gene Garber gave Herzog his first win as a Cardinal.

Al Hrabosky, a Braves reliever who played for Herzog in Kansas City, explained what made him so successful: "Whitey, being a journeyman, or scrappy ballplayer, can get down to that level. He can sit there and think in terms of the guy who's struggling at the plate. He communicates well with the players but he's not afraid to let a guy know when he's screwing up. He doesn't demand respect, he earns it. And he'll make them do things. They'll play much more aggressive. He's a fanatic in his baserunning. He's a fanatic about the hit-and-run and fundamentals."[23]

Hrabosky proved to be correct. Under Herzog, the Redbirds' fortunes began to turn. After winning two out of three against Atlanta, they did the same at home versus Cincinnati. Starting June 22, the Cards reeled off six consecutive wins, including a sweep of the Pirates. Herzog emphasized small ball and unselfish play. "We're doing different things. We're hitting behind runners. We're bunting guys over. Once you start to play good ball, you start to concentrate more," noted Garry Templeton.[24]

Players were initially reluctant to give too much credit to Herzog at the risk of slighting Boyer, though there was no denying that the managerial change corresponded to success on the field. "I'm not saying it was the manager, but it goes back to the old line 'You can't fire the players.' The change got a little spark going," said reliever John Littlefield.[25]

Herzog quickly realized that the Cardinals lacked two things he felt were necessary to win in his home ballpark: speed and a good bullpen. Busch Stadium, one of many cookie-cutter type facilities built in the 1960s, was a ballpark where fly balls went to die. The center-field wall stood 414 feet from home plate, and the right- and left-centerfield dimensions were 383 feet. Herzog recognized the need for fleet-footed outfielders to track down fly balls and cut off drives into the gaps. He knew that fast baserunners could take advantage of the same spacious outfield against a slower opposition while also beating out Baltimore chops on the infield. When he looked around at his roster, Herzog saw little speed outside of Templeton and outfielder Tony Scott. "They could hit, but they couldn't run. And those who could run wouldn't. It sometimes took four base hits to score a single run," Herzog observed.[26]

Besides lacking foot speed, the Cardinals had a clubhouse culture that the skipper found troublesome. "I've never seen such a bunch of misfits," Herzog later wrote. "Nobody would run out a ball. Nobody in the bullpen wanted the ball. We had guys on drugs—and another guy who sneaked off into the tunnel between innings so he could take a hit of vodka."[27] The situation was similar to Herzog's job as a construction supervisor nearly two decades before, only now he wielded authority to make changes.

Although the team lacked the pieces needed to contend for the pennant, it was far from devoid of talent. In fact, the lineup featured three legitimate star players who were earning among the top ten salaries in the game: Ted Simmons, Keith Hernandez, and Templeton.

Simmons debuted with the Cardinals in 1968 and became the team's everyday catcher two years later. For the next decade, he topped a .300 batting average five times and made six All-Star teams while averaging 15 home runs and 83 RBIs. He had also become a pillar in the community through charitable work and serving on the board at the St. Louis Art Museum. The Michigan native made St. Louis his offseason home and had become a fan favorite.

Hernandez was another homegrown player who had developed into one of the league's best pure hitters. He had faced ups and downs during his first few years in the big leagues before his breakout 1979 campaign, when he won the batting title, played Gold Glove defense, and earned Most Valuable Player honors.

Simmons and Hernandez were standout players, but the consensus was that the most talented member of the Cardinals roster was Templeton. The son of former Negro League shortstop Spiavia Templeton, Garry was the Cardinals' first-round draft pick in 1974 out of Santa Ana Valley High School in California. He reached the big leagues only two years later at age 20. From 1976–79, the switch-hitter batted .304 and became the first player in major-league history to record 100 base hits from each side of the plate in one season. Herzog was impressed early on by his cornerstone infielder. "If there's a better shortstop in baseball, I haven't seen him," said the skipper. "I've been in both major leagues. Maybe they've got a league on the moon that has a better one."[28] Estimable journalist Bob Broeg, who had seen his share of shortstops in 35 years scribing for the *St. Louis Post-Dispatch*, said that Templeton "with the possible exception of Honus Wagner, is perhaps the most exciting shortstop ever to play the game."[29] Templeton's preternatural physical gifts and early career success had earned him the richest contract in Cardinals history before the 1980 season.

With a defeat of the Dodgers on July 23, St. Louis had climbed to within eight games of .500, but that same day Templeton fractured his thumb sliding into first base. At the time he was leading the league with a .326 average—a point ahead of George Hendrick—and was the player the team could least afford to lose. To replace Templeton on the roster, the club recalled Tom Herr from the Triple-A Springfield (IL) Redbirds. Herr had hit only .163 in a cup of coffee earlier in the year, but he performed well enough in Triple A to earn another look. During Templeton's three weeks out of the lineup, the Cardinals lost 10 of 17. His absence magnified the need for more depth and speed, something Herzog would emphasize in future transactions.

Heading into a series against the Giants on July 29, St. Louis owned a record of 26–19 with Herzog in the dugout. Despite improved play and a winning record on his watch, the White Rat was troubled by his team's lack of aggression and hustle. Hernandez in particular was a source of the manager's ire after loafing on multiple occasions. On the other hand, Hendrick—whose effort had been questioned during tenures with Oakland and Cleveland—drew praise for buying in early to what Herzog was preaching. Hendrick's season totals of 25 home runs and 109 RBIs would lead the club.

At the August GM meetings, Claiborne made a proposal for the NL to adopt the designated hitter. The roster spot would have been a welcome addition for the Cardinals, who had a pair of excellent offensive catchers—Simmons and promising young Terry Kennedy, who clubbed 20 home runs as a minor leaguer in 1978. The measure was defeated by a 5–4 vote (there were three abstentions). "We'll get it next time. We'll get it in 1981," predicted Claiborne.[30] Little did he know, executives would be expressing similar sentiments for decades to come.

The Cardinals eventually escaped the cellar, bypassing the Cubs, who lacked much talent beyond Bruce Sutter—the reigning NL Cy Young Award winner and four-time All-Star. The fireman had already defeated the Cubs in arbitration once and publicly said he would not take a pay cut, lending to speculation that he was likely to be traded. Out west, another elite closer was clamoring to be moved. Padres stopper Rollie Fingers clashed with rookie manager Jerry Coleman, called the franchise "a joke," and said that the team "can trade me anywhere they like. Just get me out of here."[31]

Though the Cardinals showed dramatic improvement following the managerial change, overall the team failed to meet the expectations of Gussie Busch. On August 18, another shoe dropped with the firing of Claiborne after only 22 months on the job. Herzog was stunned and had concerns about how it would affect his future. "I don't know who the new guy is going to be," he said. "I'd hate to have a guy come in who might not want me." Asked if he would have interest in the position, Herzog dismissed the notion. "I've been offered some of those jobs and turned them down. To be honest, I like to hunt, fish, and play golf."[32]

Injuries and inconsistency caught up with the Redbirds in the dog days of August. Templeton returned from his fractured thumb, only to break an index finger during pregame warmups nine days later. Pete Vuckovich was pitching with a sore shoulder. Silvio Martínez was hampered by an elbow injury that had kept him out of action for a large chunk of the first half and rendered him ineffective in the second half. John Fulgham—whose 1979 ledger included a 10–6 record, 2.53 ERA, and 10 complete games—was diagnosed with a career-threatening rotator cuff tear. The offense, meanwhile, was perplexingly streaky, scoring double-digit runs six times and two runs or fewer 11 times in August. The Cardinals' slew of maladies and all-or-nothing tendencies added up to a 12–16 month despite a +28 run differential.

Busch interviewed seven candidates for the GM vacancy, but there was one person at the top of the list: Herzog. The owner had developed an excellent rapport with his field manager. On several occasions, Herzog dropped by the Busch estate and the pair would talk baseball, play cards, and throw back a couple of adult beverages. Busch appreciated Herzog's straight-shooting analysis of the team and the direction he wanted to take it, so much so that on August 29, it was announced that Herzog had agreed to step into the GM role. Busch had invited Herzog to Grant's Farm a few days earlier to offer him the job. "I was impressed that he thought enough of me to ask me," said Herzog, "but I didn't know if I was ready to get off the field … to come here in the wintertime and sit behind a desk every day." He talked it over with Mary Lou and came to the conclusion that being GM would give him the best opportunity to implement his vision for the team. The uncertainties of an outside hire also factored in the decision. "I feel I'm the right guy for the job," said Herzog. "I don't know how anybody could be better qualified for it than me."[33] Busch announced the deal in a written statement, citing Herzog's previous experience in the front office of the Mets. "As soon as the general manager position became open, we began to consider him immediately as an obvious candidate," wrote Busch.[34]

Herzog relinquished field manager duties to Red Schoendienst on an interim basis and immediately started utilizing his newfound authority. During his first day on the job, he hashed out a six-year, $3.5-million deal with reliable starter and soon-to-be free agent Bob Forsch. Some players heard the news of Herzog's promotion while driving to the ballpark, while others did not find out until they arrived at the stadium. He received universal support from his players.

Under the new front office alignment, Busch attorney Lou Susman would help write contracts, but Herzog was given ultimate control over personnel decisions. When it came to the hiring of a permanent field manager, Susman said the organization would like to hire someone "just like Whitey."[35] Herzog's first choice was Gene Mauch, who had earned his admiration and respect when the two managed against each other in the American League. However, Mauch had just resigned from the Twins' post and was not ready to jump into another managerial job. Just as he had dismissed the possibility of taking the GM job, Herzog shot down any notion that he would assume the dual role of field manager and general manager. "I don't think a manager should know what a player's salary is," he told the *St. Louis Post-Dispatch*.[36]

Herzog promptly got to work familiarizing himself with the organization's young talent, going on the road to watch Triple-A Springfield and Double-A Arkansas compete in their respective league playoffs. He was particularly impressed by prospects Tom Herr and Andy Rincon. Herr filled in admirably for Templeton at shortstop in September, hitting .337 and putting himself in the conversation for a more prominent role in 1981. Rincon, a right-handed pitcher, had what Herzog assessed was the most promising arm in the system and was given a big-league audition for the season's final weeks. There was one problem. Rincon, a California native, was already driving back home before the Cardinals could notify him of his promotion. As he cruised down a Texas highway at 72 miles per hour—well over the speed limit of 55—Rincon saw the flashing lights of a police car in his rearview mirror. In the Lonestar State, traffic violations resulted in an immediate appearance in court before a judge. "You're the guy we've been looking for," said the judge. "Here, call this number." A flummoxed Rincon dialed the number and Whitey Herzog answered. "Report to Philadelphia as soon as you can," he said. "We want to see what you can do."[37] When the judge found out he was going to the big leagues, he cut Rincon some slack and fined him only $23. Rincon made a strong first impression, spinning a five-hitter against the Cubs in his major-league debut and winning three of his four starts down the stretch.

The Cardinals went 18–19 under Schoendienst to finish the season 74–88, good for fourth place and 17 games behind the division-leading Phillies, who edged the Expos by one game. Team rules became lax during the season's final weeks, as evidenced by one veteran bringing a tumbler full of vodka on the team bus during the final road trip. Rick Hummel of the *St. Louis Post-Dispatch* equated Schoendienst's role to that of a substitute teacher.[38]

Reminiscent of the 1970s, the Cardinals had little to celebrate except for individual accomplishments. Templeton and Hernandez remained neck and neck with Cubs first baseman Bill Buckner for the batting title in the season's final days. In the end, Buckner (.324) beat out Hernandez (.321) and Templeton (.319). Former Cardinal Bake McBride finished fourth while Simmons (.303) and Hendrick (.302) also finished in the top ten. Ken Oberkfell and Dane Iorg also topped .300 but did not have enough at-bats to qualify for the batting title. "When you've got six hitters .300 or better and when you lead the league in hitting and runs scored, and yet finish 14 games under .500, something is not only wrong. Someone has to go," wrote Bob Broeg in the *St. Louis Post-Dispatch*.[39]

While the Cardinal positions players littered the league leaderboard, the team's pitchers were nowhere to be found. As a team, St. Louis finished last in the league in ERA (3.93), saves (27), and strikeouts. Only two pitchers—Forsch and Vuckovich—topped 130 innings and recorded double-digit wins.

The Cardinals' 18–30 record in one-run games highlighted the need for an upgrade at the back end of the bullpen. In the waning days of the season, Herzog indicated relief pitching would be a priority. "We could win it next year if we get the bullpen straightened out," said Herzog optimistically. Though he would not declare any specific player as off-limits in trade talks, he conceded that Templeton was "as untouchable as anybody."[40] Hernandez, who was rumored to be a potential trade candidate, stated his preference to stay in St. Louis but agreed with Herzog's assessment for the need of relief help. "I would trade somebody for a stopper," said Hernandez. "All the teams who win have them."[41]

Weeks of speculation followed surrounding who would be hired as field manager. Names such as Dick Williams, Dick Howser, and Don Zimmer were bandied about, but in the end, Herzog named himself to his old post in an announcement on October 24. Serving the concurrent role of GM and field manager was an uncommon practice. Since the days of Connie Mack, who owned and managed the Philadelphia Athletics for decades, only Paul Owens had assumed both jobs with the Phillies for a brief period in 1972. Busch and Herzog had discussed the possibility at an earlier meeting. When Herzog decided he would fill both duties, the search turned to someone who could serve as his executive assistant and handle tasks such as contracts, monitoring the waiver wire, and trade negotiations. Bing Devine was offered the job, but by then he was entrenched with the St. Louis Football Cardinals. So, Herzog hired Joe McDonald, whom he had worked with in the Mets organization.

Early in the offseason, Herzog re-signed Jim Kaat and added a pair of minor-league prospects, pitcher John Stuper and catcher Glenn Brummer, to the 40-man roster. Herzog also spent time laying the groundwork for a trade with the Padres involving Rollie Fingers. Because the 34-year-old closer had only one year remaining on his contract, Herzog insisted that a contract extension be ironed out before agreeing to a trade. One rumored package had the Cards sending five players—including Terry Kennedy and Herr—to the San Diego.

Herzog selected Dave Winfield and Darrell Porter in the November free agent reentry draft. The system, put in place in 1976, limited the number of free agents that teams could negotiate with in order to prevent big-market clubs from hoarding players.* The potential addition of Porter, Herzog's former catcher in Kansas City, could serve as an insurance policy in case Simmons and Kennedy were needed to acquire pitching. Winfield indicated he had no desire to play for a club in the Midwest, rendering his selection moot.

Simmons was one of the game's top hitting catchers, bus Herzog was not enamored with his defense. "Teddy is a switch-hitter with a lifetime batting average of near .300, but he gave up a lot of passed balls and couldn't throw worth a damn," Herzog bluntly wrote in retrospect.[42] The skipper observed that teams tended to steal bases off Simmons rather than attempt to sacrifice runners over, giving them three opportunities to score instead of two. Indeed, Simmons had allowed 116 stolen bases in 1980 and threw out only 31 percent of runners attempting to steal. In contrast, Porter had posted a 46 percent caught stealing percentage in his prior two seasons with the Royals.

Besides Porter's strong arm, Herzog had appreciated his leadership and ability to handle a pitching staff after coming to the Royals in 1977. The left-hand hitting backstop could also hold his own at the plate, as evidenced by a career .251 batting average and .356 on base percentage at the time. He did not come without baggage, however. Porter had missed the

---

*The free agent reentry draft would be scrapped in 1981 and replaced by a free agent compensation draft.

first month of the 1980 season after checking himself into treatment for drug and alcohol addiction. "Knowing Darrell as I did, I was sure that if he said he was okay, he was okay," recalled Herzog.[43]

On the eve of the Winter Meetings in Dallas, the Cardinals announced the surprise signing of Porter to a five-year, $3.5 million-dollar pact, making him the highest paid catcher in the game. Herzog's idea was to move Simmons to first base and Hernandez to left field. "I like Ted Simmons," said Herzog. "I think he's a winner. Not many guys on this team understand what I am trying to do here, but he is one of them. But.... Darrell Porter is my catcher."[44] Both Simmons and Hernandez indicated they were willing to go along with the plan.

Weeks of trade talks culminated with a flurry of activity at the start of the meetings on December 8. The first shoe to drop was the Cardinals' much-speculated acquisition of Fingers from the Padres as part of a massive 11-player deal. Besides Fingers, St. Louis received catcher-first baseman Gene Tenace, left-handed pitcher Bob Shirley, and a player to be named later (catcher Bob Geren) for seven players: Kennedy, pitchers John Urrea, John Littlefield, Kim Seaman, and Al Olmstead, infielder Mike Phillips, and catcher Steve Swisher. "At least I'll be catching the same pitching staff," quipped Kennedy.[45]

Fingers was a five-time All-Star, three-time world champion, and one of the game's premiere late-inning relievers. Yet, there was another pitcher Herzog coveted more: Bruce Sutter. "I hadn't given up on getting [Sutter], but with Fingers in the fold, I knew I had some insurance if the deal didn't come off," reflected Herzog.[46]

Cubs GM Bob Kennedy, whose son Terry had just been traded by St. Louis, knew of Herzog's strong desire for Sutter. He wanted three prospects for the all-star reliever: Herr, Leon Durham, and Ty Waller. Herzog did not want to part with the fleet-footed Herr and instead talked Kennedy into taking the comparably slower Ken Reitz, who agreed to waive his no-trade clause for $50,000.[47] Within a matter of hours, Herzog had acquired the game's two best relief pitchers. With Sutter on board, Fingers could be used as a trade chip.

Just when things were falling into place, Herzog's plan of moving Simmons to first and Hernandez to the outfield fell apart when Simmons had a change of heart. His agent, LaRue Harcourt, asked that his client be traded to a team where he could catch and DH—in other words, an American League team. "I think that [Simmons] was afraid that Keith was so good at first—one of the best I had ever seen—that if he made a mistake people would compare him to Keith," said Herzog, looking back.[48] Harcourt also made it clear that Simmons, who had 10 years of big-league service and the right to veto any deal, would need to be compensated if traded. "I think we can win with Ted Simmons at first base," said Herzog at the time. "But if he wants to be traded, we'll trade him."[49]

Herzog asked around and initially found two AL clubs willing to deal for the all-star catcher: Oakland and Milwaukee. Simmons, however, did not want to play on the West Coast, leaving the Brewers as Herzog's only option. After exchanging names with Brewers GM Harry Dalton, Herzog agreed to part with Simmons, Fingers, and Vuckovich but insisted that the Brewers' top prospect—outfielder David Green—be part of the return. When Yankees owner George Steinbrenner heard about the Brewers' impending coup, he told Herzog, "You can't make that deal with the Brewers. You'll trade them into the division championship!"[50] Steinbrenner swooped in and made an effort to land Simmons and Vuckovich by offering a package centered around Ron Guidry and Ron Davis, but Herzog preferred the return from Milwaukee. In the end, the Cardinals sent Simmons, Fingers, and Vuckovich to the Brewers for Green, outfielder Sixto Lezcano, and pitchers Lary Sorensen and Dave LaPoint. Milwaukee also agreed to supplement Simmons' current three-year contract by an additional $250,000 per year. The Brewers asked the Cardinals to pay part of the sum, but Herzog shot down that possibility. Dalton was reluctant to include Green, considered one of the best prospects in baseball, but Herzog insisted that without him there would be no deal. Not wanting to risk losing out on Simmons to the rival Yankees, Dalton conceded.

It was an earthshaking trade. Though Sorensen was three years younger than Vuckovich, they were both solid starting pitchers with nearly identical career win-loss records. Removing them from the equation, the Cardinals had ostensibly traded two of the best players in baseball at their respective positions—not to mention future Hall of Famers—for an above-average corner outfielder (Lezcano) and two prospects (LaPoint and Green). Many in the industry lauded the Brewers' end of the deal and felt the talent heading to Milwaukee—a third-place team in 1980—made them a top contender in the AL.

When it was all said and done, Herzog had traded 13 players from the Cardinals' 40-man roster within a matter of days. "I might be back home fishing by June if this doesn't work out," he said at the time. "But we had to make changes. This club hasn't won anything in 13 years."[51]

Besides turning over the roster, Herzog also made changes to the coaching staff. Chuck Hiller, a former coach with Herzog in Texas and Kansas City, was hired to coach third base. Hiller's claim to fame was hitting the first grand slam by a National Leaguer in World Series history, a feat he accomplished in Game Four of the 1962 Fall Classic. Hal Lanier, whose father Max pitched for St. Louis in the 1940s, was promoted to first-base coach from Springfield, where he had piloted the Triple-A club to the American Association title in 1980. Hub Kittle, in his sixth decade of professional baseball, was brought in to replace Claude Osteen as pitching coach. Red Schoendienst (bench coach) and Dave Ricketts (bullpen coach) would be holdovers.

"By God, the Cardinals were ready," Herzog wrote years later. "They hadn't won a damned thing since 1968, so I figured what the hell. We might as well shake things up and see what happens."[52] What happened next was one of the more bizarre seasons in baseball history.

3

1981

The Bearded Prophet and a Split Season

Whitey Herzog hoped his offseason wheeling and dealing would position the Cardinals for playoff contention in 1981, but the possibility of a players' strike left some question as to whether there would even be a postseason. The players and owners had been embroiled in several years of bitter labor relations surrounding free agency and the corresponding hot-button issue of compensation, which remained a point of contention as the season approached.

Until 1976, players were bound to their respective teams by baseball's reserve clause. Players were essentially property of the team they played for until they were released or traded. When it came to contract negotiations, a player's only leverage was to hold out. Curt Flood's attempt to defy the system had been unsuccessful, but it galvanized the players' union, under executive director Marvin Miller, to further the cause. Pitchers Andy Messersmith and Dave McNally challenged the reserve clause by playing the 1974 season without a contract, which the players' union felt entitled them to be free agents the following year. The case ultimately went before an arbitrator, who sided with the union, thus paving the way for the establishment of free agency for players with six years of service time at the end of the 1976 season.

At the same time, a compensation system was implemented whereby teams received a first- or second-round pick in exchange for losing a free agent. That was not enough to dissuade some teams from paying big bucks to lure players in. In the four years after free agency was enacted, player earnings nearly tripled. When the collective bargaining agreement came up for renewal in 1980, the owners sought to revamp compensation as a way of keeping free-spending owners in check and suppressing soaring salaries. Under their proposed plan, teams losing a free agent would be entitled to a player of equal caliber from the team signing that player.

3. 1981—The Bearded Prophet and a Split Season

While hashing out the 1980 CBA, the two sides averted a strike but failed to find middle ground on the contentious matter of compensation. Instead, they agreed to push the issue to 1981 while a committee of two players (Sal Bando and Bob Boone) and two executives (Frank Cashen and Harry Dalton) studied its implications. There was an agreement in place that if the two sides could not reach a compromise based on reports from the committee, the owners had the ability to unilaterally enforce their own re-entry draft plan in February 1981. The owners' convoluted plan dictated that if a free agent was chosen by eight or more teams in the postseason reentry draft and ranked among the top 50 percent at their position, the team that signed that player would have to give up a player from its roster. Teams could protect anywhere from 15 to 18 players, leaving the rest of the roster up for grabs. As part of the basic agreement from 1980, if the owners took the step of implementing their plan, the players had the ability to reopen talks on free agent compensation and strike by June 1, 1981.

Commissioner Bowie Kuhn tried to sell the owners' plan at the Winter Meetings by pointing to the fact that 15 out of the 26 major-league teams allegedly lost money in 1979. "Foolish player contracts signed by a few have aggravated the situation," crowed Kuhn.[1] A rise in league-wide attendance from 29 million in 1975 to 43 million in 1980, not to mention new revenue streams from the emergence of cable television, suggested that the owners were a long way from financial ruin.[2] Kuhn and the owners also argued that free agency was creating a competitive imbalance, though holes could easily be poked in that argument as well. For example, not one of the four division winners from 1979 had repeated in 1980.

Kuhn warned that the only way forward was for players to give in. "Bowie, they'll get compensation over my dead body," retorted Miller, who believed the owners' proposed plan would serve as a de facto salary cap.[3] The players' union set a new strike deadline of May 29 if there was no agreement reached.

The owners were positioned to weather the financial implications of a strike—at least temporarily. They had accumulated a $15 million mutual assistance fund and took out a $50 million strike insurance policy from Lloyd's of London at the cost of $2 million. Underwriters were unaware of the fact that the owners could essentially trigger a strike by installing their own compensation plan. The policy would kick in after 152 games were canceled and would reimburse owners $100,000 for each game lost until the fund was exhausted during the first week of August.

Despite the ongoing labor dispute, it was business as usual between the white lines as teams reconvened at their respective spring training sites in preparation for the 1981 campaign. At the Cardinals' camp in St. Petersburg, Florida, Herzog addressed his reconfigured roster on the first full day of workouts and emphasized the need for improved baserunning, pointing out that St. Louis led the league in hitting the previous year but somehow managed to score three runs or fewer in 79 games. He also mentioned the 17 games in which the team recorded double-digit hits and scored two runs or fewer. "How does that happen?" he asked. "I'll tell you. It's because you don't bust your rear going down to first base. It's because you don't break up double plays. It's because you don't bust your rear going from first to third. You stand out there shooting the bull."[4]

With so many new faces, the Cardinals were—as the *St. Louis Post-Dispatch* put it in its season preview—a team "shrouded in mystery."[5] Besides Darrell Porter and the plethora of players acquired via trade, Herzog brought in a pair of Steves—Busby and Braun—to compete as non-roster invitees. Both had played for Herzog in Kansas City. Busby won 56 games with the Royals between 1973 and 1975 and was attempting a years-long comeback from rotator cuff surgery after becoming the first major leaguer to undergo the novel procedure. Ultimately, he would fail to regain his all-star form and was cut at the end of camp. Braun, who hit .284 as a semi-regular with the Twins from 1971 to 1976 before being drafted by the expansion Seattle Mariners, had been converted to a pinch-hitting specialist by Herzog in Kansas City. Later in the spring, the Redbirds signed Julio González, a glove-first infielder who had hit .235 in four seasons with Houston. He could reliably fill in at any infield position, versatility that was lacking outside of utilityman Mike Ramsey.

A worrisome development cropped up early on in camp. Porter, the catcher whom Herzog had just committed to for five years, was suffering from stabbing pain in his shoulder each time he lifted his right arm. Because of his inability to throw, Porter was primarily limited to DH during Grapefruit League play while receiving cortisone injections, acupuncture, and physical therapy. The ailment emphasized the importance of newly-acquired Gene Tenace, who had 12 big-league seasons and three championships under his belt. He had a reputation as a tough-as-nails gamer who called a good game from behind the plate. The additions of Porter and Tenace created a positive attitude change in the clubhouse that was palpable. George Hendrick, a former teammate of Tenace with the Athletics, told Tito Landrum, "I feel the way that I did when I was with Oakland and we were winning championships. I sense that kind of attitude in here."[6] Tenace, who possessed an outspoken style of leadership, told reporters during camp: "I don't know how it was here before, but when you lose, you lose as a group. I don't like it when clubs lose and after the game the jukeboxes start going on. It'll be different. I don't believe in that."[7]

3. 1981—The Bearded Prophet and a Split Season

With Ken Reitz jettisoned to Chicago, Herzog was able to move Ken Oberkfell from the keystone to the hot corner, opening a starting role for Tom Herr while adding more speed to the lineup. Garry Templeton and Keith Hernandez remained stalwarts at shortstop and first base, respectively. New acquisition Sixto Lezcano, coming off a down year with Milwaukee, was expected to play left field with Tony Scott in center and Hendrick in right. Dane Iorg, Landrum, and Braun provided outfield depth. The highly-touted but inexperienced David Green spent most of camp with the minor leaguers and was earmarked for Triple A.

A combination of injuries and inexperience left the composition of Herzog's pitching staff uncertain as spring training unfolded. John Fulgham, who followed Busby as one of the early recipients of rotator cuff surgery, was already lost for the year. Mark Littell was coming off elbow surgery and Bob Sykes had missed a large chunk of the 1980 season due to a blood clot in his shoulder. Both struggled during the spring slate. Two youngsters on the 40-man roster—John Stuper and Dave LaPoint—had strong showings but were ticketed for Springfield to gain more experience. This left Herzog with an unimposing starting rotation of Bob Forsch, Lary Sorensen, Silvio Martínez, and Andy Rincon. Ex-Padre Bob Shirley and rookie John Martin competed for the final spot in the five-man rotation. The one certainty heading into the season was who would be pitching in the late innings of tight ballgames. Bruce Sutter was the lockdown closer Herzog had long desired.

By the time Bruce Sutter pulled on his nylon Cardinals jersey for the first time, he had already built an impressive résumé. In his five major-league seasons with the Cubs, he was a four-time All-Star, Cy Young Award winner, and had led the league in saves twice despite pitching for a losing club. To that point in his career, Sutter had struck out nearly a batter per inning using a pitch he made famous—the split-fingered fastball, also known as the splitter. He learned the dominant pitch from another hurler who donned Cardinal red decades earlier.

Howard Bruce Sutter was born in the southeastern Pennsylvania town of Lancaster and inherited a modest, even-keeled personality from his father, an accountant. Sutter led Donegal High School to the county title as a senior in 1970 and impressed scouts enough that the Washington Senators selected him in the 21st round of the June amateur draft. Sutter was only 17 years old, however, and rules at the time prohibited players from signing until the age of 18. He enrolled at Old Dominion University, but he had a much greater affinity for baseball over books, and shortly thereafter he dropped out. Back in his hometown, he went to work at a printing company and pitched for a Lancaster semipro outfit called Hippie's Raiders, where he caught the attention of Ralph DiLullo, a Cubs scout. DiLullo, who noticed Sutter's unusually large hands, had an inkling about the young hurler and signed him to a contract with a bonus of only $500.[8]

Sutter was assigned to the Cubs' rookie level team in the Gulf Coast League in 1972. He tried to learn a slider, but after pitching in only two games developed right elbow pain that halted his season. His problem was a pinched ulnar nerve in the elbow, and that offseason he underwent surgery to decompress the nerve. Sutter paid for the procedure out of his own pocket without telling the Cubs for fear of getting released. When he arrived at spring training in 1973, he could not even throw the ball from the mound to the catcher. The Cubs were about to cut the 20-year-old when he pulled up his sleeve and showed his surgical scar. They had a change of heart and decided to give him a chance to work his way back.[9]

The Cubs assigned Sutter to their Single-A affiliate in Quincy, Illinois, for the 1973 season. He mostly served the role of mop-up reliever and posted a pedestrian 4.13 ERA. The Cubs at the time employed Fred Martin as pitching coach for the entire farm system. Martin, who toiled in the minor leagues as a pitcher for 17 years, toed the rubber in parts of three seasons for the Cardinals between 1946 and 1950. His big-league career could have been much longer, but he missed four seasons serving during World War II and then was banned from the majors for a time after jumping his contract to play in the Mexican League.

Martin, remembered Sutter, "was from Oklahoma, and he was always real suntanned, looked like his skin was dried out. Looked like one of those Old West cowboys, always had a cigarette hanging out of his mouth."[10] Martin paid visits to each Cubs affiliate once a month, offering advice and then leaving his pitchers to work on their craft until his next visit. He showed all of the organization's minor-league pitchers how to throw the splitter, though most were not able to master the pitch, which is thrown with the ball gripped between the index and middle fingers. Because of Sutter's unusually long phalanges, the pitch felt natural to him and broke right away. "I could see immediately what it could do," explained Sutter. "It was just a question of getting consistent with it…. I had to learn it. It was either that pitch or sayonara."[11]

Following Sutter's middling performance at Quincy, the Cubs were again on the verge of cutting him during spring training in 1974, but Martin advocated for his pupil. Cubs brass let Sutter know he needed to impress with their Single-A team Key West, or he would be released following the June draft when an influx of young players would need roster spots. "The thing about Bruce's demeanor, then and now, is that he's at his best when his back is against the wall," recalled minor-league teammate

3. 1981—The Bearded Prophet and a Split Season

Mike Krukow. "That's why he's perfectly suited for his position. He went to Key West and dazzled them."[12]

Sutter harnessed control of the splitter in the Florida Keys, striking out 50 batters in 40 innings while posting a sparkling 1.35 ERA. After recovering from a knee injury, he moved up to Double-A Midland in the Texas League, where he was equally effective. He advanced to the big leagues during the 1976 season and before long established himself as the Cubs' closer, or fireman in 1970s parlance. In that era, it was common for closers to earn saves by throwing two or three innings. As such, late-inning relievers routinely topped 100 innings in a season. In 1977—Sutter's best season statistically—he struck out 129 batters in 107⅓ innings while sporting a microscopic 1.34 ERA. In his Cy Young season of 1979, he tied an NL record with 37 saves despite the Cubs being sub-.500.

An example of Sutter's character came late in the 1979 campaign. He was approaching the saves record, but with a limited number of games remaining on the schedule it was not assured he would get the chance to reach the milestone. Saves were only credited if a reliever closed the game with a lead of three runs or fewer—or if he pitched the final three innings with his team ahead, regardless of the score. Cubs manager Herman Franks told Sutter he wanted to put him in for the final three innings to make sure he notched a save. "He refused to do it," remembered Cubs catcher Barry Foote. "He wanted to do under normal circumstances with the game on the line."[13]

Sutter's dominance could be squarely attributed to the splitter he learned from Martin, who became like a second father to the young pitcher. The two remained close, and Sutter was at Martin's side when he died of cancer in 1979. The splitter baffled hitters, even when they were expecting it. The pitch was thrown with the arm speed

The unflappable Bruce Sutter used his famed split-fingered fastball to shut down opposing hitters in the late innings (National Baseball Hall of Fame and Museum, Cooperstown, NY).

of a fastball, but the ball traveled at around 80 miles per hour with devastating downward movement. "I had never seen a pitch like that ever—nor had anybody, because his was thrown with incredible vertical variance," described Ted Simmons.[14]

From a hitter's perspective, a Sutter splitter that appeared to be head-high would sink to the strike zone, and a pitch that looked to be down the middle would drop to the dirt. "Every time the hitter took it, it was a strike. And every time they swung at it, it was a ball. It was uncanny," recalled Foote, who caught Sutter for two seasons in Chicago.[15]

Other players and reporters often asked Sutter how he threw his untouchable pitch. Spilling the beans could have given others a competitive advantage, so he abstained from revealing too much. "I know for a fact he always told 'em something different than what he actually did," recalled Foote with a chuckle. "He didn't want anyone else to perfect that pitch. I'd listen the him explain it, and I knew that's not really what he was doing."[16]

Eventually, use of the splitter would become more widespread in the game, though decades later Sutter's is still considered perhaps the best of all time. His presence in the Cardinals bullpen allowed Herzog to sleep a little more soundly. After his quest for a championship with the Royals had been thwarted repeatedly by shaky relief pitching, the skipper had finally procured the lockdown reliever he had longed for.

Sutter and his new teammates finished spring training with a major-league worst record 9–17 record. Inconsistent pitching resulted in a 4.55 team ERA, and lackluster hitting translated to a .243 batting average during Grapefruit League play. The games began to count on April 11 when the Cardinals opened the season at home against the Philadelphia Phillies. It was St. Louis fans' first look at the man who replaced their beloved "Simba," as Ted Simmons was known. Rather than giving Darrell Porter a warm reception, the home crowd greeted him with a chorus of boos. "Terry and Ted, We Love You, Wherever You Are," read a large banner hanging in the stadium, in reference to the two departed catchers. It would not be the last time Porter was met with derision from the home crowd. The game featured a rare triple play turned by the Cards, but Mike Schmidt's three-run homer off Bob Forsch supplied all the runs Dick Ruthven and the Phillies needed.

Herzog turned to Sutter for a three-inning save in the second game. The love that fans failed to show Porter was provided to Sutter in spades. Pitching to chants of his first name, Bruce!, Bruce!, the Redbirds' new stopper retired 9 of the 10 batters he faced, including four strikeouts, to record the save. His split-fingered fastball was so nasty that Schmidt—the

National League's reigning MVP—tried to bunt his way on. Herzog was impressed at how easily Sutter navigated the vaunted lineup of the defending champions. "The Phillies aren't exactly the Fort Wayne Daisies," he said afterwards.[17]

The Cardinals lost to the Mets in their next game—a forgettable contest in which they committed five errors and walked eight—but then rattled off eight straight wins. During the streak, the pitching staff allowed only 13 runs and remained well rested thanks to several rainouts. The Cards finished the abbreviated April slate with a 9–3 record. Sutter was a key contributor to the club's the early success, allowing only one hit in his first five outings while converting all four of his save opportunities. "There have been some great Cardinals relievers … but none matched the bearded prophet," wrote Bob Broeg in the *St. Louis Post-Dispatch*.[18]

Because of the weather-related postponements, St. Louis finished April having played six fewer games than the Phillies and four less than the Expos, who equaled St. Louis' .750 winning percentage with a 12–4 mark. Montreal had fallen just short of making the playoffs the previous two seasons but were well positioned to break through in 1981 because of established stars Andre Dawson and Gary Carter and a young stud named Tim Raines. Dawson, winner of the 1977 Rookie of the Year Award, had blossomed into one of the game's elite position players. He possessed the ability to hit for average and power, played a graceful outfield, and was a threat on the basepaths. Though playing on Olympic Stadium's rock-hard surface had taken its toll on his knees, he was still a force to be reckoned with. Carter, an ebullient and curly-haired all-star catcher known as "The Kid," usually wore a smile and earned his nickname for the way he played the game. But it was the rookie, Raines, who was turning heads early in 1981. The stout speedster hit .355 and averaged a stolen base per game in April.

In the AL, Billy Martin's Oakland Athletics, playing a similar style of baseball to Herzog's Cardinals, tore out of the gate with 18 wins in their first 21 games. Like the Expos, the A's had a lightning-fast table setter at the top of the batting order. Rickey Henderson, an Oakland native, had burst on the scene in 1980 with 100 stolen bases. Oakland's starting rotation featured five workhorses who were each coming off 200-inning seasons, including 22-game winner Mike Norris. After losing 108 games only two years earlier, the A's looked like a shoe-in for the playoffs.

The biggest story of the young season, however, came out of Los Angeles by way of rural Mexico. Dodgers pitcher Fernando Valenzuela, a 20-year-old lefty, was baseball's biggest sensation. The portly hurler with an unorthodox windup and unhittable screwball started the season with 36 scoreless innings. The young phenom attracted huge crowds wherever he pitched. In his first visit to New York on May 8, the scuffling Mets, averaging less than 12,000 fans a game, set up extra ticket booths to meet the demand of walkup customers. A crowd of nearly 40,000 showed up to watch Valenzuela throw a 1–0 shutout, in the process lowering his ERA to an absurd 0.29 through seven starts.

The Cardinals posted a mediocre 14–14 record in May, in part because of injuries to two important cogs. Starting pitcher Andy Rincon, who had won three of four decisions, suffered a broken arm on May 9, a result of being struck by a Phil Garner line drive. Darrell Porter, meanwhile, was prescribed two weeks of rest after a second opinion with Dr. Frank Jobe for his persistently sore shoulder revealed a rotator cuff tear. To fill their roster spots, southpaw John Martin and catcher Glenn Brummer were summoned from Triple A.

Besides Forsch, who remained effective despite nursing a sore shoulder of his own, the Cardinal rotation remained suspect. Sorensen and Shirley started a combined 8–0 but then lost their next seven decisions. Martínez was 1–4 with a 4.71 ERA through his first eight starts. The Cards had Sutter waiting to nail down the late innings but opposing teams could neutralize the fireman by scoring early and often against the starters.

As the season marched along, ongoing negotiations between the players' union and owners failed to make any progress. The union indicated a willingness to compromise and allow for free agent compensation from a pool of players rather than the signing team directly losing a player, but the owners rejected the idea. The union asked the owners to open their books to prove they were in the dire financial state they claimed to be. When they refused, Marvin Miller filed a case with the National Labor Relations Board with the hope that an injunction would force the owners to share financial data, postpone their unilaterally imposed compensation plan, and push the issue to 1982. With the two sides at an impasse, the only hope at avoiding a strike was in the hands of the United States government. "It's not two rams butting heads anymore. It's two rams standing off to the side making a plea to a rational third party. And I assume a federal judge would be rational," said Ted Simmons.[19] Bob Sykes, the Cardinals' union rep, was frequently approached by teammates wondering if they should start looking for other jobs. On May 28, a federal judge granted a preliminary injunction that froze the dispute between players and owners for one week.

In addition to the labor issue, Garry Templeton was making headlines with subpar play and eyebrow-raising comments. By the end of May, he was hitting a substandard .258, led the Redbirds with 32 strikeouts, and had played shaky defense. Templeton had also ticked off Herzog by voicing his displeasure at not batting leadoff. The skipper had a closed-door

3. 1981—The Bearded Prophet and a Split Season   41

meeting with his disgruntled shortstop on May 29 in Philadelphia. Rick Hummel described the one-on-one as a both "a pep talk and a chewing out" for what Herzog perceived as a less than adequate effort in recent games.[20]

On May 31, the Cardinals lost to nemesis Steve Carlton for the 10th consecutive time. Afterwards, Templeton remarked that he would like to come back in a similar fashion to Carlton. When a reporter asked him to elaborate, Templeton did just that: "I'd like to be traded. Put Tony Scott and me in a package deal and send us to San Diego for Ozzie [Smith] and [Gene] Richards." Going further, the shortstop said, "I'm serious. This organization has had enough of me. I'm tired of this. I want to go somewhere else. Send me to the West Coast. Back home." When Herzog got wind of Templeton's comments, he kept his response brief: "We'll see."[21] After Templeton's quote hit the press, Smith asked Padres GM Jack McKeon about it. "[McKeon] told me there was nothing to it," said Smith. "I've got a no-cut, no-trade contract so I've got the last say anyway. And St. Louis is too hot."[22]

Templeton backpedaled his comments the next day. "The trouble with the press is that if you don't talk to them, they get on your case—and if you do talk them, you are either misquoted or misunderstood or exaggerated. Sure, I'd like to play on the West Coast where I live—who wouldn't?"[23] He added that any differences he had with his manager could be worked out. Herzog continued to insist that he had no plans to trade his cornerstone infielder, who was in the second year of a six-year contract. Templeton then went out and responded to boos from the Busch Stadium crowd with three hits and a pair of RBIs against Montreal.

The drama was far from over, however. Just a few days later, the Expos and Cards, fighting to keep pace with the first-place Phillies, wrapped up their four-game series with an afternoon affair. Templeton declared he was too tired to play. "I guess he doesn't like playing day games after night games," said Herzog when asked why the shortstop asked out of the lineup.[24] His teammates were furious, and there was building tension in the clubhouse. To make matters worse, Mike Ramsey—Templeton's replacement at shortstop—suffered a broken bone in his hand during the game.

The following day, St. Louis made a trade, though not the one Templeton proposed. The Cards sent Scott and his .227 batting average to Houston for right-handed pitcher Joaquín Andújar. Scott was expendable, particularly given that he had won his arbitration case and nearly tripled his salary before the 1981 season despite coming off a season in which he hit .251 with zero home runs. Andújar, a two-time All-Star with sporadic success, was described as "talented, competitive, temperamental, and eccentric."[25] He was known to clash with managers and had fought with opponents and teammates alike. However, Hub Kittle had managed Andújar for five years in the Dominican Winter League and felt he knew how to handle him. He was expected to provide pitching depth as a middle reliever and spot starter.

Any hope that a players' strike would be avoided was dashed on June 10 when a judge denied the union's injunction request, ruling that it was "without reasonable cause that the owners committed unfair labor practices." In a 23-page document, the judge called the union's request for the owners' financial data a "tactic" and declared that free agent compensation was not an economic issue. "The entire decision was delusional," wrote Jeff Katz in his book *Split Season: 1981*.[26] The clock was ticking; the players' union had the ability to strike within 48 hours of the ruling.

On June 11, Silvio Martínez outdueled Valenzuela—fresh off a White House visit with Ronald Reagan and Mexican president José López Portillo—in front of 39,250 fans at Busch Stadium. After winning his first eight decisions, Valenzuela had come down to earth, going 1–4 with a 6.16 ERA in his next six starts. Following the game, players learned that the strike was on after last-ditch negotiations proved unfruitful. For the first time in major-league history, there would be a midseason work stoppage. The Redbirds (30–20) were in second place—one and a half games behind Philadelphia—when the season was halted. The Cards still had played five fewer games than the Phillies due to early-season rainouts that had yet to be made up. Whether there would be anymore baseball in 1981 was anyone's guess.

The owners painted Marvin Miller as the villain and suggested that an agreement could have been reached without his interference. Miller allowed the owners to prove it by stepping aside and leaving negotiations to the players, who were led by a quartet of Bob Boone, Doug DeCinces, Mark Belanger, and Steve Rogers. Federal mediator Kenneth Moffett called a series of meetings between the players and owners during the first week of the stoppage. The owners underestimated the players' resolve.

"The players weren't smooth or eloquent, but the owners confused that with being unintelligent," wrote Katz. "They never quite realized how well thought out the players' ideas were. Miller's great strength had been in education. He didn't lead them around by the nose and would never have gone against what they wanted, even if he thought it was wrong. Miller wore blinders; his sole purpose was what was best for the players and creating in them a principled group."[27]

Once the strike began, the players—except for a small minority who had a stipulation in their contract—forfeited their paychecks. Bruce Sutter lost $5,000 per day in wages.[28] Less established players making the league minimum salary of $32,500 had less to lose—but also less in their bank accounts to start with. The owners, on the other hand, could more easily withstand the lost revenue thanks to their shrewd purchase of a $50 million strike insurance policy. The windfall would last until August 5, and owners were sure the players would cave well before then. Besides the financial implications, early August also served as a timetable by which the strike needed to be resolved in order for players to get back in shape and complete a meaningful number of games.

While major-league stadiums sat empty, the minor leagues played on. Herzog took the opportunity to pay visits to Little Rock and Springfield to see prospects Andy Rincon, David Green, Dave LaPoint, and John Stuper. Rincon had been astutely optioned to the minors before the strike, a move that allowed the young hurler to pitch down on the farm once his arm healed and potentially be in top form if and when the strike ended. Coaches Hiller, Ricketts, and Lanier were sent to work with the Cardinals' Single-A affiliates.

Players scattered to their homes as if it were the offseason. Ken Oberkfell planned to mow his lawn and do some fishing. Bob Sykes took a job as a car salesman. Kansas City Royal Clint Hurdle served drinks as a bartender while Richie Hebner of the Tigers labored as a gravedigger. Dodger Ron Cey landed an acting gig in a low-budget horror film called *Q: The Winged Serpent*. Many less-established big leaguers took factory and construction jobs to make ends meet. Then there was Giants slugger Jack Clark, who had inked a lucrative five-year contract and grumbled about having to scrape by to make payments on his Rolls-Royce *and* his Jaguar. Bill "Spaceman" Lee of the Expos took off from Montreal on his bicycle. "I'm off to Toronto ... and after that to Prince Edward Island for the Shakespeare Festival. Then I'm going where there are no telephones or newspapers. I don't want to know when this strike is over," said the free-spirited pitcher.[29]

Without live action to call, Jack Buck and Mike Shannon recreated broadcasts of the Cardinals World Series clinching games from 1946, 1964, and 1967 for KMOX. The San Diego Padres broadcast team of Jerry Coleman and Dave Campbell called fictitious games in front of 3,200 baseball-starved fans in the Jack Murphy Stadium parking lot.[30]

A month into the strike, the players and owners remained at a tense impasse, and Marvin Miller returned to the negotiating table. Americans, meanwhile, were finding other ways to occupy their time. One poll found that 46 percent of respondents did not miss baseball.[31] In mid–July, negotiations moved from New York to Washington, D.C. Pressure was mounting from the federal government to resume the national pastime.

A breakthrough came on July 23 when the owners dropped direct compensation and showed a willingness to adopt the union's plan of a player pool. Behind closed doors, the sides were close to a settlement. At the same time, some impatient players around the league—unaware of the progress in negotiations—spoke out to reporters, indicating some loss of support for the union's cause. Their comments stalled talks as owners sensed that the union might be breaking. The lead player reps called for urgent meetings in Los Angeles and Chicago to hear the players' concerns and provide facts about the negotiations. The 120 players who attended emerged in unanimous support of the union.

A settlement was finally reached on July 31. Under the agreement, a team signing a free agent ranking in the top 30 percent of the league statistically could protect 24 players. Other teams could protect 26 players and the rest went to a compensation pool. Teams losing a ranking free agent got to choose a player from the pool. In the end, the players had forfeited $28 million in wages during the strike. The owners reportedly lost $116 million, though the $44 million received from strike insurance lessened the blow.[32] It was no coincidence that the two sides settled just as the insurance policy was about to run out. Some questioned whether the 50-day work stoppage had been worth it for either side. White Sox owner Jerry Reinsdorf called the strike "inane, insane, and asinine."[33]

The owners had gained little, though some players voiced sentiments of disappointment. "I'm not happy with the settlement," said Bob Forsch. "I'm not militant but I think we should have gone a little longer on the compensation thing. I didn't feel there should be any. We started out that way. We lost our salaries during the strike and [gave up on] compensation. The owners made out a lot better than we did ... we were in a no-win situation."[34] Gene Tenace echoed Forsch's comments: "I don't think it was worth it. This should have been settled a long time ago. A little common sense would have taken care of it."[35]

When the owners met to ratify the deal, Busch tore into his fellow owners. "What did we end up with? If the Cubs lose a player to the Phillies through free agency, then possibly I have the honor of giving the Cubs my 27th best player—marvelous compensation." Busch was one of three owners—joining Clark Griffith of the Twins and Dick Wagner of the Reds—who voted no.

With the strike over, the owners had to decide how to handle the playoffs. Some favored picking up the season where it left off while others, including Kuhn, desired a split-season format where the first-place teams before and after the strike would meet for an extra playoff round. If the first and second half winners were the same team, that club would play the team with the second-best overall record. Proponents of the plan felt that two separate halves would spark more fan interest. After all, the strike had been a disastrous public relations fiasco. The split season would give teams

3. 1981—The Bearded Prophet and a Split Season

who had played poorly in the first half a second chance to salvage the season. Another key factor in the decision was the additional revenue that an extra round of divisional playoffs would bring in. The Cardinals joined the Reds and Phillies as teams who opposed the unconventional structure, but the majority won out. The split season was adopted.

The plans' flaws were immediately evident. First, it would be possible for a team to have the league's best overall record and not make the playoffs. There was also the potential for a scenario in which a team would benefit from losing a game. Katz explained in *Split Season: 1981*: "Take the Yankees and Orioles, scheduled to play on the last day of the year. Suppose the Orioles, second-place finishers behind the Yankees in the first half, were set to finish a close third in the second half behind New York and Boston. If the Yankees trailed the Red Sox by mere percentage points going into the finale, the Orioles, by losing on purpose, could give the Yankees their second title, while ensuring themselves the second-best record and a spot of their own in the postseason."[36]

The Cardinals gathered at Busch Stadium for a brief "summer training" on August 1. In an attempt to earn some goodwill with the fanbase, practices were open to the public at no cost. The Cardinals and Royals met up for a pair of home-and-home exhibition games, the first time the two teams had met outside of spring training. No team was happier to have a clean slate than the underachieving Royals, who were 12 games out of first place when the strike began.

The All-Star Game, which had been wiped out by the work stoppage, was rescheduled for August 9 in Cleveland to kick off the season restart. A record-setting crowd of 72,086 fans flocked to Municipal Stadium. Sutter—the lone representative from the Cardinals—entered in the bottom of the ninth with the NL ahead, 5–4, and retired Frank White to start the inning. With Dave Stieb due up, AL manager Jim Frey found himself out of position players, in part due to Fred Lynn's departure from a knee injury. Frey had no choice but to send the pitcher up to hit. Stieb, who had never stepped foot in a big-league batter's box, struck out on three pitches. Sutter then induced a fly ball off the bat Dave Winfield for the third out to earn the save. It was the NL's 10th straight Midsummer Classic win and 18th out of 19.

The Cardinals started the second half in Philadelphia the next day. Phillies first baseman Pete Rose entered the game tied with Stan Musial as the NL's all-time hits leader. Rose reached on an error by Templeton in his first at-bat and then grounded out in his next two plate appearances versus Forsch. In his fourth at-bat, Rose pulled a Mark Littell slider through the left side of the infield for hit number 3,631 to break Musial's mark. Stan the Man was on hand to congratulate Charlie Hustle. Though Rose's accomplishment grabbed the headlines, the Cardinals won the game, 7–3. The Redbirds showed no signs of rust, belting four home runs, which would account for eight percent of their season total of 50.

St. Louis started the second half 8–5 and were concluding a homestand against the Giants on August 26 when things with the Cardinals' tempestuous shortstop came to a head. It was an afternoon getaway game and Ladies' Day promotion at Busch Stadium. Templeton, back in his preferred leadoff spot post-strike, came to the plate in the bottom of the first inning against Gary Lavelle. Templeton swung and missed at a ball in the dirt for strike three and took a few half-hearted steps to first base while catcher Milt May threw to first for the out. Templeton would later blame a sore ankle and knee as to why he was not running hard. The crowd of 7,766 saw a player who appeared to be loafing and voiced their displeasure with loud boos as he returned to the dugout. Templeton responded by displaying the middle finger of his right hand.

When Templeton came out to the on-deck circle in the third inning, the booing commenced—even louder than before. Templeton later said that several men behind the Cardinals dugout yelled racial slurs at him.[37] He responded to the taunts by grabbing his crotch. Home plate umpire Bruce Froemming ejected Templeton on the spot. Herzog came to the top step of the dugout and dragged him off the field by his jersey like a parent disciplining a toddler. The pair tussled in the dugout and had to be separated by coaches and players. "Get out of here," yelled Herzog. "I don't want you on the road trip. I don't want you around my players. I don't want to see you. You make $690,000 and you go and make an ass of yourself. I don't need that, and my boys don't need that!"[38]

Mike Ramsey replaced the wayward shortstop, and the Cardinals—furious at their teammate and rallying behind their skipper—scored nine runs in the next two innings to rout San Francisco. "We can win with Ramsey," said Tenace after the game. "At least you'll know he'll give you 100 percent. With Templeton, you never knew. You never knew if he'd even talk to you or not."[39]

Gussie Busch wanted to release Templeton that day, but Herzog recognized that such a drastic move would hurt the team and talked the owner off the ledge. Instead, Templeton was fined $5,000 and suspended. While his teammates flew to the West Coast, he stayed behind in St. Louis and agreed to a psychiatric evaluation. "I think he has got some real deep emotional problems," assessed Herzog after tempers had cooled. "I think he's very emotionally distressed."[40]

As fans and teammates grew frustrated with Templeton's antics, there

3. 1981—The Bearded Prophet and a Split Season   47

was sentiment from those who knew him well that he was misunderstood and lacked a certain level of maturity needed to cope with the expectations placed upon him. "I'm not really making excuses, but I think you have to recognize that just because a guy is now 25 years old, making hundreds of thousands of dollars—most of us are not that lucky—doesn't necessarily mean that he automatically becomes a mature, stable guy," said Bing Devine—the GM who had drafted Templeton.[41] Some teammates theorized that he could not handle the fact that the team was doing well while personally he was not achieving his previous level of success.

Herzog insisted that a public apology was needed before Templeton could return to the team. He maintained that his preference was to not trade his talented shortstop, but he said he would be open to the idea if an equivalent shortstop could be acquired in return. Following his mental health evaluation, Templeton was admitted to the hospital, reportedly treated for depression and placed on the disabled list. He would later tell a different story to Brad Balukjian, author of *The Wax Pack*. "They put me in the psych ward," recalled Templeton. "They gave me this plush room. All I did was go in there and play ping pong!" Furthermore, he claimed that he flushed the medication doctors prescribed down the toilet.[42]

Even without Templeton and Rincon—who had yet to pitch since the strike because of shoulder inflammation—the Cards managed to win six out of ten on the West Coast swing and returned home in first place. Their 15–9 second-half record had them two and a half games ahead of Montreal.

A disappointing three-game sweep at the hands of the Cubs followed in which Cardinal pitchers allowed 21 runs, six of them by reliever Joe Edelen, whose ERA ballooned to 9.17. After the third loss, Herzog attempted to fortify the bullpen by acquiring right-handed reliever Doug Bair from Cincinnati in exchange for Edelen and infielder Neil Fiala. Bair had been one of Sparky Anderson's more dependable arms three years earlier, when he saved 28 games and posted a 1.97 ERA. His ERA rose to above four in the subsequent two seasons, however, and he had struggled to the tune of a 5.77 ERA in 1981. Cardinals scout Mo Mozzali felt Bair might benefit from a change of scenery and recommended him to McDonald and Herzog. The Cards snapped a five-game losing skid with a three-game sweep of the Mets that concluded on September 13. Bair contributed immediately, picking up a win in the middle game and throwing two scoreless frames as a setup man for Sutter in the finale.

Templeton returned to the club on September 15 after issuing a well-received apology to teammates. Tenace expressed regret over the critical comments that he gave on record in the aftermath of the Busch Stadium incident. "I was fully unaware of his problem at the time that I said those things," said the esteemed catcher. "Sometimes you say things you regret. This was one of those times for me."⁴³ The Cards traveled to Montreal for an important five-game series at Olympic Stadium that included back-to-back doubleheaders. With all eyes on him after three weeks of inaction, Templeton singled in each of his four at-bats. "He has got the most awesome talent ever given to an athlete," said an awestruck Hernandez. "He got four hits after being in a hospital for three weeks. He didn't even swing a bat."⁴⁴ Templeton went 10-for-20 in the series, helping the Redbirds take three of five. St. Louis left town with a three-and-a-half-game lead over Montreal with 17 to play. It appeared that the Redbirds may snap their playoff drought.

The Cards' road trip concluded with three games in New York and a pair at Chicago. Subpar outings by Bob Shirley and John Martin and then a rare blown save by Sutter cost the Redbirds all three contests at Shea Stadium. St. Louis won the first game at Wrigley Field behind a masterful performance by Joaquín Andújar, who had won five of six decisions since being acquired from Houston. The outing was marred by the fact that Andújar pulled a hamstring in the eighth inning, calling into question his availability for the stretch run. St. Louis dropped the second game when Chicago rallied late against Sykes and Littell. The Cards limped home clinging to a half-game lead over the Expos.

St. Louis fans greeted Templeton warmly in his first home game since the previous month's ugly incident. There was little else for the Redbird faithful to cheer about. The Phillies scored 23 runs in executing a two-game sweep. Herzog was so desperate for starting pitching that he turned to 43-year-old Jim Kaat—making his first start in nearly a year—in the series opener against Pittsburgh on September 25. The result was a 5–4 defeat. While the reeling Cardinals had lost seven of eight games, the Expos had won seven of eight to pull ahead by two and a half games atop the NL East standings.

Just when it looked as though the Redbirds had squandered away their playoff chances, they pulled out consecutive victories against Pittsburgh, including a win by Dave LaPoint in his Cardinals debut. Montreal, holding a one-and-a-half-game advantage, then came to town for an all-important two-game showdown. In the first tilt, John Martin pitched the Cards to a 6–2 triumph. In the second, Ken Oberkfell's four hits paced the 'Birds to an 8–4 victory. The sweep gave St. Louis a half-game lead over the Expos with five to play.

The Cardinals followed by splitting a pair with the Phillies, who were already playoff-bound after winning the first half. Meanwhile, Montreal beat Pittsburgh twice to pull back ahead. The second-half division title came down to the last weekend of the season. St. Louis visited Pittsburgh while Montreal traveled to New York.

3. 1981—The Bearded Prophet and a Split Season

The Cardinals could ill afford to lose the first game against the Pirates. On a cold, wet night with a wind chill of 25 degrees and only 2,348 fans in attendance, things looked bleak after the Bucs mounted a 7-2 lead through five innings. The Redbirds cut the deficit to 7-5 with three unearned runs in the top of the sixth. The score remained unchanged until the top of the ninth when George Hendrick and Darrell Porter each belted solo homers off Rod Scurry to tie the game. Sutter entered the game in the bottom of the inning hoping to send the game to extra innings. A leadoff walk to the speedy Omar Moreno proved to be his undoing. After Moreno was sacrificed to second, Mike Easler doubled home the winning run. Montreal defeated the Mets that night, dropping their magic number to one.

The Expos won again the following day, officially eliminating the Cards from the playoff picture. Ironically, the Cardinals' victory that day ensured they would finish with the NL East's best overall record (59–43), two games ahead of Montreal and two and a half games better than Philadelphia. In yet another cruel twist of fate, the Expos had played one more game than St. Louis in the second half after the Cardinals-Cubs suspended game from April 29 had been lopped off the schedule post-strike. The NL West's Reds posted baseball's best overall record (66–42) and would also be left out of the playoffs. The Dodgers and Astros were first- and second-half winners, respectively. Herzog joked that his club should fly to Hawaii to take on the Reds in their own version of the playoffs.

The Expos and Dodgers each overcame 0–2 deficits to win their respective five-game division series over the Phillies and Astros. In the NLCS, Burt Hooton's knuckle-curve and Fernando Valenzuela's screwball propelled Los Angeles past Montreal to the World Series.*

In the AL, the Yankees had led the East division in the first half with a 34–22 record. With little to play for in the second half, the Bronx Bombers posted a sub-.500 record, spurring an impatient George Steinbrenner to fire Gene Michael and replace him with Bob Lemon. The Brewers won the second half on the shoulders of Pete Vuckovich (14–4, 3.55 ERA) and Rollie Fingers (6–3, 1.04 ERA, 28 saves). Fingers' masterful season would earn him both the American League Cy Young and MVP Awards. From Milwaukee's perspective, the infamous trade with Herzog and the Cardinals was already paying huge dividends.

The AL West's Athletics posted baseball's best record in the first half and finished second to the Royals in the second half. Kansas City benefited from the split season more than any other team, making the playoffs

---

*It would be the Expos' only playoff appearance before the team eventually relocated to Washington D.C. after the 2004 season.

despite finishing with the division's fourth-best overall record (50–53). The A's summarily swept the Royals in three games.

The Yankees got past Milwaukee in the division series, setting up a much-hyped ALCS matchup between Billy Martin's A's and the team that had fired him twice. The Yankees, anchored by Dave Winfield and Reggie Jackson, outscored Oakland 20–4 in a resounding sweep.*

The Dodgers-Yankees World Series was a rematch of the 1977 and 1978 Fall Classics, each won by New York. The Yankees were poised for another title after winning Games One and Two at home behind the strong pitching of Ron Guidry and Tommy John. Los Angeles then pulled out three consecutive one-run victories at Dodger Stadium, starting with Valenzuela's gutty complete-game performance in Game Three. Back in the Bronx for Game Six, Lemon made the controversial decision to pinch-hit for John in the fourth inning with two runners on base and the game tied, 1–1. The Dodgers jumped on the Yankees bullpen with eight runs and cruised to a 9–2 win to capture the crown.

Bruce Sutter finished the season with 25 saves and earned his second Rolaids Fireman of the Year Award. The prize was calculated based on two points for wins and saves with a point subtracted for each loss. The award meant a bonus of $125,000. From Sutter's perspective, the personal achievement was tarnished by the split-season format, which he called a "farce."[45]

The split-season issue aside, Herzog was pleased with how his team played. "If you had told me that I would lose Andy Rincon and Darrell Porter for three and a half months and that Tempy would play like he played before he became part of the team, I wouldn't have given us a chance of finishing higher than fifth," said the skipper.[46]

Forecasting his offseason, Herzog indicated plans to seek out starting pitching and add a right-hand hitting outfielder. On the topic of trading Templeton, he said, "We've got him signed for three more years.† And where are you going to find another shortstop?"[47] Herzog would soon answer his own question.

Herzog's first transactions of the offseason were seemingly minor roster moves. The club added three players to the 40-man roster from Springfield: catcher George Bjorkman, infielder Kelly Paris, and pitcher Ralph Citarella. They also agreed to a trade, sending Bob Sykes to the Yankees for Double-A outfielder Willie McGee. Sykes developed arm trouble and

---

*The series gave birth to the wave, first started by A's fans at the Oakland Coliseum.
†Templeton had four years left on his deal.

would never throw a regular-season pitch for New York. McGee's career, on the other hand, would take a much different trajectory.

Herzog's second hot stove swap came on November 19 with pitchers Lary Sorensen and Silvio Martínez going to Cleveland in exchange for 25-year-old outfielder Lonnie Smith. The exchange was ostensibly part of a three-way deal in which Philadelphia sent Smith to Cleveland for catcher Bo Díaz. In Philadelphia, Smith had been stuck behind established outfielders—Greg Luzinski, Gary Matthews, Bake McBride, and Garry Maddox, among others—and had not cracked the Phillies' everyday lineup until the end of the 1981 season, when he finished with a torrid 23-game hitting streak. Smith had been an integral part of the Phillies' 1980 World Series championship club in part-time duty, hitting .339 with 33 stolen bases. Though considered an average defender, at best, he was penciled in as the Cardinals' starting center fielder for 1982. In the event David Green proved himself ready for the big leagues, Smith could slide over to left field. "He's really the kind of ballplayer I had in mind coming up with," said Herzog of Smith. "He was the number one guy on the priority list."[48]

With a pair of outfielders added to the fold and two starting pitchers subtracted, Herzog went to the Winter Meetings in Hollywood, Florida, on a search for arms. Besides mainstay Bob Forsch and John Martin—who had impressed as a rookie in 1981—the starting rotation was full of holes. Joaquín Andújar was a free agent whom the Cardinals wanted to bring back—but at the right price. Herzog was also shopping Sixto Lezcano and Garry Templeton. One rumor had both players going to Baltimore for a package that included pitchers Mike Flanagan or Sammy Stewart, but that potential transaction would not solve the Cardinals' shortstop dilemma. Herzog thought he was close to a deal that would send Templeton to the Cubs for pitcher Mike Krukow and shortstop Iván DeJesús, but new Cubs general manager Dallas Green instead traded Krukow to Philadelphia for Keith Moreland and middling pitchers Dickie Noles and Dan Larson. Herzog offered a blunt assessment of his rivals' swap: "I don't want to criticize anyone else's players. Dallas knows the Philadelphia players better than anyone else, but all the Cubs got was a bunch of crap for their best pitcher."[49]

With the Cubs seemingly unwilling to deal DeJesús, Herzog turned his attention to the Padres' Gold Glove shortstop—Ozzie Smith. San Diego GM Jack McKeon indicated that a straight up trade was not in the cards. "I've got a guy [Smith] who plays 162 games. You've got a guy you can't get rid of. I need a little bit more," said McKeon.[50] By the fourth day of the meetings, talks advanced as the two general managers figured out what players would be added to get the deal to the finish line. Herzog offered to include Lezcano, and the Padres were willing to part with either Steve

Mura or Juan Eichelberger, both pitchers. Herzog sought the advice of former Padre Bob Shirley, who recommended Mura.[51]

There was one complication, however. Smith had a blanket no-trade clause in his contract, giving him the right to refuse any deal. Smith's agent, Ed Gottlieb, indicated that his client was "vehemently opposed to going anywhere else," wrote Hummel. "He's very troubled and upset over the whole thing," said Gottlieb.[52]

While the logistics of compensating Smith for waiving his no-trade clause were being ironed out, Herzog responded to media criticism of the pending deal at a speaking engagement in Belleville, Illinois, on December 16. "It's amazing how the media talks. [Templeton] doesn't want to play in St. Louis. He doesn't want to play on [artificial] turf. He doesn't want to play when we go into Montreal. He doesn't want to play in the Astrodome. He doesn't want to play in the rain. The other 80 games he's all right."[53]

Gottlieb arranged for Smith and Herzog to link up in San Diego on December 28 so the two parties could get a feel for one another and discuss financial considerations. The meeting lasted six hours, after which Herzog publicly expressed doubts that a deal would be finalized. "Ozzie is a great fielder and baserunner," said Herzog. "I'd like to have him, but if he doesn't want to come to St. Louis, I don't want him. No .230 hitter is worth what he's asking."[54]

As negotiations with Smith stretched into the New Year, the Cardinals filled another rotation spot by securing the services of Andújar with a three-year deal worth $1.2 million. The righty had amassed a mediocre career record of 48–49 but had impressed since coming over from the Astros, posting a 6–1 mark and 3.76 ERA in 11 appearances, including eight starts.

By late January, Smith/Gottlieb and the Cardinals remained at a stalemate. In exchange for Smith's waiving his no-trade clause, Gottlieb sought a salary of $750,000, a figure commensurate with the game's other elite shortstops. The Cardinals' brass, pointing out most of the comparable players had been in the league longer than Smith's four years, offered $450,000 plus $50,000 worth of incentives.[55] Smith's contract with the Padres would have paid him a minimum of $240,000, and he indicated that he was willing to leave a substantial amount of money on the table to remain in San Diego. It appeared that the trade could be off. With Templeton still available, the Orioles reached out to reopen talks for the shortstop.

Another meeting with Herzog persuaded Smith to reconsider. "Whitey told me that with me playing shortstop for the Cardinals, we could win the pennant," recalled Smith. "He made me feel wanted, which is something everybody wants, and which was a feeling I was quickly losing from the Padres."[56] Smith ultimately agreed to waive his no-trade clause

3. 1981—The Bearded Prophet and a Split Season

if the Cards agreed to submit the case to an arbitrator to settle his salary. On February 11, 1982—two months after the framework of the trade was first agreed to—the deal finally become official. In addition to the swap of Smith/Mura for Templeton/Lezcano, each team also received a player to be named later. Subsequently, pitcher Luis DeLeón was announced as the player going to San Diego while St. Louis re-acquired Al Olmsted to complete the transaction. With the trade finally consummated, Herzog had accomplished his goals of adding starting pitching depth and speed while ridding the club of its controversial shortstop. Whether it would be enough to bring postseason baseball back to St. Louis remained to be seen.

4

Spring Training
The Wizard Arrives

> *"Last season was an atrocity, but I'm trying to get it out of my mind. We had the best record and got nothing. You only hope they don't come up with any more split season baloney. This year, we could win, maybe win it all."*
> —Whitey Herzog[1]

On February 25, 1982, morning fog gave way to sunshine as Cardinal pitchers and catchers convened in St. Petersburg, Florida, for the start of a new season. Position players trickled in as the calendar turned to March. The camp comprised 37 roster players and six non-roster invitees, including utilityman Steve Braun, ex–Cardinal pitcher Eric Rasmussen, and 38-year-old right-hander Vicente Romo, who had spent the previous seven seasons in the Mexican League. Unlike Herzog's roster overhaul of the previous offseason, the NL East division's winningest club returned nearly all of its key pieces and added the athleticism of the Smiths—Lonnie and Ozzie. While the two new faces with the same surname got to know their teammates, their meeting was a reunion. The pair grew up together in the Los Angeles area and played on the same youth summer-league team.

All members of the 1981 coaching staff returned, and Dick Tettelbach, an old minor-league teammate and longtime friend of Herzog, served as a guest baserunning instructor.* Tettelbach observed games and worked with players on getting more effective leads. Though his short-lived big-league career included a .150 batting average across 80 at-bats with zero stolen bases, Herzog claimed that Tettelbach was the rest baserunner he had ever seen. "He was a big guy, about 200 pounds, but he was a hell of a baserunner, a very intelligent person," said Herzog. "He stole 77 bases

---

*Former Cardinal Joe Cunningham, who worked in the front office as director of sales in 1982, donned a uniform briefly as a hitting coach near the end of the season.

4. Spring Training—The Wizard Arrives

at Joplin before base stealing was the 'in' thing."[2] Tettelbach would later recall how he and Herzog alternated batting second and third for Joplin. When one reached second base, the other would bunt the ball down the third-base line. While the two umpires followed the ball, the baserunner at second would cut inside the third-base bag and dash home.[3] Tettelbach, a former teammate of George H.W. Bush at Yale University, worked in the pavement-sealing and tennis court-coating business and had been out of professional baseball for a quarter century.

Darrell Porter showed up to camp able to throw without pain, an encouraging sign after a shoulder injury had kept him out of action for a large chunk of the 1981 season and contributed to a subpar .224 batting average. He had spent the offseason weight training instead of, as Rick Hummel wrote, "his usual offseason exercise program of casting his fishing rod."[4]

Ozzie Smith's work ethic quickly earned him the respect of his new teammates. "He's won two Gold Gloves and he still takes more ground balls out there than anybody," noted Tom Herr.[5] Things had not changed since Gene Tenace first observed Smith at Padres camp years earlier. "He took 200 or 300 extra ground balls every day," said Tenace. "I'll tell you. He can do things with that glove that you didn't think were possible."[6] Smith did not want to be a one-dimensional player and worked hard to improve himself at the plate as well. He spent extra time in the batting cages with coaches Chuck Hiller and Dave Ricketts working on a downward swing in order to hit more balls on the ground. "Topspin," said Ricketts repeatedly as he fed balls into a pitching machine. "Think AstroTurf, fly balls are nothing in St. Louis … think ground balls, with your speed."[7]

The wizardry of Osborne Earl Smith's defense can be traced back to the Los Angeles neighborhood of Watts during the 1960s. His parents and five siblings had moved west from Mobile, Alabama, when Smith was six. He grew up with a ball in his hands nearly every day, joining football, basketball, and baseball teams through the YMCA. One of the few times he was not outside playing ball was during the Watts riots in 1965. "We had to sleep on the floor because of all the sniping and looting going on," Smith later recalled.[8]

On days when there were no organized sports, Smith entertained himself by bouncing a ball off concrete steps and the garage wall, practice that helped build quick reflexes and excellent hand-eye coordination. On occasion, he and other kids in the neighborhood went down to the local sawmill and practiced doing flips into piles of sawdust. Later, Smith would utilize these skills to thrill fans with his signature backflip.

By the time Smith got to Locke High School, he was an outstanding shortstop and played guard for the school's cagers. Scouts came out to watch the Locke baseball team, but they were there to see Smith's teammate—Eddie Murray. Ozzie, who weighed less than 135 pounds in his prep days, was overlooked by talent evaluators and went undrafted. He passed up basketball scholarship opportunities and enrolled at California Polytechnic State University in San Luis Obispo on a partial academic scholarship. He walked on to the baseball team and worked his way into the starting shortstop role while learning how to switch-hit.

Following his junior year at Cal Poly in 1976, Smith was drafted in the seventh round by the Detroit Tigers. He wanted $10,000 to sign, but the Tigers were only willing to offer half that amount, so he returned for his senior season. In 1977, he was a fourth-round selection of the Padres. Without the leverage of returning to college, Smith found his offer even lower than the year before. He ultimately signed for the same $5,000 the Tigers had offered and used his bonus to buy a new burgundy Chrysler LeBaron.[9]

Ozzie Smith's legendary shortstop defense stemmed from years of hard work and unwavering dedication (National Baseball Hall of Fame and Museum, Cooperstown, NY).

Smith was assigned to the Padres' rookie-level affiliate in Walla Walla, Washington, for the summer of 1977. In 68 games, the 22-year-old hit .303 with one home run and 30 stolen bases. The Friars then sent him to the Arizona Fall League, where he caught the eye of Padres manager and former big-league shortstop Alvin Dark. Smith's glovework earned him an invite to big-league spring training in 1978, where he immediately impressed teammates. "Ozzie was a recognizable talent as soon as he showed up in spring camp," recalled Padres pitcher John D'Acquisto. "First of all, he was a great teammate and a great person. He was quick, sure-handed, smooth as silk, and had an accurate throwing arm."[10]

Dark announced that the job was Smith's to lose and told him not to worry about his hitting. "All I want you to do is pick up the ball and throw it across the diamond," Dark told his young shortstop.[11] The Padres fired Dark midway through spring training, but Smith had already shown enough to win the starting shortstop job under new manager Roger Craig.

Smith's glovework quickly captured the attention of the league. Just ten games into his career, he made what many consider one of the most spectacular plays ever seen on a baseball diamond. Atlanta's Jeff Burroughs hit a hard groundball that was bound for center field. Smith dove to his left, but the ball took a bad hop and careened behind his glove. While in mid-air, he adjusted and grabbed the ball with his bare hand before jumping to his feet and throwing to first base for the out. When the MLB Network counted down the 75 all-time best defensive plays in 2017, Smith's gem ranked number one.

Smith's rookie season nearly took a tragic turn on September 25. At around nine in the morning, he was riding in D'Acquisto's Porsche Turbo on Boundary Street in San Diego. Overhead, Pacific Southwest Airlines Flight 182 was descending to San Diego International Airport when the Boeing 727 collided in midair with a private Cessna. "I could see the flash of light and the plane in my side view mirror," recalled D'Acquisto, who floored the gas pedal of his Porsche to narrowly avoid the falling debris. All 137 occupants of the two planes as well as seven people on the ground were killed. Nine others on the ground were injured and several houses were destroyed. At the time, it was the worst air disaster in American history. "We dodged a bullet that day," said D'Acquisto.[12]

Smith's spectacular defense and solid offensive production in 1978—a .258 average and 40 stolen bases—helped the Padres to the franchise's first winning season. He finished runner-up to Atlanta's Bob Horner in the Rookie of the Year voting and set his sights on hitting .300 in his sophomore season. However, an abysmal start in which Smith was hitless in his first 32 at-bats dashed any chance of achieving his goal and contributed to a .211 batting average. The Padres' 93 losses cost Craig his job. In his place, the Friars hired former Yankee Jerry Coleman, one of the team's broadcasters. Smith improved his batting average in 1980, hitting .233 while drawing 71 walks and winning his first Gold Glove, but San Diego endured another last-place finish.

The offensive-starved Padres lost their best hitter—Dave Winfield—to the Yankees before the 1981 season. "A lot of players were upset about losing Dave," recalled Smith in his memoir *Wizard*. "We knew he was the franchise's best player, and when he left, it told the rest of us about the organization's commitment to winning."[13] The Yankees' acquisition of Winfield added to an outfield logjam that would eventually lead to the trade of Willie McGee to the Cardinals.

Smith was arbitration-eligible for the first time in 1981. He and the Padres settled on a contract that included a no-trade clause, an unusual inclusion at the time. Smith was hitting .259 when play was halted due to the players' strike. The Wizard was named to his first All-Star team when play resumed in early August. He hit a dismal .184 in the second half, dropping his season average to .233.

In order to encourage Smith to keep the ball out of the air and utilize his speed, Herzog made a wager with his new shortstop. He would pay Smith a dollar for every ground ball and line drive he hit. Each time Smith struck out or hit a fly ball, he would owe his manager a buck. "That's one of the special qualities of Whitey Herzog and why he's able to bring out the best in his players," Smith later explained. "He created a fun deal, but it also made me a better hitter and a greater asset to the team."[14]

While the infield foursome of Oberkfell, Smith, Herr, and Hernandez was set in stone, the back end of the starting rotation remained largely unsettled as spring training commenced. Bob Forsch, Joaquín Andújar, Steve Mura, John Martin were penciled in at the first four spots. Andy Rincon, coming off an injury-plagued season, had a leg up for the fifth and final rotation spot if he proved to be healthy. Swingman Bob Shirley and youngsters John Stuper and Dave LaPoint were also in the mix. Stuper was coming off a rough 1981 season that included a 6–14 record and 4.92 ERA in Triple A. LaPoint, on the other hand, had registered a 13–9 record and 3.19 ERA in Springfield and impressed as a September callup. John Fulgham was also in camp looking to reestablish his place on the roster following rotator cuff surgery. Herzog sought additional pitching depth and attempted to pry Dave Stieb from Toronto or Floyd Bannister from Seattle. He dangled a package of George Bjorkman, Gene Roof, and an unnamed pitcher, but neither club would bite.*

David Green turned heads in camp with his raw athleticism and improved plate discipline. There was never any question about his speed, fielding, and throwing arm, but the 21-year-old phenom had appeared overmatched at the plate during his brief big-league stint in 1981. A strong spring showing put him in the conversation to crack the opening day roster.

---

*Toronto made a wise decision. Stieb would lead the AL in innings and shutouts in 1982 and average 15 wins for the next nine seasons.

4. Spring Training—The Wizard Arrives

The first significant injury of the spring cropped up on March 22 when Gene Tenace suffered a fractured right thumb. The projected backup catcher was playing first base when he leaped in the air for a ball that caromed off his glove. While trying to reach for the ball, his sunglasses fell and obscured his vision, causing him to jam his hand into the ground. The 35-year-old veteran was placed on the 21-day disabled list. Eight days later, Herzog lost his starting third baseman in a similar manner. Ken Oberkfell dove for a ball and jammed his glove hand into the ground, fracturing his left thumb. Like Tenace, he would be sidelined to start the season. The pair of sore-thumbed Redbirds surmised they could take infield practice together. "I'll catch 'em and you throw 'em back," quipped Tenace.[15] Herzog looked internally for substitutions at the hot corner. Dane Iorg, who was tearing the cover off the ball and positioning himself for a more prominent role as a left fielder, saw time at third base during the final week of spring games. Backups Mike Ramsey, Julio González, and Braun were also options. Oberkfell's injury all but cemented a roster spot for Green.

On March 31—three days after Wayne Gretzky astonished the sports world by netting his record-setting 92nd goal for the National Hockey League's Edmonton Oilers—Ozzie Smith attended his long-awaited and much-discussed arbitration hearing. The date had been delayed because of his agent's five-week European honeymoon. Smith was eager to put the matter behind him. The 5-foot-11, 150-pound shortstop failed to hit his weight during the Grapefruit League slate, finishing with a .139 batting average. "I'm not concerned about average," he said. "I think I've been hitting more balls on the ground than in the air, which is what they want."[16] Smith lost his arbitration case but nevertheless received a 50 percent raise from his 1981 salary.

The makeup of Herzog's 10-man pitching staff crystalized near the end of camp. Shirley—who allowed 14 runs in 18 spring innings—was shipped to Cincinnati for Triple-A pitchers Jeff Lahti and José Brito. The trade cleared a roster spot for LaPoint, a lefty Herzog wanted as part of his five-man relief corps. Jim Kaat, Doug Bair, Mark Littell, and Bruce Sutter filled out the rest of the bullpen. Along with a five-man starting rotation of Forsch, Andújar, Martin, Rincon, and Mura, the opening day pitching staff was set.

The Cardinals concluded the Grapefruit League schedule on April 4 with a victory over the Mets, improving their record to 13–11. Porter was drilled with a pitch to the elbow in the game, but there was a collective sigh of relief when x-rays came back negative. With Tenace and on the shelf to start the season, Orlando Sánchez would serve as Porter's backup to begin the season. The other catchers in camp—Glenn Brummer and Bjorkman—were dispatched to Triple A.

With outfielders Braun and Iorg in the mix to fill in at third base, Herzog kept seven outfielders on the opening day squad. Lonnie Smith, George Hendrick, Green, Roof, and Tito Landrum comprised the rest of the group. Willie McGee, the quiet outfielder who turned in an impressive spring, was sent to Louisville, the Cardinals' new Triple-A affiliate.

When spring training ended, the 26 major-league teams decamped their respective training facilities in Florida, Arizona, and California. With a collective bargaining agreement in place, the focus was finally back on runs, hits, and errors instead of the labor dispute. A survey found that three-quarters of teams reported ticket sales greater than or equal to the previous year's figures, an indication fans were willing to forgive and forget the loss of 712 games from the 1981 schedule.[17]

Besides Ozzie Smith and Templeton, several other stars had switched teams; Reggie Jackson (Angels), George Foster (Mets), Ken Griffey (Yankees), and Davey Lopes (Athletics) all donned new uniforms. Johnny Bench had not switched teams but was manning a new position for the Reds—third base. Six teams had new managers, and the Minnesota Twins were set to move into a new downtown facility—the 57,411 seat Hubert H. Humphrey Metrodome. Twins fans would appreciate the comfortable environs when outside temperatures on opening night dipped into the 20s.

A number of 40-somethings sought milestones to punctuate their already distinguished careers: Gaylord Perry—the gray-haired hurler who had taken his spitball to Seattle—was three wins shy of 300; Carl Yastrzemski entered his 22nd season with the Red Sox looking to add to his career total of 3,192 hits; Phillies first baseman Pete Rose was inching closer to Ty Cobb for the all-time hits title; and Willie Stargell was set to close out his 20-year career with the Pirates. "Baseball is like a good meal," said Stargell, "and right now I feel that I'm on the dessert."[18]

In a preseason poll of 218 members of the Baseball Writers' Association of America, the Expos were the consensus pick to win the NL East and also received the most votes to win the World Series. "Everybody has picked Montreal," said Tom Herr at the time. "To hear them talk, we shouldn't even play. Just hand the title to Montreal. That's ridiculous as far as I'm concerned. We had the best record in our division last year and we were 9–6 versus Montreal. We're not afraid to play them."[19]

The writers narrowly chose the defending champion Dodgers over the Astros to take the NL West. The reigning AL champion Yankees were picked to repeat as East division champions, though the power-hitting Brewers and strong-armed Orioles were also considered potential contenders. Billy Martin's Oakland A's—led by 23-year-old speedster Rickey Henderson—were heavy favorites to win the AL West. By the end of the season, the writers would wear the collar, going 0-for-4 in their predictions.

5

April

A Dozen Straight W's

"Big-league ballplayers are mostly men, normal men with insecurities, doubts and weaknesses, not the gods you thought they were."—Keith Hernandez[1]

The National League's 107th season commenced on April 5, 1982, in Cincinnati, where the Cubs squeaked by the Reds in a weather-shortened, eight-inning affair. The American League—baseball's junior circuit—kicked off in Baltimore, where the Orioles routed the Royals. A rare spring blizzard dropped over a foot of snow on many parts of the upper Midwest and Northeast, forcing the cancellation of six of the 11 games scheduled for April 6.

Weather was not a factor for the Cardinals and Astros, who began the 162-game season in Houston under the roof of the Astrodome—dubbed the "Eighth Wonder of the World" when it opened in 1965 as major-league baseball's first indoor ballpark. Coming off back-to-back playoff appearances, the Astros had high hopes heading into the 1982 campaign. Houston's strength was its pitching corps, which had posted a major-league best 2.66 ERA the preceding year. The ace of the staff was Nolan Ryan, a 35-year-old workhorse and native of Alvin, Texas, who led the AL in strikeouts seven times between 1972 and 1979 as a member of the California Angels. The Ryan Express had rolled into Houston two years before, and in 1981 the righty with a high leg kick and devastating heater registered a league-best 1.69 ERA. Behind Ryan in the rotation were a pair of wily 37-year-olds—Don Sutton and Joe Niekro—who were stalwarts in their own regard. Sutton had recorded double-digit wins in all 16 of his major-league seasons, whereas Niekro was a knuckleballer with a pair of 20-win campaigns under his belt. The seasoned trio to that point had racked up 575 wins in their combined 46 years in the big leagues.

Things were not all rainbows and sunshine in Space City, however. Sutton, who inked a four-year contract with Houston before the 1981 season, made headlines during spring training when he asked to be traded to the West Coast so he could be closer to his Laguna Hills home. He verbally sparred with Astros general manager Al Rosen, who adamantly refused the request. "We dot the i's and cross the t's of every contract, and we worked our butts off to sign Sutton," said Rosen. "So, as a GM I have the responsibility to the owners, stockholders, and fans. I'm not letting him go, period."[2]

Sutton's trade demands would elicit jeers from Astros fans in his first start of the season, but on Opening Day it was all cheers for Ryan, who drew the assignment in opposition to Bob Forsch. In front of a half-full Astrodome, the visitors donned their powder blue road uniforms with the classic "birds on the bat" logo across the chest while the home team wore the polarizing "tequila sunrise" jerseys with horizontal stripes of yellow, orange, and red across the abdomen. Lonnie Smith was grazed by a pitch to leadoff the game and promptly stole second base. After Tom Herr struck out, Keith Hernandez drew a walk. Cleanup man Darrell Porter, a .164 hitter career hitter against Ryan in 75 career plate appearances, came to the plate. After falling behind in the count 0–2, Porter's chances looked even more bleak. However, Ryan hung a breaking ball and the bespectacled catcher jumped on it, clubbing it over the right-field fence for a three-run homer. Three consecutive hits by George Hendrick, Dane Iorg, and Steve Braun plated another, and Ozzie Smith's groundout scored the Cardinals' fifth run of the inning. It took Ryan 43 pitches just to record three outs. The Cardinals added a sixth run in the second inning, and Ryan hit the showers after only three frames. He called it his worst outing since joining the Astros.[3]

St. Louis batters pummeled the Houston bullpen with equal disregard. By the end of the game, the Cards had scored 14 runs on 18 hits, seven of which went for two bases. Each of the St. Louis starting nine was represented in the hit column. Forsch allowed all three Houston runs while scattering seven hits in eight innings to earn the win. Jim Kaat pitched a scoreless ninth, becoming the first player in major-league history to pitch in 24 seasons. "The way the Cardinals hit the ball was really an awesome display," said Astros catcher Alan Ashby. "If they keep it up, the whole league is going to be in trouble."[4]

Porter's contributions in the resounding victory—2-for-5 with a home run, double, and three RBIs—were surely gratifying given the struggles he had endured both on and off the field in previous years. The second-year

Cardinal was born in Joplin, Missouri, the third of five children born to Ray and Twila Mae Porter. During Darrell's early childhood, the family moved to Bonner Springs, Kansas, and then to Yakima, Washington, as Ray followed work with a trucking company. The Porters eventually settled in Oklahoma City, where they rented a modest two-bedroom home in a working-class neighborhood. All five children shared a bedroom until Ray and Twila Mae, who worked in the high school cafeteria, saved enough money to buy a three-bedroom house on the next block. The larger dwelling seemed like a palace to seven-year-old Darrell. Ray was a strict disciplinarian who taught his children to be humble and work hard but rarely offered praise. He used alcohol to cope with the stresses of a mortgage and life on the road, as Darrell later described in his autobiography *Snap Me Perfect! The Darrell Porter Story*.

Darrell started playing organized baseball at the age of nine. The day before Little League tryouts, Ray asked him what position he wanted to play. When Darrell answered that he was not sure, Ray encouraged him to try catcher. "It's easy to progress in the game as catcher, because good catchers are hard to find," explained Ray. "And if you're a good catcher, you can go all the way to the major leagues."[5]

When he was a freshman at Southeast High School, scouts began taking notice of Porter's strong arm behind the plate. As a sophomore, he joined the football team as a defensive end and took over the reins of starting quarterback as a junior. He was named all-state catcher his junior and senior years and enjoyed the accolades that came with being a star quarterback. As he neared graduation, Porter was faced with the difficult decision of choosing between the grid iron and the baseball diamond. He signed a letter of

Darryl Porter followed Herzog to St. Louis from Kansas City and provided solid defense behind the plate (National Baseball Hall of Fame and Museum, Cooperstown, NY).

intent to play football for the University of Oklahoma in February 1970 and then was chosen by the Milwaukee Brewers with the fourth overall pick of Major League Baseball's June amateur draft. The prospect of a six-figure signing bonus—life-changing money for the Porter family—had Darrell leaning toward baseball.

When Brewers scout Bob Mavis showed up to negotiate a contract, Ray and Darrell were dismayed by the team's initial lowball contract offer of $15,000. "That's chicken feed, Mr. Mavis!" exclaimed Ray. "Why, 37 colleges have offered him football scholarships ... if you don't come up with a better figure, my boy might just accept one of those scholarships."[6] Mavis returned two days later with his boss, Bobby Mattick. The pair made, in their estimation, a very generous offer of $35,000. Ray insisted on $70,000 with incentives, but Mattick stood firm with a final bid of $65,000. Darrell observed in disbelief as Ray turned down the offer. "Well young fellow, I guess you'll be playing football for OU this fall after all," said Mattick. As a stunned Darrell watched the scouts drive off, Ray confidently said, "They'll be back." Within minutes, Ray's prediction came true and Darrell signed a contract for $70,000 plus incentives.[7]

The Brewers sent Porter to Baltimore to work out with the big-league club for a few days before he was to report to their Single-A affiliate in Clinton, Iowa. Porter felt like royalty as he was transported from the airport in a limousine and put up in a luxury hotel. At the ballpark, he impressed Brewers' brass with his throwing arm and batting practice power. In the clubhouse after the game, Porter looked on in astonishment as players smoked and drank beer, habits he had not associated with being a professional athlete.

After getting a taste of the majors, Porter was dispatched to Clinton, where the stuffy locker room smelled like dirty laundry and the showers were covered in mildew. Besides the unpleasant clubhouse conditions, the young catcher found the breaking pitches in professional baseball baffling and struggled to the tune of a .200 batting average. On the advice of a couple of teammates, he began to drink alcohol a few nights a week to help himself relax.

Porter, who threw right and batted left, found his footing in his second season of Single A playing in Danville, Illinois, where he hit .271 and mashed 24 home runs. The Brewers wanted to get a look at the young catcher some compared to Johnny Bench, so Porter was called up to the major-league squad in September 1971. After spending most of the following season gaining more experience at Triple A, he became the Brewers' starting catcher in 1973. Though only 21, Porter acquitted himself well as a rookie, batting .254 with 16 home runs and an impressive .820 OPS.

Porter was named to the AL All-Star team his sophomore season of

1974, but his personal and professional life began to spiral out of control. Along with alcohol, he had gradually begun to use marijuana, Quaaludes, and cocaine. His substance use escalated as he dealt with marital problems to the point where he even smoked marijuana during games. His on-field performance suffered as a result. The Brewers sought ways to help the scuffling youngster and had him meet with a psychiatrist. Porter complied but admittedly did not take the consultation seriously. By 1976, his batting average barely topped the Mendoza line and his power had all but vanished. The last-place Brewers ran out of patience and traded him to the Kansas City Royals.

Porter was on the precipice of sliding into baseball obscurity. "I had a growing sense that I was really messing up in baseball, the one thing I could do and do well," he later reflected.[8] The year 1977 had the potential to be a make or break year for Porter. To that end, he cut out cocaine and limited his use of Quaaludes and marijuana to after games. He set out to reestablish himself as a big leaguer, and the Royals clubhouse proved to be an excellent fit. Whitey Herzog, then in his second full year in Kansas City, led a group that was at tightknit as it was talented. And the Royals were certainly talented. The lineup featured George Brett, Hal McRae, Frank White, Al Cowens, and John Mayberry, just to name a few.

Teammates found Porter to be affable and big-hearted. As a catcher, he emboldened and mentored the young pitchers he worked with. In his first spring with the Royals, a couple of similarly-surnamed minor leaguers—Dan Quisenberry and Randy McGilberry—were called over to big-league camp one day to throw batting practice and show their wares in front of Herzog and pitching coach Galen Cisco. Porter caught McGilberry, a hard-throwing righty from Alabama. "Darrell was my kind of catcher," recalled McGilberry decades later. "He was very articulate in his encouragement from behind the plate. After practice, he came up to me and said, 'Man, you have a live fastball, and that slider is awesome!'"[9] Coming from a guy who had several big-league seasons under his belt, Porter's words carried a lot of weight.

Later that summer, McGilberry, 23, earned a promotion to the big leagues. The first person to greet him in the clubhouse was Porter. "Welcome to the big leagues, McGilla!" exclaimed Porter while offering a welcoming embrace. Porter immediately took the rookie under his wing. After the game the pair met up for a couple of drinks at the hotel bar. Porter informed McGilberry that his luggage had been moved to the room next to his and that the two were going fishing the next morning. "As promised, we went fishing and I had the time of my life," recalled McGilberry. "Darrell and I bonded like brothers, and it was like nothing I could have dreamed up." On the field, Porter knew how to get the most out of

McGilberry's two pitches—fastball and slider—and calm him down when necessary. "I was anxious, and he would just take his hands and motion for me to slow down. We were a team," said McGilberry, looking back.[10]

With the Royals, Porter rediscovered joy in playing baseball that had faded in preceding years. Both he and the team enjoyed mutual success. Kansas City won 102 games in 1977 and ran away with the AL West crown. In 130 games, Porter hit .275 with 16 home runs. Ultimately, the Royals' championship hopes were dashed in the ALCS by the Yankees for the second straight year.

Playing catcher took a physical toll on Porter. "He was in tremendous pain in his knees and throwing arm," observed McGilberry. "I knew he was taking drugs for the pain and would just play in spite of it."[11] In 1978, Porter started 141 games behind the dish, but the heavy workload did not diminish his offensive production. His ledger included a .265 average, 18 home runs, 78 RBIs, and a second All-Star nod. The disappointment of another ALCS loss to the Yankees put a damper on an otherwise standout season.

Porter was even better in 1979, hitting .291 with a career-high 20 home runs, 112 RBIs, and a league-high 121 walks. He was named to his third All-Star team, surpassing the likes of Thurman Munson and Carlton Fisk in fan voting, and finished ninth in the AL MVP balloting. The Royals came up short in their bid for a fourth straight division title, however, and as a result Herzog was fired. Porter—his own harshest critic—felt a sense of failure for his team's shortcomings.

That offseason, Porter dove headlong back into using drugs and alcohol. "Get up and make coffee, do a Quaalude, drink beer, sniff cocaine, and smoke cigarettes," is how he described his daily routine.[12] He became increasingly paranoid that the Royals were aware of his substance abuse and thought that people were following him and spying on him. In reality, management had no idea about his habits.

By the time he got to spring training in 1980, Porter was near rock bottom. Things came to a head when former big-league pitcher Don Newcombe, whose own career had ended prematurely because of alcoholism, visited the team to speak on the topic. Players were given a questionnaire with 15 queries about their use of alcohol. "Read them over," said Newcombe. "If you can answer three of the questions with a yes, then you may have a drinking problem."[13] Porter answered yes to 14. He sought out Newcombe and, for the first time, admitted he had a problem and needed help. At Newcombe's encouragement, Porter talked to Royals GM Joe Burke. "I was at my locker getting ready for the exhibition game when Darrell grabbed my shoulder, crying his eyes out," remembered McGilberry. "He said, 'McGilla, I'm going to get help, man.'"[14] The next thing Porter knew

5. April—A Dozen Straight W's   67

he was on a plane to The Meadows, a substance abuse treatment center in Wickenburg, Arizona.

Porter spent six weeks at The Meadows before rejoining the Royals on April 26. It took him time to work himself back into playing shape. In 118 games, he batted .249 with only seven home runs. Though Porter's statistics had dropped off, the Royals flourished and won their fourth AL West division title in five years and finally overcame the Yankees to reach the World Series. Kansas City fell to the Phillies in six games with Porter managing only two hits in 14 at-bats.

Porter became a free agent after the 1980 season, and the Cardinals were among eight teams that selected him in the free agent draft. Herzog felt a defensive upgrade was needed at the catcher position, and he was very familiar with Porter's skill set from his years in Kansas City. "He was one of those special kinds of players who just had a knack for playing baseball," recalled Herzog years later. "He was just a winner."[15] Porter was on his honeymoon when his agent called with the news of the Cardinals' generous five-year, $3.5 million offer. Porter's preference was to re-sign with Kansas City, but when the Royals' best offer fell $1.5 million short of the Cards' proposal, it became an easy choice.

When he reported to St. Petersburg for his first spring training with St. Louis, Porter developed a sore throwing shoulder. The malady would be far from his only challenge. When the regular season began, fans took their frustration over the trade of Ted Simmons out on his replacement, showering Porter with boos whenever he failed to succeed on the field. "This vendetta by the St. Louis fans really hurt me," wrote Porter. "Things got worse and worse, and gradually it affected my game to the point that I hated coming to the stadium."[16] He found solace in road trips and was relieved when the players went on strike, allowing him a reprieve from the wrath of the home crowd. Porter ended the abbreviated 1981 season hitting only .224. Despite his subpar offensive production during his first year in St. Louis, Porter offered intangibles like those described by McGilberry. His strengths as a catcher were easily overlooked by the average spectator. "People aren't aware how good a catcher Porter is, how good a game he calls, and how well he handles pitchers," said scout Jim Russo.[17]

"To think he accomplished so much with the internal struggles, it makes you wonder what he might have done otherwise," said McGilberry in retrospect. "I just know he was a man you could count on no matter how much pain he was in or what his struggles were."[18]

Porter continued his strong start to the 1982 season with three more hits—including a solo home run—in the second game of the season. The venerable Niekro stymied Porter's teammates, however. Providing quite a contrast from Ryan in terms of repertoire and results, Niekro allowed only two earned runs in 8⅓ innings before yielding to reliever Joe Sambito for the final two outs. Free-swinging centerfielder Tony Scott, whom Herzog had traded to Houston for Joaquín Andújar a year earlier, contributed two hits and a walk for the victors. Herzog knew Scott was susceptible to breaking pitches, but starter John Martin had trouble getting his curveball over the plate, issuing five walks over six innings in the Cardinals' 3–2 defeat.

Joaquín Andújar drew the starting assignment in the rubber match against his former club. To that point, Andújar's career had been erratic, but Hub Kittle, who had managed him for several years in winter ball, knew how to untap his potential. Andújar kept the Houston lineup off-balance by alternating between sidearm and overhand deliveries and allowed only one unearned run. Opposing starter Bob Knepper was even better, however, using his sweeping curveball to limit St. Louis to only four singles over eight shutout innings. Dave Smith pitched a flawless ninth to seal a 1–0 victory and series win for Houston. Andújar took the loss, the first of many tough-luck defeats he would suffer as the season wore on.

The recent snowstorm and near-freezing temperatures lingering in the Midwest forced the cancellation of a scheduled exhibition between the Cardinals and St. Louis University on April 9. Several players used the day off to receive treatment from trainer Gene Gieselmann. Bob Forsch would later write about the time that Andújar asked for tips about driving in the snow. "First of all, you've got to drive kind of faster than you usually would," said Forsch with a straight face. "Then you've got to get right behind the car in front of you. If you start sliding, you'll bump into the car in front of you and that'll slow you down." Andújar burst into laughter once he realized the advice was in jest.[19]

Before the home opener on April 10, the Cardinals announced that Whitey Herzog would relinquish his GM role to Joe McDonald, who had held the title of executive assistant since October 1980. The pair had worked together with the Mets when Herzog was farm director and McDonald his assistant. In reality, McDonald was already doing much of the duties of a GM, negotiating contracts and trades with Herzog having the final say. The restructuring of titles had been decided in a February meeting between Gussie Busch and Herzog, who felt the GM job was too consuming and left no time for fishing.[20] "I'll be very honest with you," Herzog told the *St. Louis Post-Dispatch*, "A lot of times, I thought I was crazy for sitting in the office instead of fishing and skiing."[21] He explained that one of the drawbacks of filling both roles was that he was unable to talk to his players at contract time. "All you do is talk to their agents, and I don't like talking to agents," said Herzog.[22]

McDonald took a circuitous route to the GM desk of the Cardinals. He was born on Staten Island, New York, and attended Brooklyn's St. Francis Prep, the alma mater of such notables as Vince Lombardi and Joe Torre. McDonald demonstrated decent ability as a first baseman on sandlots and his high school team, but scouts could not look past his slender 6-foot, 140-pound frame.[23] He graduated from Fordham University with an accounting degree and went to work crunching numbers and doing public relations work for an aerospace and defense corporation. McDonald's next job involved helping direct professional golf tournaments on the women's circuit. His boss at the time, Fred Corcoran, happened to be the agent to such major-league stars as Stan Musial and Ted Williams. Through this connection, McDonald met George Weiss, who had been named team president of the expansion Mets. McDonald was hired as the team statistician in the team's inaugural season of 1962 and eventually worked his way up the organizational ladder, serving as director of scouting, director of player development, and then GM.

Herzog and McDonald usually agreed on player personnel decisions, so it made for a natural transition. During the press conference announcing the change, the team disclosed that Herzog's field manager contract had been reworked as a three-year deal. "Here I am, giving up half my job, and [Busch] gives me a two-year extension and a $75,000 a year raise," wrote Herzog years later. "And I don't have to listen to any more bullshit. Who needs an agent?"[24]

The Cardinals kicked off the home portion of their schedule against the Pirates, who had been idle since spring training after snow forced postponement of their two-game opening series versus Montreal. The Bucs had been the NL East's most successful team during the 1970s, capturing six division titles and two World Series crowns. After a third-place finish in 1980, they ended the 1981 season 10 games under .500, the franchise's worst winning percentage in 24 years. Willie Stargell was in the twilight of his distinguished career, but the Pittsburgh lineup still had the potential to do damage. Among the Pirate regulars were a pair of former batting champions—Bill Madlock and Dave Parker—as well as Mike "The Hit Man" Easler, young slugger Jason Thompson, and second-year catcher Tony Peña. It remained to be seen, however, if Parker could bounce back from an injury-riddled 1981 and if unproven middle infielders Johnny Ray and Dale Berra—son of Yogi—would rise to the challenge. Pittsburgh's pitching staff was middle of the pack, and most prognosticators were skeptical that they had the arms to compete with division foes Montreal, Philadelphia, and St. Louis. To improve their chances, the Pirates enlisted a community college professor to perform hypnosis during spring training. He had the players repeat the mantra, "the Pirates are going to win the pennant."[25]

A crowd of 40,878 watched Steve Mura make his Cardinal debut in the home opener. A trio of early walks contributed to three Pirate runs, and Mura hit the showers after requiring 47 pitches to record five outs. The bullpen was equally wild and ineffective, walking another six and yielding eight more runs, including two on a home run by opposing hurler Rick Rhoden—one of the game's best hitting pitchers.* The Cards made four defensive miscues, including one each by relievers Jim Kaat and Mark Littell, further adding to the misery of an 11–7 defeat. Lonnie Smith's first career grand slam provided one of the few highlights for the home team. *St. Louis Post-Dispatch* columnist Tom Barnidge called the display "an April Fool's joke, only nine days late."[26]

Ozzie Smith and Keith Hernandez received their 1981 Gold Glove Awards before the April 11 contest, an Easter Sunday matinee in front of a sparse congregation of 14,819. The Cardinals pounced on Pirates starter Ross Baumgarten with four runs in the first two innings. "What Baumgarten didn't throw in the dirt, the Cardinals hit," wrote one Pittsburgh scribe.[27] Bob Forsch delivered another solid outing before turning the game over to Bruce Sutter in the top of the eighth with a 5–2 lead. Sutter had trouble putting hitters away and surrendered three runs—one on a Thompson double and two on a Madlock single—which tied the game. Pittsburgh took a 6–5 lead against Kaat in the ninth. The Cards were down to their last out with many fans already heading to their cars when backup catcher Orlando Sánchez coaxed a base on balls off Enrique Romo to stave off defeat for at least one more batter. Reserve infielder Julio González, in the game as a late-inning defensive replacement, then came to the plate. The Puerto Rico native, known more for his glove than his bat, had posted a meager .294 slugging percentage through his first five big-league seasons but connected on a hanging slider from Romo. The ball sailed into the left-center field gap for a triple, scoring pinch-runner Gene Roof from first. After Ozzie Smith walked, Dane Iorg slapped a single to left field that scored González with the winning run. The Cardinals narrowly avoided a fourth defeat in five games.

The series concluded with an afternoon tilt on Monday, April 12. A recipe that the Cards would use time and again plated their first run. Lonnie Smith led off the game with a walk, stole second, advanced to third on a groundout, and scored on Keith Hernandez's single. Smith later

---

*Rhoden would finish his 16-year career with a batting average of .238 and nine home runs.

stole another base, giving him six in as many games. Speed accounted for another St. Louis tally in the fourth. Tony Peña tried to throw out Ozzie Smith on an attempted steal of second, but the throw got by shortstop Dale Berra and rolled all the way to the center-field wall, allowing Smith to scamper home. George Hendrick supplied two solo home runs to further the St. Louis cause. Sutter redeemed himself with a two-inning save for John Martin, who pitched well enough to earn a win in the 5–4 victory.

Having split their first three contests, the Cardinals headed north to the friendly confines of Wrigley Field to take on the rival Chicago Cubs for a three-game series that commenced on April 13. The Cubbies had been perennial cellar dwellers for several seasons, finishing a combined 128 games below .500 between 1973 and 1981. However, the Northsiders had a new look after hiring GM Dallas Green the previous fall. Green, who had managed the Phillies to a World Series title in 1980, had made a Herzog-esque slew of transactions in his short tenure. He handpicked his former third-base coach, Lee Elia, to be his manager and traded for several players he had in Philadelphia: Larry Bowa, Keith Moreland, Dickie Noles, and a young infielder named Ryne Sandberg. With returning productive hitters Bill Buckner, Steve Henderson, and Leon Durham, the Cubs had the makings of an improved offense, but they lacked starting pitching talent needed to be serious playoff contenders. When seven *Chicago Tribune* writers made their predictions on how the 1982 standings would shake out, none had the Cubs finishing higher than fourth in the NL East.

Andújar took the mound in the series opener wearing short sleeves despite blustery winds and temperatures in the 40s. Unaffected by the brisk climate, he pitched into the ninth inning before departing with a 4–3 lead. The imperturbable Sutter relieved and escaped a bases-loaded, one-out jam to pick up a well-earned save. One of Chicago's five hits was Sandberg's first as a Cub after going hitless in his first 20 at-bats. Stolen bases by Lonnie Smith and Tom Herr led to the first two Cardinal runs, but a rare home run by Ozzie Smith proved to be the deciding blow. Ozzie's first and only career round-tripper to that point had come on September 4, 1978. He had batted 1,774 times without hitting another before redirecting Willie Hernandez's first pitch of the ninth inning over the left-field bricks. Rick Hummel reported that the news of Smith's home run was so shocking that the national ticker service called the Wrigley Field press box to confirm that it was in fact Ozzie, and not Lonnie, that hit the home run.[28]

The next day, Andy Rincon made his first start in 340 days and outpitched future Hall of Famer Fergie Jenkins with a 104-pitch complete-game effort. Rincon's performance helped overcome a frustrating day for the offense, which amassed 16 baserunners but scored only three runs.

In the series finale on April 15, Mura atoned for his uninspiring

Redbird debut and authored a complete-game gem of his own. Solo home runs by Hendrick and Lonnie Smith provided all the runs Mura needed in the 6–1 win. In his postgame comments, Elia accused Herzog and the Cardinals of violating baseball's unwritten rules when Herr attempted to steal second with two outs in the seventh and St. Louis leading, 5–0. "You can tell him that if he promises me the Cubs won't score six runs, I'll stop trying to run," responded Herzog.[29] The victory improved the Cardinals' record to 6–3. St. Louis pitchers held Cubs hitters to a .141 average in the three-game sweep.

Through nine games as a Cardinal, Lonnie Smith was making a strong first impression, hitting .297 with a pair of homers, eight RBIs, and seven stolen bases. In terms of Baseball Reference's "Wins Above Replacement" (WAR) calculation—which measures a player's total on-field contribution in relation to his peers—no one was more valuable to the 1982 Cardinals than Smith. By the end of the regular season, he would accrue a WAR of 6.2.

Lonnie Smith's on-base skills and aggressive baserunning made him the ideal top-of-the-order catalyst (National Baseball Hall of Fame and Museum, Cooperstown, NY).

A former first-round (third overall) draft pick of the Phillies, Smith had spent several seasons trying to crack the Philadelphia lineup without much luck. He was born in Chicago and raised by an aunt and uncle in Compton, California, following the death of his mother when he was only three. Smith managed to avoid the gangs that were prevalent in his neighborhood by keeping busy with sports. He ran track but did not find running lap after lap particularly enjoyable, so he turned his attention to baseball.[30] Playing for Compton's Centennial High School, Smith's speed—four seconds flat to first base—is what initially caught attention of scouts. Had it not been for a shoulder injury that required an operation during his senior year, he likely would have been taken first overall in the amateur draft. Still, he was selected ahead of such talented contemporaries as Garry Templeton, Dale Murphy, and Rick Sutcliffe.

Smith spent two years in Single A, hitting .311 with a combined 12 homers and 68 stolen bases. At age 20, he was promoted to the Triple-A Oklahoma City 89ers. He spent most of four seasons in the Sooner State, where he consistently hit over .300, reached base at a high rate, and demonstrated elite speed. Despite these abilities, Smith was viewed as a defensive liability because of poor jumps and a below-average throwing arm. After working doggedly to improve his defense, he finally made the Phillies' opening day roster in 1979. Manager Danny Ozark inserted Smith in the leadoff spot playing right field, a position he had never played. The rookie misplayed two balls into extra-base hits and was hitless in three at-bats before Ozark replaced him with a pinch-hitter in the seventh inning. Smith did not start again for two weeks and when he finally did was removed from the game in the third inning. The dejected outfielder made the unusual request to be sent back to Triple A. "I felt better there, I felt relaxed," he explained.[31]

Back in the more comfortable environs of Oklahoma City, Smith hit .330. By September, Ozark had been fired and replaced by Dallas Green, and Smith was recalled to Philadelphia. In 1980, Smith spent the entire season in the big leagues, eventually earning more playing time. In 100 games as a semi-regular, he hit .339 and stole 33 bases. He continued his superb hitting in the postseason, batting .333 (8-for-24) and helping the Phillies capture the franchise's first championship. His impressive showing earned him a third-place finish in the Rookie of the Year voting behind Steve Howe and Bill Gullickson. After the season, Philadelphia traded left fielder Greg Luzinski but acquired Gary Matthews to replace him, again leaving Smith without a starting spot. The move was a gut punch to Smith, who, according to the *Philadelphia Daily News*, "ate himself out of shape and reported to Clearwater 15 pounds overweight" in 1981.[32] "Ever since this talk of Matthews started, I've been in limbo," said Smith at the time.

"I can't concentrate, I can't have the fun on the baseball field that I usually have."[33]

Relegated to a part-time role during most of the strike-shortened 1981 season, Smith eventually played himself into the starting center-field job, ending the year with a 23-game hitting streak during which he hit .415. Phillies GM Paul Owens parlayed Smith's hot finish into an offseason trade with Cleveland for young catcher Bo Díaz. The Indians then flipped Smith to St. Louis for a pair of pitchers. The Phillies trade of Smith did not go over well with their fans, who lit up the team's phone lines and sports talk radio with outrage, some vowing to cancel their season tickets. "Lonnie is tough, That's the one thing I'll say about Lonnie Smith. You're not going to intimidate him," remembered Dane Iorg of his 5-foot-9, 180-pound teammate.[34]

The Cardinals returned home to face the Phillies on April 16, giving a motivated Lonnie Smith the opportunity to show his former club what they were missing. Philadelphia's five losses in their first seven games and Smith's blistering start only added to the ire Phillies fans had over the trade of the talented 26 year old. "Already, the magnitude of the Phillies' blunder in getting rid of Lonnie Smith is becoming embarrassingly evident," wrote Frank Dolson in the *Philadelphia Inquirer*. "He is more than just a good, young ballplayer. He has the look, the feel, the drive of a right-handed Lou Brock—another young outfielder the Cardinals 'stole.'"[35]

The struggling Phillies were without the services of two-time reigning MVP Mike Schmidt, who was on the shelf with a fractured rib. After rain delayed the series opener nearly two hours, first-inning triples by Lonnie Smith and Darrell Porter provided Bob Forsch with early run support. Keith Hernandez recorded his 1,000th career hit with a 2-for-3 effort while raising his average to .459. Forsch limited the Phillies to two earned runs, and Bruce Sutter retired all six men he faced for his third save in the Redbirds' 3–2 triumph.

The Cardinals then faced a familiar and formidable opponent in the form of Steve Carlton, who toed the rubber for the Phillies in the middle game. After St. Louis regrettably traded the lefty in 1972, he had dominated his former club with a 30–9 record. A three-time Cy Young Award winner at that point in his career, Carlton had ruled the roost against most NL teams since joining the Phillies, but his numbers versus St. Louis were particularly jarring.* Carlton possessed an overpowering fastball, sweeping

---

*Carlton would pick up his fourth and final Cy Young Award after the 1982 season. He ended his career with a 38–14 record versus St. Louis. His .731 winning percentage against the Cardinals was his highest among NL opponents.

curveball, and devastating late-breaking slider that made him one of the game's elite hurlers. On the relatively rare instance that an opposing hitter reached base, his deceptive pickoff made it very difficult to steal bases. Carlton toed the line between a legal pickoff move and a balk. To this day, he still holds the major-league record for pickoffs (144) and balks (90). Despite Lefty's reputation, the Redbirds' kinetic running game remained in motion. Following a leadoff double by Lonnie Smith, Herr walked, and both advanced on a double steal. George Hendrick's sacrifice fly scored Smith and advanced Herr to third. Gene Tenace, fresh off the disabled list after recovering from a broken thumb, drew a walk. With Julio González at the plate, the slow-footed Tenace attempted to steal. When the catcher's throw went to second, Herr broke for home. Phillies second baseman Manny Trillo prepared to throw to the plate but dropped the ball as Herr scored for his third career steal of home, giving St. Louis a 2–0 lead. The Cards added four more runs in support of Andújar, who tossed a three-hit shutout in an expeditious two hours flat.

In the series finale on April 18, a Sunday afternoon affair, Lonnie Smith again served as the offensive catalyst for the Cards, contributing another four hits against his former club. Andy Rincon—pitching on three days' rest—threw seven innings and departed with the game tied at three. Sutter allowed a pair of runs in the top of the ninth inning, but the Cardinals evened the score in the bottom half on run-scoring singles by Hendrick and David Green. With the game still tied the bottom of the 11th, Green singled off Warren Brusstar to drive in Hernandez with the winning run. Green, who had appeared in all 12 contests, was hitting .400 (10-for-25) and showing why he was regarded as one of the game's top prospects. The victory extended the Cardinals' winning streak to eight games and improved their record to 9–3. Philadelphia, meanwhile, had dropped eight of their first 10. Though the Phillies were swept out of town, Schmidt provided bulletin board material by declaring that the Cardinals' pitching wasn't "worth a darn."[36]

On April 20, cold air from the North collided with warm air from the South across the Midwest, causing baseball-sized hail in Central Texas and 16 inches of snow in Weyerhaeuser, Wisconsin. The Cardinals, partaking in a two-game set in Pittsburgh, avoided the extreme weather, continuing their winning ways in the Steel City before traveling across Pennsylvania for a trio in the City of Brotherly Love. Contributions from players up and down Herzog's roster resulted in a sweep of the Pirates. Tom Herr stroked four hits in the first game. Tenace and Green chipped in with three apiece in the second. As well as the Cardinals were playing, they were not the hottest team in the league, however. The upstart Atlanta Braves, under new manager Joe Torre, had reeled off a record 13 consecutive wins to start the season.

With a flashy new shortstop and Lonnie Smith's charge out of the gate, it was easy to overlook the contributions of Keith Hernandez, the Cards' stalwart first baseman who occupied the third spot in the batting order. He had hit in 12 of the team's 14 games, batting .420 while averaging a walk per game.

───

Keith Hernandez's Cardinal roots were sown in his childhood. His father, John Hernandez—the son of Spanish immigrants—was a promising 18-year-old first baseman when he signed with the Brooklyn Dodgers in 1940. Like many in his generation, John's baseball aspirations were put on the back burner while serving in the United States Navy during World War II. He was stationed at Pearl Harbor, where he served on the same ship repair unit as Stan Musial. The two played on a Navy team together and struck up a friendship. After the war, John spent four more years languishing in the minor leagues, including time with the Houston Buffaloes, a Cardinals' Double-A affiliate. A beaning earlier in his career affected his vision, and he was never the same player after that. While in Houston he met Jacquelyn Jordan, who was working as a secretary with an oil company. The two married and settled in Pacifica, California, near John's hometown of San Francisco. John worked as a fireman, and the couple raised two sons: Gary and Keith. When the Cardinals visited Candlestick Park to play the Giants, Musial would leave tickets for the Hernandez family. John and the boys got to go in the clubhouse and talk with Musial, an experience that turned an impressionable young Keith into a Cardinal fan.[37]

The Hernandez boys were bred to be ballplayers and, specifically, first basemen. "Baseball was like Dad's vocation," Gary once explained. "The fire department was something that put food on the table and paid the bills. His passion was baseball and teaching us to play it."[38] John set up a batting tee in the garage by placing a tennis ball in an athletic sock that was hung by the rafters by a rope. He critiqued his sons' swings until they had they had it down pat. Young Keith would take 500 to 1000 swings a day. "I just absolutely loved it," he recalled.[39]

Even when the boys resisted, John dragged them out to the ball diamond, spending hours on batting practice and fielding. He even went as far as giving them written tests on playing first base. "He would write out situations and read them to us, and we had to answer where we'd be on the field, where the first baseman was supposed to be on field at all times. On cutoffs. Double plays. I knew fundamentals when I was eight years old," said Keith.[40]

Jacquelyn was also heavily involved in the boys' development as ballplayers. "She never missed a game," said Hernandez. "At times she would come to our batting practice sessions with a nine-millimeter camera and film motion pictures of us swinging. Dad would set up the screen in the living room, and we would have a critique and tutorial of our swings. From the very beginning, baseball was a family affair."[41]

Though John's instruction during Little League fostered Keith's development into an outstanding player, the relationship took a turn when Keith was a teenager. "Once I got into high school, he was so petrified that a coach wound ruin me," said Hernandez. "In other words, he lost control. And that's when things started to get a little dicey between me and him."[42] Their relationship remained complicated even as Hernandez became a successful major leaguer. John's obsessiveness and overbearing presence weighed on Keith, but at the same time John knew the intricacies of Keith's swing to the point where he was often the only one who could help him out of a slump.[43]

"Intense, hyper, introverted, and driven to succeed" is how one *Sports Illustrated* profile described Hernandez during his adolescent years.[44] These traits and years of preparation translated into three-sport stardom at Capuchino High School in San Bruno, California. Hernandez was a left-handed quarterback and challenged the school's scoring record on the basketball court. Near the end of his final game, he was just a few points shy of the mark but opted to dish the ball to an open teammate for an easy basket. His team won the game as a result of Keith's selfless play, but John berated him for passing the ball, leaving him in tears.

Hernandez sat out his senior baseball season after an argument with the coach. As a result, scouts questioned his attitude and passed him over for the first 41 rounds of the 1971 June amateur draft. The Cardinals finally selected him in the 42nd round but showed little motivation to sign him. That changed after Hernandez spent the summer dominating the Joe DiMaggio League, an amateur circuit in the Bay Area. John negotiated a contract with the Cardinals that netted Keith a $30,000 signing bonus. Bob Kennedy, the Cardinals' director of player development, sent Keith across the country to the Florida State League in order to "cut the apron strings" from his father.[45]

Former Cardinal pitcher Greg Terlecky vividly recalled the first time he saw Hernandez: "It was his first spring training and we were in minor-league camp. Bob Kennedy grabbed me and said, 'Come here, I want you to look at that first baseman. He's going to be in the Hall of Fame someday.'"[46]

Though Hernandez's potential was evident to the farm director, his first two seasons in pro ball were a struggle. After growing accustomed to hitting around .500 in the amateur ranks, dealing with failure for the first time, on top of the grind of playing every day, took its toll. "I hit .256 in A-ball. I hit .260 in Double A the next year. And, you know, it was tough. It was depressing," said Hernandez years later.[47]

What stood out to Terlecky looking back was that as Hernandez went up the minor-league ladder, he got better. "Most hitters settle back down. They might have a great first pro ball season, hitting maybe .300, then they'll start trickling down," said Terlecky. "Keith went the opposite direction. As he faced better competition, he became a better hitter."[48] Indeed, Hernandez's average jumped to .351 with the Triple-A Tulsa Oilers in 1974, resulting in a cup of coffee in St. Louis at the end of the season.

Hernandez entered 1975 as the Cardinals' starting first baseman, but swing changes recommended by hitting instructor Harry Walker brought unfavorable results. Walker recommended that Hernandez try to hit every pitch to the opposite field, regardless of where the pitch was in the strike zone. The lefty-swinging Hernandez lost the ability to pull the ball and his swing was zapped of power. Adding to the stress of his on-field struggles were feelings of insecurity and loneliness. One day in the clubhouse, he overheard a conversation between Bob Gibson and Al Hrabosky and interjected a thought. "Shut up, rookie," bristled Gibson. "You're just a rookie. Speak when you're spoken to."[49]

"It was a tough clubhouse—I was the youngest guy there," remembered Hernandez. "And I felt like I was a sapling in a forest full of oak trees. And I just didn't feel like I belonged."[50] By early June, he was hitting .203 with only one home run and was demoted back to Tulsa. There, he found his old swing with the help of manager Ken Boyer, hitting .330 in 85 games and earning his way back to St. Louis when rosters expanded in September. He continued his hot hitting with the Cardinals, batting .350 and cementing his status as the team's starting first baseman. Years of

Keith Hernandez was a perennial .300 hitter who played elite defense at first base (National Baseball Hall of Fame and Museum, Cooperstown, NY).

working on fundamentals with his father paid off in 1978 when Hernandez captured the first of 11 Gold Gloves, though his batting average that year dipped to .255.

Hernandez credited the mentorship of Sizemore and Brock with helping him to overcome his self-doubt. "[Lou] would just get in my face and be stern and say, 'Get mad at the pitcher. Don't feel sorry for yourself. That pitcher's out there trying to get you out in the real world and away from the game you love. Get mad at him,'" recalled Hernandez.[51]

Hernandez's best season was 1979, when he made his first All-Star team, led the league in runs (116), doubles (48), and batting average (.344) and was named the NL Most Valuable Player, an honor he shared with Willie Stargell. Hernandez proved that the breakout was no fluke, hitting over .300 in the next two seasons.

Despite his successes, questions lingered about Hernandez's attitude. A turning point came during the 1980 season after Whitey Herzog had taken over as manager. Hernandez failed to break up a double play in a game at San Francisco, and Herzog chastised his first baseman after the game. "I told him, 'I'm not picking on you, I just want you to be the player you can be,'" said Herzog.[52] The two developed a mutual respect from that point on.

Herzog effusively praised Hernandez early on in the 1982 season. "He's the best first baseman that I've ever seen at making plays to the bases. Bunts, force plays, he gets rid of the ball so quick. That's why he takes all of our relays from right field. He's so good at it." The skipper was equally complimentary about Hernandez's offensive prowess: "What he really does well is the hit-and-run. That sonofabuck is just a great hitter."[53]

———

Hernandez and his teammates strode into Philadelphia's Veterans Stadium on April 23 with growing confidence. The Schmidt-less Phillies, meanwhile, were losers in 10 of 13 games to start the season. First-year skipper Pat Corrales was already taking heat from fans, some of whom held signs calling for erstwhile Cardinal catcher Tim McCarver—a Phillies broadcaster—to be installed as manager. In search of some needed offensive production, Philadelphia called up top prospect Julio Franco from Oklahoma City.*

Aided by four walks from Phillies starter Mike Krukow, the Cards claimed an early advantage in the series opener. George Hendrick and Ozzie Smith padded the lead with homers off reliever Sid Monge. Smith's round-tripper, his second in 30 at-bats, would account for his season total.

---

*Remarkably, Franco would still be playing in the big leagues 25 years later—at age 49.

Bob Forsch hurled eight strong innings to pick up his third win in the 9–2 trouncing.

In the middle game, the Cardinals overcame Bo Díaz's 4-for-4, two-home run performance, which perhaps made the bitter pill of the Lonnie Smith trade easier for Phillies fans to swallow. Dane Iorg, another former Phillies outfielder, stepped up for St. Louis. A lifetime .298 hitter entering the season, Iorg was off to a slow start at the plate. However, he had been contributing in a different way. One day, Herzog asked him to take out the lineup card, a task usually reserved for managers and coaches. The Cards went on a winning streak, and a superstitious Herzog had sent him out every day since. With a chance to provide more than just luck, Iorg reached base safely in all four trips to the plate. Lonnie Smith added a pair of singles and drove in three, continuing his torrid hitting versus Philadelphia pitching. The 7–4 victory increased the Cardinals' run of consecutive triumphs to 12, the franchise's longest streak since 1943.* When asked how much of the streak was luck versus skill, Herzog opined, "Well, it's amazing that in any endeavor how lucky you are when you're good and when you're horse manure, how unlucky you are."[54]

The Redbirds' early success was an entirely new experience for Ozzie Smith. "It wasn't that I didn't like the feeling of winning, but it took a little while to get used to it and to know how to handle it," he later wrote. "During that streak, I realized that winning was almost completely a mental thing. I had never experienced it, but it bred more confidence in everybody, including me."[55]

The starting rotation that had its share of doubters was largely responsible for the April surge. Andújar in particular was effective in his first three starts, limiting opponents to 14 hits and two walks in 25 innings while sporting a 1.08 ERA. "Hub Kittle tells me the name of the game is throwing strikes," said Andújar. "I can throw 95 to 97. But I'm just throwing 90 or 92 and trying to win games."[56]

Steve Carlton finally snapped the winning streak in the series finale on April 25. Though he had been winless in four decisions entering the game, Carlton returned to his customary form. He was perfect for the first four innings as the Phillies amassed an 8–1 lead. The Cards rallied in the top of the ninth, sending Carlton to the showers after 138 pitches, but the comeback fell short.

The Cardinals, atop the NL East with a 13–4 record, returned to Busch Stadium for a brief three-game homestand with the Astros, who were off to a disappointing 6–12 start. Dollar Night drew an impressive

---

*The franchise's longest winning streak at the time was 14, set by the 1935 Gas House Gang.

5. April—A Dozen Straight W's   81

Monday weeknight crowd of 24,295 for the opener on April 26. After having to face Carlton the previous day, the offense had another tall task in the form of Nolan Ryan, who entered the game with an uncharacteristic 0–4 record and 7.97 ERA. Like Carlton the day before, Ryan put his early season struggles behind him, going the distance in a 6–2 victory. Lonnie Smith added two more stolen bases to his league-leading total in a losing cause. Vern Ruhle kept the Cardinal bats quiet the following night, combining with Joe Sambito for a five-hit shutout. St. Louis caught a break in the third game of the series to avoid being swept. Joe Niekro had cruised through five innings when he attempted to field a ground ball with his bare hand. With his hand numb, Niekro continued to pitch, allowing a single to Herr and walk to Hernandez before being pulled from the game by manager Bill Virdon. Niekro's replacement, Dave Smith, walked the next three hitters, including two with the sacks loaded. David Green greeted Houston's second reliever of the inning, Frank LaCorte, with a two-run single that gave the Cards a 5–3 lead. An atypically wild Bob Forsch pitched around six free passes to earn his fourth win.

Following an off day on April 29, the Cards hit the road again for four games versus the Cincinnati Reds, a team that had undergone significant roster turnover during the offseason. Their entire starting outfield from 1981—Ken Griffey, Dave Collins, and George Foster—were all now playing in New York. The Reds' front office was optimistic that a revamped outfield of Paul Householder, Eddie Milner, and César Cedeño would provide defensive upgrades to offset the loss of offensive production. Starting pitching was the Reds' strength, led by 37-year-old Tom Seaver and young Mario Soto, who combined for a win-loss record of 26–11 in 1981.

Little went right for the Redbirds in the first game of the series. Playing without Hendrick (injured) and Ozzie Smith (away for the birth of his first child), the offense could not solve Reds starter Frank Pastore, who stymied St. Louis despite admittedly having poor command of his pitches.[57] The Cardinals' middle-relief trio of Jim Kaat, Mark Littell, and Dave LaPoint—perhaps rusty from lack of use early on—was roughed up for a combined five runs in the 8–2 loss. St. Louis wrapped up April with a 14–7 record and entered May two games ahead of the second-place Expos. Herzog could hardly have hoped for a better first month of the season.

6

May

The Injury Bug Bites and McGee Debuts

"This was Whitey's team. We didn't have any team captains or any 'rah-rah' speeches. We just tried to kick ass and take prisoners."—Mark Littell[1]

The Cardinals resumed their series at Riverfront Stadium on May Day and fell behind early. Cincinnati scored three runs on six hits against Andy Rincon, resulting in the starter's third-inning exit. Reds righty Mario Soto, on the other hand, mowed down the Redbirds with ruthless efficiency, scattering five harmless singles over nine innings. Ozzie Smith, Keith Hernandez, and Jim Kaat—each among the best defensive players in the game at their respective positions—all committed errors. A seventh-inning grand slam by first baseman Dan Driessen off Kaat turned the game into a 10–1 laugher. Later in the inning, a bench-clearing incident made things more interesting. Soto, perhaps oblivious of the score or baseball's unwritten rules, tried to bunt for a hit off Mark Littell with the bases empty and two outs. The transgression was not lost on Littell, who sailed the next pitch under Soto's chin. The Reds hurler took exception and advanced toward the mound with bat in hand. Pushing and shoving ensued, but that was the extent of the hostilities. "We wrote the book on how not to play today," said Tom Herr to reporters afterwards. "Whatever could go wrong, did go wrong."[2]

Reds starter Charlie Liebrandt threw 6⅓ innings of one-run ball in the lid-lifter of a Sunday doubleheader on May 2 to defeat Steve Mura and the Cardinals, 5–1. The loss was the Cards' sixth in seven games. Michigan native John Martin was tasked with turning the team's fortunes in the second game. Martin was a former college teammate of fellow big leaguers Bob Welch and Bob Owchinko at Eastern Michigan University and 27th-round pick of the Detroit Tigers. He asserted himself as a legitimate prospect in the Tigers system in 1979, posting a 9–1 record and 1.57 ERA in 48 minor-league relief outings. Martin was dealt to St. Louis the following season in exchange for outfielder Jim Lentine and joined the Cardinals' starting rotation in 1981, logging eight wins—two of which came opposite Nolan Ryan and Steve Carlton down the stretch. Martin struggled through his first four starts of the 1982 season and owned a 5.64 ERA. He was sharp in the nightcap of the twin bill, however, and through six innings had yet to allow a hit. Keith Hernandez's two-run single and Gene Tenace's three-run homer in the top of the seventh provided Martin with a six-run cushion. He ultimately lost the no-hitter in the seventh and ran out of gas in the ninth, ceding back-to-back home runs to Dave Concepción and César Cedeño. With the game suddenly a 6–4 nail-biter, Sutter was called on to get the final two outs for his eighth save.

The Redbirds returned to St. Louis and began an eight-game homestand with a series against the Chicago Cubs on May 3. After struggling to score against top-flight hurlers for the better part of a week, the Cardinal offense found the Cubs' offerings more to their liking. The Redbirds exploded for 23 runs on 37 hits in a three-game sweep. Lonnie Smith continued to spark the lineup from his place atop the batting order, contributing eight hits in 12 at-bats. The return of several injured players also buoyed the Cards. Ken Oberkfell, recently recovered from his broken thumb, went 6-for-9. Cleanup man George Hendrick, who had missed time nursing a sore elbow, belted three home runs. And Doug Bair, limited in April due to pneumonia, threw six scoreless innings of relief and picked up a pair of wins. With a 0.61 ERA through his first nine outings, Bair was settling in as Herzog's number two righty out of the pen. The sweep left the lackluster Cubs ten games under .500 and nine and a half games behind the first-place Redbirds.

Elsewhere, Gaylord Perry became the 15th major-league pitcher—and first since Early Wynn in 1963—to notch a 300th career win in the Mariners' 7–3 victory over the Yankees on May 6. The feat offered a rare moment of celebration for baseball fans in the Pacific Northwest, who had yet to experience a winning season in the Mariners five-plus years of existence. The 43-year-old Perry, who did not look a day under 50, had notoriously baffled hitters for years with his alleged use of a spitball.

George Hendrick, one of the few sources of power in Whitey Herzog's batting order, was clearly a difference-maker in the early going. With him, the Cardinals were 16–2; when he was out of the lineup, they had lost seven of nine. His presence in the cleanup spot forced opposing hurlers to provide better pitches to hit for Keith Hernandez, who was hitting .351

(19-for-54) with Hendrick hitting behind him and .265 (9-for-34) without him. The reticent Hendrick downplayed the correlation between his name on the lineup card and the team's record at an annual dinner of the Knights of the Cauliflower Ear, an organization of sports-loving business professionals founded by Gussie Busch in the 1930s. "About the references to the amount of games we won with me in the lineup ... we're a 25-man team. No one makes the team, and certainly not with so many quality people to come in, like Dave Green and Tito Landrum and the others. I'd just like to get the record straight about that."[3]

It was a rare public comment from the man nicknamed Silent George. Hendrick's tight-lipped approach to the media began in 1976 while playing for Cleveland after he was burned by reporters on two occasions for what he thought were off-the-record conversations. "When I have something to say, I say it," said Hendrick to a reporter in 1979. "My policy has been to let you write whatever you want to write and just deal with it ... it's worked out all right."[4] Amongst teammates, Hendrick enjoyed talking cars and his beloved Los Angeles Lakers.

George Hendrick let his bat do the talking, leading the 1982 Cardinals in home runs and runs batted in (National Baseball Hall of Fame and Museum, Cooperstown, NY).

"As a person, he's one of the nicest guys on the club. Easygoing, levelheaded," described Tenace. "He's a leader by example. With a runner on second base and none out, he'll hit to the right side and move the runner to third. Lots of fourth-place hitters won't do that."[5]

Like Ozzie Smith and Eddie Murray, Hendrick grew up in the Watts neighborhood in South Los Angeles. He was discovered by scouts, including Herzog (then with the Mets), while playing for a sandlot team. Hendrick, who did not play organized sports in high school, took the field in blue jeans and a white T-shirt. "I remember I saw him on a Saturday before the first Super Bowl," recalled Herzog. "He was the only guy out there of any consequence. He had great tools. If Oakland hadn't picked him, we would have gotten him in a minute."[6] The A's took Hendrick with the first-overall pick in the 1968 January free-agent draft.

Hendrick debuted with Oakland three years later and served as a reserve outfielder his first two seasons, though he did start five games in the 1972 World Series, filling in for an injured Reggie Jackson. The A's defeated Cincinnati in a tightly-contested series that was decided in seven games. In 1973, Oakland traded Hendrick and Dave Duncan to the Cleveland Indians for Ray Fosse and Jack Heidemann.

During his four seasons in Cleveland, Hendrick averaged 22 home runs and was named an All-Star twice. Despite his success, he had his share of detractors along the way. Hendrick played a smooth, effortless-appearing outfield defense that some perceived as a lack of hustle. As Herzog wrote in his book, *You're Missing a Great Game*, early in Hendrick's career he "had a lot of problems not running balls out, jogging to flyballs in the outfield, that kind of stuff."[7] Gaylord Perry, a teammate of Hendrick's on the Indians, once thought Hendrick took a lackadaisical approach on a missed fly ball that cost Perry and the team a win. Using colorful language, Perry said that he never again wanted Hendrick in center field when he pitched. Hendrick also clashed with Cleveland manager Ken Aspromonte.

During the winter before the 1977 season, Cleveland traded Hendrick to San Diego, where he mentored Ozzie Smith during the shortstop's rookie year. "What a class act George was," recalled Padres teammate John D'Acquisto. "We used to sit next to each other during games until I had to go to the bullpen, and he would talk to me about hitters and their weaknesses, so he was preparing me for my duties in the game ... one of the most underrated players in baseball."[8]

The Padres dealt Hendrick to St. Louis in May 1978 for Eric Rasmussen. Hendrick was a welcome addition to a Cardinals lineup sorely lacking power. He led the club with 25 home runs in 1980 and was the only player on the team to reach double-digit homers in the strike-shortened season. Hendrick had a strong, accurate throwing arm and received praise from Herzog for his defensive acumen. Aside from one particular instance, Herzog had no issues with Hendrick's effort during his tenure with the Cardinals. The manager recalled a play in which Hendrick stopped at first when he could have had a double. "After the inning, I brought him in, sat him down, gave him an earful of what I thought, and fined him a few dollars," remembered Herzog. Hendrick promised his skipper it wouldn't happen again, and he was true to his word. "By the time 1982 rolled around, and we brought in some younger guys to play around him, he had become kind of the elder statesman, and he really responded to that," wrote Herzog.

"George helped out those younger players, set a good example, and became one of the most respected players on the team."[9]

Hendrick carried a .300 average, seven homers, and 18 RBIs into a series with the NL West-leading Braves on May 7. After a 13–0 start under new manager Joe Torre, Atlanta had come back down to earth with eight losses in their next 13. The Braves' record-setting streak came as a result of hot starts from middle-of-the-order hitters Dale Murphy, Bob Horner, and Chris Chambliss and near-flawless relief pitching from Steve Bedrosian and Gene Garber.

Atlanta came away with a 6–3 win in the series opener, the deciding blow a 10th inning, bases-loaded double by Chambliss. The Cardinals lost the game as well as David Green, who pulled a hamstring while trying to avoid a collision with Bedrosian at first base. Green winced in agony as he was carried off the field by Hal Lanier and Chuck Hiller. Green had been deployed as a part-time center fielder and frequent defensive replacement, hitting .316 at the time of his injury. To take his place on the roster, the Cardinals looked to a fast, rail-thin outfielder named Willie McGee.

Willie Dean McGee was born in San Francisco, California, and grew up in the East Bay town of Richmond. His father, Hurdice, worked in a naval shipping yard and helped makes ends meet for his wife, Jesse Mae, and their six children by working nights as a janitor. Hurdice also served as a deacon in the Pentecostal Church, a denomination that frowns upon sports on Sundays. Willie, obsessed with baseball from an early age, would notoriously wait for his father to take his usual nap after Sunday services and slip out of the house to play the game he loved.

As a child, McGee was described as shy, timid, scrawny, and quiet. Because he lacked self-confidence, he initially did not bother to try out for the baseball team at Henry Ells High School. The coach finally talked him into giving it a shot in the 10th grade. One preternatural skill McGee exhibited early on was blazing speed. After one of his high school teammates, Eddie Miller, was drafted by the Texas Rangers, the idea of playing professional baseball seemed within reach. McGee dedicated himself during his senior season and made the All-Northern California Baseball team. By then, scouts had taken notice of the athletic outfielder from Richmond. Yankees scout Wayne Morgan recalled that McGee did not make a lot of contact, but when he did the ball jumped of his bat.[10]

The Chicago White Sox selected McGee in the seventh round of the

1976 draft. "I came pretty close to signing with the White Sox, but I didn't feel ready," McGee later explained. "I thought I should play for another year."[11] After passing up Chicago's offer of $12,000, McGee enrolled at Diablo Valley College. The Yankees then selected him in the secondary phase of the January 1977 draft, a separate selection process for players who had previously been drafted but did not sign. McGee fulfilled his commitment to Diablo Valley that spring and then signed with the Yankees for $7,500.

McGee spent his first two years in the Yankees farm system with Single-A affiliates in Oneonta, New York, and Fort Lauderdale, Florida. Though he displayed little power, he rated as the fastest player from home to first in the organization. When he moved up to Double A in 1979, McGee dealt with a foot injury, couldn't hit a curveball, and was flustered by a long-distance relationship with a girl back home. Following a demotion back to Fort Lauderdale, he considered walking away from the game and returning to Richmond until his father gave him a pep talk over the phone. "Boy, you want to be a ballplayer? Be a ballplayer! Ain't nothin' for you here," said Hurdice to his son.[12] McGee took the words to heart and his fortunes began to turn.

McGee moved back up to the Double-A Nashville Sounds in 1980 and suffered more maladies. He sustained a foot injury and then a fractured jaw from a collision with a teammate, yet still managed to hit .283 in 78 games. Despite showing improvement, his progress up the minor-league ranks stalled. The Yankees tended to prefer big-named free agents over unproven youth, as indicated by their signing of Dave Winfield before the 1981 season, adding to a crowded outfield group that included Jerry Mumphrey, Bobby Brown, Oscar Gamble, Reggie Jackson, and Otis Nixon. The Bronx Bombers needed a 40-man roster spot, and McGee became the odd man out. "I started seeing guys with lots of ability year after year have good years and not get moved up," McGee told the *New York Times* in 1982.[13] He realized that his path to the major leagues may be to impress another organization.

With no room at Triple-A Columbus, McGee was sent back to Nashville in 1981, where he found himself on the shelf early in the season after dislocating his hip running the bases. Once he recovered, he put up his most impressive numbers yet, batting .322 with seven home runs and 24 stolen bases. McGee was named to the Southern League All-Star team along with teammate Don Mattingly. "I loved Willie. He was a great guy and a hell of a ballplayer," recalled Nashville teammate Stefan Wever. "He was an outstanding defensive outfielder, had a good arm, was very intelligent on the bases."[14]

Because McGee was not on the Yankees' 40-man roster, he was eligible for the minor-league draft following the 1981 season. Cardinals scout Hal Smith was high on McGee, but St. Louis had a low draft pick. Rather than risk losing out on McGee to another club, Herzog asked McDonald to call Yankees GM Bill Bergesch to work out a trade. From the Yankees' perspective, it made sense to deal McGee and get a player in return rather than lose him in the draft for $20,000.[15] New York settled on Bob Sykes, and the trade was consummated. McDonald and Bergesch also made a gentleman's agreement that the Cardinals would give the Yankees "future considerations" if McGee turned into a contributing member of the club. McGee did not find out he was heading to a new organization until seeing the transaction listed in his local newspaper. When he did not hear from either side for two weeks, he finally called the Cardinals to confirm what he had read.

Willie McGee came up from the minors as a short-term fill-in and never looked back. His humble demeanor and electric talent made him a fan favorite (National Baseball Hall of Fame and Museum, Cooperstown, NY).

McGee's abundance of talent was evident during spring training, as was his free-swinging hitting style. "He had a world of talent but was unorthodox," observed Bob Forsch. "He would swing at terrible pitches, then you throw the same bad pitch and he would rake it someplace. He did it so humbly, like he was embarrassed. When he came up, I knew he wouldn't hurt us."[16]

A crowd of 49,062, the sixth largest since Busch Stadium opened in 1966, packed the ballpark for Bud Light Mug Night on May 8, the same day that "Chariots of Fire" dethroned Joan Jett and the Blackhearts' "I Love Rock N' Roll" atop the *Billboard* Hot 100 chart. Cardinal pitchers, starting with Bob Forsch, allowed seven runs on 14 hits and four walks, but the offense picked them up with some come-from-behind magic. The Braves

6. May—The Injury Bug Bites and McGee Debuts 89

took the lead in the seventh and eighth innings, and in each frame the Cards tied the game in the bottom half. In the ninth, Lonnie Smith's legs nearly single-handedly accounted for the deciding run. Smith walked to lead off the inning and stole second. The next man up—Ozzie Smith—bunted back to pitcher Rick Camp, whose high throw to first was dropped by Chambliss. Smith never stopped running and slid head-first across home plate for a game-winning tally. "That ought to bring some of those 50 [thousand] back," said Herzog afterwards.[17]

Atlanta improved to 20–9 with a 3–0 win in the rubber game on May 9 as a quartet of Braves pitchers combined for a three-hitter. Horner blasted his ninth home run of the season on a low and outside slider from Joaquín Andújar, who suffered the loss. "Not too many guys hit that pitch," said Andújar. "Only one I saw before—[Roberto] Clemente."[18]

The homestand concluded with a two-game set against the Reds. With the help of Johnny Bench's 366th career home run, Frank Pastore won the first game and bewildered the Cardinal offense for the second time in 11 days. In the second game, the Cards had an impressive showing versus Mario Soto, who would lead the major leagues in 1982 with a strikeout rate of 9.57 per nine innings. Tom Herr, Ken Oberkfell, and George Hendrick each managed a pair of hits off the strong-armed righty, leading to five St. Louis runs. Doug Bair earned the save with three scoreless innings of relief. McGee—making his first career start—went 0-for-3 but walked and stole a base. Following the series split, the Cardinals owned a 20–12 record; Cincinnati stood at six games below .500.

The schedule makers next sent the Cardinals on a four-city, 13-game road trip, starting with four against the Braves. Atlanta–Fulton County Stadium, known as the "Launching Pad" for its hitter-friendly reputation, lived up to the moniker in the first game. Braves starter Ken Dayley, making his major-league debut, was chased in the second inning after giving up four runs, including a surprising home run off the bat of reserve outfielder Tito Landrum, who entered the game with only one hit in 18 at-bats on the season and zero career home runs.

Landrum was a late bloomer who had demonstrated impressive perseverance to that point in his career. He was discovered by Cardinals scout Joe Ford and signed out of a state college in Oklahoma as an undrafted free agent in the fall of 1972. Landrum, whose given name was Terry, spent seven full seasons in the minors before finally getting a cup of coffee in 1980 and then sticking with St. Louis for the entire 1981 season. He acquired his nickname during his first year of pro ball. "I was living with a couple Latin guys in a house trailer. The Jackson Five was big, and I liked to go out and dance. Ever since it's been Tito in the summer and Terry Lee in the winter," Landrum once explained.[19] "He was a good bench player because he kept his mouth shut and he knew his role. He was just happy to be there," recalled Herzog years later.[20]

Besides Landrum's long ball, another career first came in the fifth inning. With Keith Hernandez on third and Gene Tenace at second, Joe Torre elected to intentionally walk the hot-hitting Ken Oberkfell to get to McGee. Al Hrabosky was then summoned from the bullpen. The former Cardinal pitcher and future team broadcaster was known as the "Mad Hungarian" for his on-field antics and demeanor. Hrabosky had a ritual of psyching himself up to pitch by stomping around on the mound and then suddenly whipping his body around to face the hitter. The display did not intimidate McGee, who fell behind 1–2 before fighting off several fastballs and ultimately delivering a two-run single to left field for his first career base hit. Bruce Sutter, who already had five multi-inning saves, was asked to get the final eight outs after Andy Rincon—pitching in middle relief—ran into trouble. The bearded stopper allowed home runs to Dale Murphy and Claudell Washington in the ninth but managed to preserve a 10–9 victory.

Joaquín Andújar and Phil Niekro engaged in a pitcher's duel on May 14. Phil, like his brother, Joe, was a knuckleballer. The matchup was the Cardinals' fourth against one of the Niekro brothers on the young season. For some players, like Hendrick, the knuckleball was like kryptonite. He claimed the pitch would throw his swing out of whack for a week.[21] Niekro's knuckler danced, fluttered, and held St. Louis scoreless for eight innings. The Cards managed to push across a run against sidewinding righty Gene Garber to tie the game in the top of the ninth, but Atlanta's backup catcher—the fantastically-named Biff Pocoroba—hit a walk-off home run off Doug Bair in the bottom of the inning. The Cardinals lost the game and their starting catcher in the process. Darrell Porter took a foul tip off his finger and suffered a fracture that would keep him out of action for several weeks.

The Cards and Braves played another close game in front of a packed crowd of 48,433 on Saturday, May 15. John Martin started for St. Louis, but Herzog had a lightning-fast hook, pulling the southpaw after he loaded the bases in the first inning. "He was aiming the ball and I didn't want to get down early," said the skipper post-game.[22] Herzog had no tolerance for walks, and Martin would not receive another starting assignment that season. It would be a busy day for the relief corps, starting with Littell, who had been buried in the bullpen for two weeks with an ERA near eight. The Missouri Bootheel native allowed two inherited runners to score but otherwise held down the Braves for three innings. By the top of the ninth, St. Louis trailed, 3–2, when Hernandez doubled off Garber to tie the game. Sutter pitched a scoreless ninth, sending the game to extras.

6. May—The Injury Bug Bites and McGee Debuts

Ken Oberkfell and McGee singled to start the 10th inning, bringing up Sutter in an obvious sacrifice situation. The Cards closer laid down a hard bunt to the right of the mound. Garber and first baseman Bob Horner both converged on the ball, leaving no one to cover first base. Garber tried to throw out Oberkfell at third, but his errant throw nailed third-base coach Chuck Hiller, allowing Oberkfell to score. Two batters later, Lonnie Smith homered off Rick Camp to give the Cards a 7–3 lead. Sutter returned to the mound for his third inning of work but, in his words, "didn't have anything."[23] He punched out Murphy, but then Horner singled, Bob Watson doubled, and Chambliss smoked a three-run homer that cut the lead to 7–6. Herzog, having exhausted his bullpen, called on Bob Forsch to get the final two outs. The veteran starter came through, recording his first career save. "I used eight pitchers and I've only got 10," said Herzog. "The only ones I didn't use was the one who pitched yesterday and my starter tomorrow."[24]

The "starter tomorrow," Steve Mura, took the mound for the Sunday getaway game on May 16. He felt he had his best stuff of the season, but luck was not on his side. The Braves plated five runs in the first inning, in part because of a pair of bloop hits and a questionable 3–2 pitch to Murphy that was called a ball. Mura managed to settle in after the rocky start and gave his team a much-needed five innings. Hendrick's ninth homer of the year accounted for the Cards' only two runs. Rick Mahler went the distance for the victorious Braves. The loss continued a troubling trend; it marked the 11th time in 36 games the Cards had scored two or fewer runs. The pitchers weren't faring much better. Following the 12-game winning streak, St. Louis had dropped 11 of 20, a stretch during which they posted a 5.40 ERA. Herzog offered a blunt assessment: "We're going horsecrap."[25]

The Cardinals spent their "off day" on Monday, May 17, playing an exhibition game against the Triple-A Louisville Redbirds. Glenn Brummer—despite managing just three hits in 28 at-bats as Louisville's backup catcher—was added to the major-league roster in place of Porter. John Martin yielded three home runs to Louisville designated hitter Mike Calise. The minor leaguers defeated the parent club, 6–5. Following the game, the Cardinals jetted west to San Diego.

On May 18, Detroit Tigers outfielder Larry Herndon hit home runs in his first three at-bats versus the Oakland A's at Tiger Stadium. He had also homered in his last at-bat the previous game, making him only the 14th player in major-league history to homer in four consecutive plate appearances.* Herndon's big day helped move Detroit into a tie with the Boston

---

*Herndon was a third-round draft pick of the Cardinals in 1971. He debuted with St. Louis in 1974 and singled in his only official at-bat as a Cardinal. In his 14-year major-league career, Herndon hit 107 home runs.

Red Sox atop the AL East. The Brewers were in third place with a record of 18–16.

The San Diego Padres (18–15) were another team that impressed early on. The Friars' new skipper, Dick Williams, had a reputation for turning downtrodden teams into winners. Williams led the Red Sox to the AL pennant in 1967 and piloted the Expos to the franchise's first winning season in 1979. San Diego, having been willing trade partners with St. Louis, featured a trio of former Cardinals—Garry Templeton, Terry Kennedy, and Sixto Lezcano—in their regular starting lineup.

As the Cards and Padres were set to square off at Jack Murphy Stadium, all eyes were on the shortstops at the center of baseball's biggest off-season trade. Another ex–Redbird, lefty John Curtis, got the start for San Diego in the series opener. Bob Forsch, who remained undefeated despite a 7.31 ERA in his three previous starts, toed the slab for the Cardinals. The seasoned righty got back on track, breezing through the Padres lineup with an efficient five-hit shutout. Ozzie Smith, who received more cheers than boos, doubled and helped preserve the shutout with a run-saving diving stop to his left on a would-be single off the bat of Luis Salazar. Forsch helped his own cause with an RBI single, one of two runs scored by St. Louis. Gene Tenace overcame a foul tip to the family jewels with the help of smelling salts provided by trainer Gene Gieselmann and hit a home run to account for the other St. Louis tally.

Padre pitchers surrendered nine walks in the second game, but the Friars persevered to win in extra innings, 5–4. The defeat was frustrating for the Cards, who added 11 hits to the bounty of free passes but stranded 14 on base. San Diego took advantage of Tenace's below-average throwing arm with six steals, including three by rookie Alan Wiggins. As Rick Hummel wrote in the *St. Louis Post-Dispatch*, "It was a bizarre game that demanded a bizarre ending."[26] With Sutter on the mound in the 10th inning, Wiggins singled, stole second, and was sacrificed to third. Herzog then ordered intentional walks to Templeton and Ruppert Jones, loading the bases for Lezcano. The one-time Cardinal hit a grounder to Dane Iorg, who was making a rare appearance at third base. Iorg threw home to Tenace for an apparent force out but home-plate umpire Jerry Crawford ruled that Tenace missed home and called Wiggins safe. The game was marred by injuries on both sides. The Padres' talented young second baseman, Juan Bonilla, suffered a compound fracture of his left wrist in a collision with Willie McGee while covering first base on a bunt. Tenace, hitting .414 with a Ruthian OPS of 1.506, broke a bone in his right hand while diving into third base in the ninth inning. Tenace's malady left the Cards with the inexperienced tandem of Orlando Sánchez and Glenn Brummer as their only healthy catchers. "We've just got to weather

6. May—The Injury Bug Bites and McGee Debuts

that storm until we get to the rainbow," said Tenace. "But right now, we're in a damn tornado."[27]

Dave LaPoint replaced Martin in the starting rotation and started the series finale. LaPoint had a registered a mediocre 4.34 ERA in 15 relief outings, but Herzog was searching for stability at the back end of the rotation. The southpaw responded with seven strong innings, allowing only two runs in a 6–3 victory. In a true team effort, the Redbirds received contributions from several bench players; Ramsey went 2-for-5, Landrum drove in a pair, and Brummer doubled twice. Neither shortstop made much noise with the bat in the series; Smith went 2-for-12 and Templeton 1-for-11.

Contributions from the backups would prove to be one of the more underrated aspects of the Cardinals' success in 1982. Herzog had a knack for keeping his reserves happy. "He treated all people the same, not just the marquee people. He would talk to the 24th and 25th man on the team and ask about their families," wrote Bob Forsch years later.[28]

Dane Iorg credited his skipper with helping him excel in a platoon and pinch-hitting role: "Whitey was so good with the extra men. That's who he communicated with. He would always let me know a few innings in advance to get ready. And he knew I was going to face top relievers from the other team, so he always worked me in the lineup to get three or four at-bats once or twice a week, which was so valuable. It was such a privilege to play for him."[29]

Dane and Garth Iorg (pronounced ORJ), along with Forsches, Niekros, and Bretts, were one of the more successful pair of big-league siblings during the 1970s and 1980s. Born and raised in Eureka, California, Dane was drafted out of high school by the Kansas City Royals, but he elected to instead enroll at Brigham Young University in Provo, Utah. "I wasn't ready," said Iorg years later. "There was no money. I felt like my college education was a lot more valuable to me at the time, and that turned out to be true."[30] After three years at BYU, Dane was drafted by the Phillies.

Iorg hit over .300 in each of his first three years in the Phillies minor-league system. By 1976, he was knocking on the door of the big leagues, producing a .326 average, .408 on-base percentage, and 11 home runs for the Triple-A Oklahoma City 89ers. Like Willie McGee's situation with the Yankees, the Phillies were loaded with talent that made it tough for Iorg—an outfielder and first baseman—to crack the majors. The Phillies outfield at the time consisted of Greg Luzinski, Garry Maddox, and Jay Johnstone—all in the primes of their careers. Dick Allen and Bobby Tolan were established first basemen. Lonnie Smith and Iorg, both roadblocked at Triple A, were carpool buddies.

On June 15, 1977, Iorg was traded to the Cardinals as part of five-player deal for Bake McBride. "I was so happy when I got traded to St. Louis because the Phillies were an established team, and it was hard to break in. It was good for my career," said Iorg in retrospect.[31] He spent the rest of 1977 shuffling between Triple-A New Orleans and St. Louis, serving mostly as a pinch-hitter for the parent club. Iorg hit only .143 in limited duty during the first two months of the 1978 season before being sent back to the minors. "I was so upset I broke down," said Iorg. "I literally cried."[32] The frustrated 28-year-old voiced his displeasure to the front office and press at the time. After a week, he reported to Triple A, where he took his anger out on American Association pitching with a league-leading .371 average and 24 home runs. As a September callup with the Cardinals, he got a short stint as an everyday player and hit .360 in 16 games.

In 1979, Iorg finally stuck in the big leagues for a full season as a part-time outfielder. The next year, he filled in for an injured Bobby Bonds and hit .525 (21-for-40) during the month of May and .303 for the season. In the abbreviated 1981 slate, Iorg led the Cards with a .327 average and hit a whopping .441 (26-for-59) with runners in scoring position. Despite irregular playing time, he thrived in his limited role and had a knack for coming through in clutch situations. "My key was to be aggressive," said Iorg decades later. "I remember one time Whitey put me in with the bases loaded and two outs. My attitude was to make sure to get a good pitch. I was concentrating too much on that and took a 3–2 fastball down the middle. I took that to heart, and I was never going to allow that to happen again."[33]

Iorg and his teammates made the two-hour trek north on Interstate 5 to Los Angeles for a weekend set against the defending champion Dodgers May 21–23. Despite entering the series with a 19–20 record and seven losses in their previous 10 games, the Dodgers were as talented as any team in the league. Under manager Tommy Lasorda, they had won four of the last eight NL pennants with a core group of infielders—Ron Cey, Bill Russell, Davey Lopes, and Steve Garvey—that had remained constant for an unprecedented nine seasons. Following Lopes' offseason departure for Oakland, Steve Sax had taken over at the keystone and impressed with grit and enthusiasm that drew comparisons to Pete Rose. With power-hitting outfielders Dusty Baker and Pedro Guerrero and a deep starting rotation anchored by Fernando Valenzuela, the Dodgers would be an acid test for Herzog's Cardinals.

6. May—The Injury Bug Bites and McGee Debuts 95

In the series opener, St. Louis fell behind 3–0 in the first inning but scored six unanswered runs off erstwhile Cardinal and native St. Louisan Jerry Reuss. Steve Mura had his changeup and curve working and threw 140 pitches before being lifted in the ninth inning for Sutter, who recorded the final two outs for his 12th save. A 13-hit attack by the Cardinals included multi-hit efforts by both Smiths, Hendrick, and Oberkfell. Ozzie's fifth-inning double was his 11th extra-base hit of the season, matching his entire 1981 total.

Andy Rincon made his first start in 17 days in the second game of the series. The outing was bittersweet for the young hurler, who had grown up a Dodger fan in nearby Pico Rivera and had dreamed of pitching in Dodger Stadium. While fulfilling his childhood fantasy he could not escape the control problems that had plagued him throughout the season. After walking six Dodgers, Rincon had issued 25 free passes in 40 innings. He departed in the fifth inning and took the loss after Los Angeles held on to win, 3–2. "He doesn't hold runners on, and he missed a hit-and-run sign. I don't know what the problem is," said a frustrated Herzog.[34] The outing would be Rincon's last in the big leagues.

In the Sunday matinee, Bob Welch handcuffed the St. Louis offense with a five-hit shutout. "Welch pitched good, but then we really ain't got Murderers' Row out there," admitted Herzog.[35] The running game that had been so prolific early on, had come to a halt because, as Rick Hummel pointed out, "Either the slow runners are getting on, or the ones with bad legs are getting on, or they get so far behind they can't run as often as they'd like."[36] Lonnie Smith, who had swiped 19 bases in his first 33 games, had gone eight days without attempting a steal. Forsch allowed all five Dodger runs and absorbed his first loss of the season.

The Cardinals limped into Candlestick Park down to their third and fourth-string catchers and without the services of Herr and Hendrick—both on the active roster but out of the lineup with sore legs. McGee started for just the second time since making his major-league debut two weeks earlier. He figured it was a matter of time before he would be sent back to Triple A. "Sooner or later, it's going to have to happen, when one of those catchers comes back," he surmised.[37] But for the time being, the rookie was soaking up the moment, playing just across the bay from his hometown.

The struggling Giants (19–24) sent Rich Gale to the mound opposite of Joaquín Andújar in the opener. Flanking McGee in center were Lonnie Smith in left and David Green, fresh off the disabled list, in right. The alignment made Smith the slowest member of an outfield for the first time in his life. The Cards struck first when Ramsey tripled to score Green. In the top of the fourth inning, McGee came to the plate with the bases loaded and his team up, 2–0. He ripped a Gale offering over the head of first baseman Jack Clark into the right-field corner for a bases-clearing triple. "This is the best thing that's happened to me in my life," said McGee after the game, quickly adding "except for my parents and my family. Without them, I wouldn't be where I am today."[38] Andújar was exceptional, improving his record to 4–3 with a complete-game, six-hit shutout that lowered his ERA to 2.45. When it came to Andújar's hitting, there was room for improvement. Using his usual 40-ounce bat, he struck out twice, bunted into a double play, and popped out. "But I'll tell you, when I make contact, you're not going to see that ball, it will go so far," he warned.[39]

On May 25, Cubs starting pitcher Fergie Jenkins fanned Garry Templeton on an 0-2 fastball, becoming only the seventh pitcher in major-league history to record 3,000 strikeouts. The elite fraternity included Walter Johnson, Bob Gibson, Tom Seaver, Nolan Ryan, Gaylord Perry, and Steve Carlton. Young Dave LaPoint had 26 career strikeouts under his belt when he took the mound for the Cardinals that night at Candlestick Park. Three miscues by the San Francisco defense contributed to an 8–3 St. Louis victory. Oberkfell and Brummer drove in a combined five runs to pace the visitors. Brummer's two RBIs came on a ball that did not leave the infield. With Green at third and Ramsey at second, Brummer hit a high bouncer to second baseman Guy Sularz, who made an off-balance throw to first. Brummer, hustling all the way, beat the toss. Green scored and Ramsey rounded third and kept running, scoring all the way from second base. "If we're going to win, we have to play that way," said Ramsey after the victory.[40] The running game, which had conspicuously vanished the week before, was revived by Ramsey and McGee, who combined for three steals.

St. Louis completed a sweep of the Giants on May 26 with an eight-run, 17-hit outburst. The Cardinal backups ensured that the road trip would end on a positive note. Ramsey recorded three hits, finishing the series 7-for-11 plus a pair of walks. Landrum started in right field and went 3-for-5 with a homer and three RBIs. Mura gave up four runs on 11 hits, but four double plays turned by the defense helped him survive long enough to earn a win. "They're exciting to watch," said a frustrated Jack Clark after the sweep. "We're the opposition and we're having fun watching them beat us … that's the team the guys over here want and the kind of team I want to play on."[41]

The short-handed Cards finished the long road trip 8–5 and returned home with a 28–17 record and a two-and-a-half-game lead over the surprising Mets. Besides a winning record, the most encouraging development on the trip was the emergence of Dave LaPoint, who won both of his starts while recording nine strikeouts against only one walk.

6. May—The Injury Bug Bites and McGee Debuts

LaPoint was born and raised in Glens Falls, New York, a town on the Hudson River, 50 miles north of Albany. Shortly after graduating high school, the fresh-faced 17-year-old lefty was plucked by the Milwaukee Brewers in the 10th round of the 1977 draft. He showed steady improvement as he progressed up the Brewers minor-league chain. In his third year of pro ball, LaPoint struck out an eye-popping 208 batters in 180 innings for Single-A Stockton. By 1980, he had moved up to the Brewers' Triple-A affiliate in Vancouver, British Columbia. He hurt his arm that season and lost velocity on his fastball. No longer able to overpower hitters with speed, he worked on developing a changeup, a pitch that tailed away from right-handers. John Stuper—who would go on to a long tenure coaching at Yale University—later called it the best changeup he had ever seen.[42] The pitch accelerated LaPoint's ascension to the majors. The 6-foot-3, 205-pounder earned a callup to the Brewers in September 1980, appearing in five games.

After he was acquired by the Cardinals, LaPoint went 13–9 with a 3.19 ERA in 25 games for the Springfield Redbirds in 1981. During the players' strike, Herzog was on hand for one of LaPoint's starts and told him he wanted him to throw 70 percent changeups. "I said, 'Whitey, I'm not a real math genius but if I throw 100 pitches, you want me to throw 70 changeups? He goes, 'I've already told your catcher and I'm going to be sitting behind home plate, so you better.' I did, and I had a shutout and like 13 strikeouts," recalled LaPoint years later. "He said, 'Son, when the strike is over, you're going to the major leagues.'"[43] Herzog kept his word, and LaPoint picked up a key late-season win for St. Louis during the unsuccessful playoff push. Now back in his preferred role as a starter, he had stabilized the back end of the Cardinals rotation.

Following a much-needed day off, the wearied Redbirds returned to Busch Stadium for nine games versus the three California teams beginning May 28—the same day *Rocky III* hit movie theaters. The film's theme song, Survivor's "Eye of the Tiger," became a rock anthem that blared from stereo speakers throughout the summer.

The Cards' first opponent on the homestand was Garry Templeton's Padres. The ostracized shortstop, making his first appearance in St. Louis since the infamous trade, was quoted in the publication *Inside Sports* as calling Herzog a "backstabber." Herzog, responding to the jab, said, "How can I be a backstabber? He wanted to be traded to the West Coast and he wanted to play on a grass field. I gave him both of those."[44]

Templeton was booed lustily by the crowd of 31,733 each time he came to the plate in the Friday night opener. The jeers turned to cheers when he recorded outs in all four of his at-bats. Padres manager Dick Williams called Templeton's treatment "embarrassing" and said he was "ashamed to admit that I was born in St. Louis."[45] Templeton's counterpart, Ozzie Smith, was also hitless but made multiple spectacular plays in the field. While many were curious to see how the two shortstops would fare, the Cardinals' rookie centerfielder stole the spotlight. Willie McGee tripled, singled, walked, stole a base, and scored half of his team's six runs. Forsch notched his sixth victory and Sutter saved another.

Despite his electric performance, McGee found himself back on the bench the following night. A baserunning blunder by Joaquín Andújar in the bottom of the eighth proved costly. With the game knotted at two, the Cardinal starter got caught in a rundown between second and third while trying to advance on Ozzie Smith's single. After Andújar was ruled out for intentionally knocking the ball out of Luis Salazar's glove, Smith too was thrown out on the play. Tim Flannery's ninth-inning blooper landed just out of the reach of third baseman Ken Oberkfell to break the tie. Eric Show closed it out for San Diego in the bottom half of the inning.

The series finale on the afternoon of Sunday, May 30, was a wild affair in which the Redbirds twice rallied to avoid defeat. LaPoint pitched eight innings of two-run ball before San Diego added a third run off Doug Bair in the top of the ninth. The Cards' offense, meanwhile, was blanked through eight frames by southpaw Tim Lollar and then Gary Lucas in relief. Keith Hernandez and George Hendrick, the latter recovered from a pulled hamstring, started a ninth-inning rally with back-to-back singles. Lonnie Smith doubled home Hernandez and Julio González reached on an error, scoring Hendrick. Tom Herr, still injured but on the active roster, pinch-hit and tied the game with a sacrifice fly. In the top of the 10th, Sutter allowed two runs to score, the second coming on a tailor-made double-play ball that was botched by Ramsey. In the home half of the inning, the first two Cardinals were retired. Down to their last out as storm clouds rolled over Busch Stadium, many fans headed for the exits. Hendrick kept the game alive with a single and scored on a double by Lonnie Smith. Ramsey, who committed four errors in the series, redeemed himself with a game-tying single. González was hit by a pitch, loading the bases for pinch-hitter Dane Iorg, whose broken bat flare dropped in center field to score the game-winning run.

The Cardinals ended May on a winning note the next night, blowing out the Giants 11–6 in the first game of a three-game series at Busch. Ten of the runs came in the fourth inning during a nine-hit barrage that included a pair of walks and two errors by San Francisco. McGee had two hits during the relay race of an inning and four in the game. His early

6. May—The Injury Bug Bites and McGee Debuts

success surprised Herzog. "I certainly didn't think he'd be able to come up here and handle the pitching like he has," said the skipper.[46]

Through the season's first two months, St. Louis held a 31–18 record—the best mark in the NL—and had declared themselves strong contenders in the NL East. The Mets, Expos, and Phillies were bunched at second, third, and fourth in the division. The Cubs and Pirates had fallen well off the pace, trailing the Cards by 10 and 11 games, respectively.

In the junior circuit, the Brewers' 22–24 record had them at sixth place in the seven-team AL East. Entering the season, expectations had been high in Milwaukee after four straight winning seasons and the franchise's first playoff appearance in 1981. The disappointing start cost manager Buck Rodgers his job. On June 2, Brewers GM Harry Dalton replaced Rodgers with the team's hitting coach, Harvey Kuenn. The Brew Crew's fortunes would quickly turn.

7

June

Stuper Is Super and Sutter Struggles

> *"June is when baseball really begins. Now partisanship deepens, and we come to the time when the good weather and the sights and sounds of the game are no longer quite enough."*—Roger Angell in *Five Seasons*[1]

John Stuper inherited his passion for America's pastime from his father, Frank, who labored in the coal mines of western Pennsylvania for more than 30 years. Frank would come home from work exhausted, his hands covered in grime, but he always made time to play catch with his son. As an unexceptional high school pitcher, John was not on the radar of any professional scouts or major universities. Butler Community College gave him a chance, and he flourished with a 25–3 record over two seasons while earning all-conference honors. He then transferred to Pittsburgh's Point Park College, where he helped the school's ball team to the 1978 NAIA World Series. By that time, scouts had taken notice. The Pirates—Stuper's favorite team growing up—drafted him in the 18th round.

Stuper was assigned to the Single-A Charleston Pirates of the Western Carolinas League, where he amassed a record of 4–8 with a 5.33 ERA in his first season as a pro. He walked almost twice as many batters as he struck out. After that poor showing, the Pirates traded him to the Cardinals in exchange for minor-league infielder Tommy Sandt. "When we got him, he was a strong and well-conditioned kid, but he was throwing down from the side and being used in relief," said Hub Kittle in 1982. "Gradually, we changed his mechanics and when he came over the top the ball began to jump. He was throwing his fastball at 90, 91 miles per hour."[2] Things fell into place for Stuper with the Double-A Arkansas Travelers in 1980. The 6-foot-2, 200-pound righty won seven of nine decisions and was added to the Cardinals' 40-man roster that fall. He then logged another 100 innings

7. June—Stuper Is Super and Sutter Struggles

in the Mexican Winter League, pushing his innings total for the calendar year well over 200.[3] All that pitching led to arm fatigue the next season, when he posted a 6–14 record and ERA near five at Triple A.

Stuper rested his arm during the winter and reported to spring training in 1982 looking to reestablish himself as a prospect. From the Grapefruit League, he was sent to Louisville, where he brandished a 7–1 mark and 1.46 ERA in eight starts. When the Cards looked for help from the farm to replace a struggling Andy Rincon, Stuper got the call. His debut came on June 1 versus San Francisco. Stuper worked quickly and appeared composed in front of the Busch Stadium crowd, tossing eight effective frames while surrendering just three runs. Giants starter Atlee Hammaker was equally effective, however, and Stuper took a no-decision in the Giants' extra-inning victory.

In the series finale, Ozzie Smith went 2-for-3, stole three bases, and scored the game's only run on a single by Keith Hernandez. Joaquín Andújar went the distance, outpitching Bill Laskey with a brilliant six-hitter. Andújar nearly lost his shutout with two outs in the ninth inning when Darrell Evans hit a deep blast to right field, but the ball caromed off the wall. "I knew he hit it good," said Andújar. "I thought, 'Oh, no. Bye-bye.' I put my head down, just waiting for my heart attack."[4] Having avoided a cardiac event, Andújar retired the next man up, Johnny Lemaster, to end the game. Andújar claimed afterwards that 115 of his 120 pitches were fastballs.[5] "That son of a gun has become a pretty good pitcher," said Giants skipper and soon-to-be Hall of Famer Frank Robinson. "He's been a thrower before, but now he's a pitcher. He's still relying on his fastball, but he's cutting it and getting it where he wants it."[6] Andújar's stellar outing improved his record to 5–4 and lowered his ERA to 2.37.

Rookie pitcher John Stuper debuted in June and helped stabilize the starting rotation (National Baseball Hall of Fame and Museum, Cooperstown, NY).

The Redbirds enjoyed an off day on June 3 before welcoming the scuffling Dodgers to town for a weekend series. Though the Cards had won four of the first six games on the homestand, they had yet to hit a home run. George Hendrick ended the power outage, breaking open a scoreless game in the fifth inning of the series opener with a two-run blast off Dave Stewart. The round-tripper was Hendrick's team-leading 10th of the season. The Cardinals stole an insurance run in the seventh inning off reliever Terry Forster when Glenn Brummer doubled, astutely stole third base, and scored on Bob Forsch's squeeze bunt. Forsch's workmanlike approach on the mound kept the Dodgers lineup off-balance and off the basepaths. Mixing his fastball, slider, and curveball, the crafty righty allowed only two runs and twirled his second complete game of the season in a 5–2 victory. The win improved his record to 7–1 and was the 100th of his career, placing him in elite company; Forsch became just the 11th pitcher in franchise history to reach the milestone.* "It's nice but it's just a number," said the humble hurler. "The important thing to me is that I won all 100 with the same club."[7]

Bob Forsch came from a baseball family. His father, Herbert, was a native South Dakotan who married a Canadian named Freda. The pair eventually settled in California, where Herb showed his wares as an infielder and pitcher in the San Joaquín Valley League, earning $15 a game while working at the winery that sponsored the team. He pitched on Sundays and kept his arm in shape by throwing to Freda in their backyard. "I'd smoke 'em in there pretty good, too, and she'd catch 'em," Herb once said. "I didn't have to worry about her. She could handle the glove."[8] Kenneth was born in 1946 and Robert came along in 1950. Both took to baseball an early age. Herb operated an electric motor repair shop, and the family owned a chicken farm on several acres of land in Sacramento. Herb used part of the acreage to build ball field for the boys to play on. "All I ever wanted them to do in sports was to play, so they'd stay off the streets," said Herb in 1987.[9]

By the time Ken and Bob were teenagers, they had honed their baseball skills to the point where playing professionally was a real possibility. Ken, a pitcher, played one year at Sacramento City College and then at Oregon State on a baseball scholarship. When Bob was in high school, he earned enough money working at Herb's shop to buy a pitching machine

---

*The other 10 pitchers to reach 100 wins in a Cardinals uniform up to that time were Bob Gibson, Jesse Haines, Bill Sherdel, Bill Doak, Dizzy Dean, Harry Brecheen, Slim Sallee, Mort Cooper, Larry Jackson, and Max Lanier. Since then, only Matt Morris and Adam Wainwright have joined the list.

for the backyard. Bob signed a letter of intent to follow in Ken's footsteps at Oregon State but was drafted by the Cardinals as a third baseman–outfielder in 1968 and decided to turn pro. Ken was drafted that same year by the Houston Astros.

Fresh out of Hiram Johnson High School, Bob took a red-eye flight to Florida for minor-league spring training. He arrived at eight in the morning and found out he had to report to the field only two hours later. The sleep-deprived teenager was issued a wool uniform and had to wear a helmet because they ran out of hats. "What I didn't know was that every afternoon in Florida, it rains," Forsch later wrote. "Those wool uniforms don't do well in the rain. Stink? Oh, yeah. And this was the clean one. I was standing out there in the rain, thinking, 'What am I doing here?'"[10]

Forsch played in an afternoon game that day and then overslept for the night game, barely making it before the bus pulled away. Sitting on the bench during the game, an older coach walked by and barked, "What's the count and how many outs are there?" Forsch read the numbers off the scoreboard. "Don't ever be on the bench and not know the count and how many outs!" exclaimed the coach. "You always have to be involved in the game. If you're gonna sit there, learn something!" That coach turned out to be legendary minor-league instructor George Kissell. "I found out George was always right," Forsch later recalled.[11]

Forsch played third base and posted an identical .223 average both in rookie ball and his first year at Single A. In his third year in the minors, he hit a dismal .126 and struck out in 52 of his 111 at-bats. His future in baseball looked bleak. When Cardinals farm director Bob Kennedy suggested he give pitching a try, Forsch figured he had little to lose. After all, Stan Musial had come up as a pitcher before transitioning to a position player. "We joked that he would be the next Stan Musial but the opposite," recalled teammate Greg Terlecky.[12]

Forsch, who was a slender 6-foot-4, became a full-time pitcher in 1971 and steadily progressed up the minor-league ranks. By 1973, he was pitching for the Tulsa Oilers—the Cardinals' Triple-A affiliate—and was considered among the organization's top pitching prospects, along with Terlecky. "Sometimes, it gets a little competitive in Triple A about who's going to get called up, who's going to get a shot," said Terlecky. "You could tell there were some players who weren't rooting for you, but Bob always rooted for you. He was a great teammate, a quiet leader. He wasn't a rah-rah guy but was very professional."[13] In 1974, Forsch earned a promotion to St. Louis, quickly becoming a reliable member of the starting rotation. In 1977, he turned in a 20-win season against only seven losses—a .741 winning percentage.

On Sunday, April 16, 1978, Forsch became the first Cardinal pitcher in

54 years to throw a no-hitter in St. Louis when he blanked the Phillies at Busch Stadium.* The achievement was not without controversy, however. In the eighth inning, Garry Maddox hit a ground ball that skipped under the glove of third baseman Ken Reitz. The play was ruled an error by Neal Russo, a sportswriter from the *St. Louis Post-Dispatch* who was serving in the role of official scorer. "It was an error all the way," said Reitz after the game. "But it was the first time I ever received a standing ovation for making an error."[14] Phillies third baseman Mike Schmidt and manager Danny Ozark were among those in the visitors' clubhouse who thought the play should have been ruled a hit. "That far along in the game, the first hit has to be a clean hit," said Russo in defense.[15] When Ken threw a no-hitter of his own for Houston a year later, the Forsches became the first set of brothers in major-league history to accomplish the rare feat.

Steady Bob Forsch anchored the rotation by throwing strikes and letting his defense do the rest (National Baseball Hall of Fame and Museum, Cooperstown, NY).

Bob Forsch was often described as mild-mannered, quiet, and humble. He possessed a dry wit that shines through in *Tales from the Cardinals Dugout*, a book he co-authored with Tom Wheatley. Forsch came up as a hard thrower but developed an excellent changeup and curveball that he used with pinpoint control, an understated style of pitching that matched his personality. His walk rate of 1.4 batters per nine innings in 1980 was the lowest in the league. Forsch relied on mixing speeds and utilizing his excellent defense to win ballgames. He was the longest-tenured member of the 1982 roster and the only starting pitcher still with the club following Herzog's rebuild.

---

*The Cardinals' most recent road no-hitter at the time was thrown by Bob Gibson in 1971. Jesse Haines had thrown the last home no-hitter in 1924.

7. June—Stuper Is Super and Sutter Struggles

On June 5, the Minnesota Twins (13–41), owners of the major league's worst record, hosted the Baltimore Orioles at the Metrodome. Cal Ripken Jr., Baltimore's talented rookie, batted seventh and played third base. It marked the start of the iron man's streak of 2,632 consecutive games played. By season's end, Ripken would club 28 home runs and capture AL Rookie of the Year honors.

Farther down the Mississippi River, the Cardinals faced Fernando Valenzuela, the Dodgers' 21-year-old sensation who had taken the league by storm a year earlier, using an unhittable screwball to lead the NL in strikeouts (180) and shutouts (8) while winning both the Rookie of the Year and Cy Young Awards. The phenom helped draw a throng of 46,025 to Busch Stadium for the Saturday night tilt. Valenzuela lived up to the hype and flummoxed Redbird hitters for nine innings to earn his league-leading eighth win of the season. "That sumbuck can pitch," Herzog bluntly assessed.[16] Steve Mura was roughed up for six runs in 5⅔ innings and took the loss, falling to 5–4. First baseman Steve Garvey paced the Dodgers with three hits, one of which was his 200th career home run.

Besides having his hands full with Valenzuela, Herzog was faced with some difficult roster decisions. A roster spot was needed to make room for Darrell Porter, who had recovered from his broken hand. Willie McGee had previously been viewed as a short-term callup, but he was playing so well that the team had to consider other avenues. Thus, John Martin became the odd man out, leaving the Cardinals with an unsustainable active roster composition of seven outfielders and only four relievers. The Cards attempted to solve the logjam by prying lefty reliever Gary Lavelle from San Francisco in exchange for a three-player package that inclued Tito Landrum, but the Giants rebuffed the offer, forcing St. Louis to look to the farm system to rebalance the roster. Before the next day's game, Steve Braun was placed on the disabled list with a sore shoulder, providing a temporary solution for the over-staffed outfield. Taking Braun's place on the roster was right-handed reliever Jeff Keener, who was called up from Double A.

In the homestand finale against the Dodgers on June 6, the Cards held a 3–2 lead heading to the ninth inning with Bruce Sutter on the mound. Coming into the game, St. Louis held a 29–1 record when leading after eight innings. The odds were undoubtedly in the Cardinals' favor, though perhaps they were due for a late-inning collapse. Steve Sax's two-run triple that landed just beyond the reach of McGee proved to be the decisive blow.

The 5–4 homestand left the Redbirds with a 33–21 record, four and a half games ahead of the Expos, Mets, and Phillies, who were in a three-way tie for second place. Overshadowed by the loss was another multi-hit game for McGee, his fourth in seven starts during the homestand, a stretch during which he hit .400 (12-for-30) with three stolen bases. McGee's hot bat forced Herzog's hand, and his playing time came at the expense of Green. "I hate for David to not play at all right now," said Herzog before the Dodgers series, "but I've got to find out about Willie. He hasn't shown me he can't play."[17]

Major League Baseball's June amateur draft took place on Monday, June 7. The Cubs had the first overall pick and selected Shawon Dunston, a high school shortstop and the consensus best player on the board. Dunston stole 33 bases without getting caught and hit a ridiculous .790 with six home runs during his senior season at Brooklyn's Thomas Jefferson High School.[18] With the second pick, the Blue Jays chose another shortstop, Augie Schmidt, who ultimately never made it past Triple A. With the third and fourth picks, the Padres and Indians chose pitchers Jimmy Jones and Bryan Oelkers, respectively, passing on Dwight Gooden, who fell to into the lap of the Mets with the fifth pick. The Cardinals made 6-foot-5 right-hander Todd Worrell their first rounder with the 21st overall selection. Other notables from the St. Louis draft class included Terry Pendleton (seventh round) and Vince Coleman (10th round).

While the Cardinals' scouts and team brass were looking ahead to the future, the major leaguers headed north of the border to battle the Expos, who boasted a lineup that included all-star catcher Gary Carter, five-tool outfielder Andre Dawson, perennial .300 hitter Al Oliver, and the league's defending stolen base leader, Tim Raines. With a solid rotation anchored by Steve Rogers and a shutdown closer, Jeff Reardon, it was easy to see why a majority of sportswriters had picked Montreal as the favorite to win the NL East.

Sutter faltered for the second day in a row, allowing the Expos to take the first game. The Redbirds' fireman entered the game in the eighth inning with a runner on second, one out, and the game tied, 2-2. Sutter walked the bases loaded but then escaped the jam on a pair of pop-outs—a red flag given that the downward action of his signature split-fingered pitch was intended to induce groundballs and miss bats. In the bottom of the ninth, Sutter caught too much of the plate with a first-pitch fastball to Warren Cromartie, who sent the ball sailing over the right-center field wall for off for a game-winning homer. "I think that was the only hit I got off him," said Cromartie years later.[19] Actually, Cromartie was 5-for-29 in his career against Sutter—a .172 average—but that was the only home run he managed to hit off him. Sutter bristled when reporters inquired about the fateful pitch after the game. "It doesn't matter what kind of pitch is was," he said. "It doesn't matter whether it was up or down. It doesn't matter whether it was a good pitch or a bad pitch. It was a home run. That's all that matters."[20]

7. June—Stuper Is Super and Sutter Struggles

The baseball world was dealt a blow on June 8 with the passing of Leroy "Satchel" Paige, whose legendary pitching career in organized baseball spanned nearly 40 years. In 1957, Paige and Herzog were teammates with the Triple-A Miami Marlins. One day, Herzog and his fellow outfielders were holding a long-distance throwing contest from center field to home plate. Paige—who was listed as 49 years old but rumored to be older—strolled over and, without warming up, threw the ball 400 feet on a line from the center-field fence to home plate.[21]

In the middle game of the Cards–Expos series, Herzog quite literally squeezed out a victory. The skipper had watched his team leave 11 men on base the day before and then muster only one run through six innings against Steve Rogers. Herzog pushed the envelope with his team trailing, 2–1, in the seventh. Tom Herr walked to lead off the inning and then stole second, showing no ill effects from the quadriceps strain that had sidelined him for the better part of three weeks. After Herr advanced to third on a groundout, Herzog called for a squeeze bunt. Pinch-hitter Mike Ramsey executed the play to perfection, scoring Herr to tie the game. The score remained even in the eighth when the Expos loaded the bases off Steve Mura and Jim Kaat. With two outs, Herzog summoned rookie Jeff Keener to make his major-league debut.

Keener grew up in Albion, a small town in southeastern Illinois near the Indiana border. Like many kids in towns across the Midwest in that era, he grew up listening to the voices of Jack Buck and Harry Caray. Once a year, his family would make the two-hour drive west to Busch Stadium to catch a game. Jeff's father, John, was a teacher and high school baseball coach, and the father-son duo spent countless hours playing catch in the backyard. By high school, Keener had developed into an excellent pitcher and helped Edwards County High School to the final eight in the state tournament, where his team competed against much larger schools from Chicago and Peoria. "They had more kids in their school than we had in our town," recalled Keener.[22]

Keener dealt with injuries his senior year and did not receive any baseball scholarship offers. His father called around to college coaches in the region, including Rich Hacker, who was coaching at Southeastern Illinois College in Harrisburg. Hacker gave Jeff a shot and encouraged him to throw only side-arm (he had thrown three-quarters and side-arm in high school). "In my first outing, I pitched in relief, and I didn't get an out," said Keener. "Hack came out and was very encouraging. From there, I steadily got better."[23]

After two years at Southeastern Illinois, Keener transferred to the University of Kentucky. He compiled a 7–4 record as a starting pitcher with the Wildcats his junior year and went 13–1 his senior season as a reliever while breaking an NCAA record with a 0.57 ERA.[24] Cardinals scout Virgil Melvin invited Keener to Busch Stadium for a tryout, and the Cardinals selected him in the seventh round of the 1981 draft. Keener spent spring training in minor-league camp and was assigned to Arkansas to start the 1982 season. He had heard from Cardinals farm director Lee Thomas that he might be getting the call up to Triple A but was surprised when Thomas gave him the news that he was going all the way up to the parent club.

Keener's adrenaline was pumping as he stood on a big-league mound for the first time in front of more than 37,000 Olympic Stadium fans with the game on the line. "I looked down at my chest, and I was so nervous you actually could see my jersey moving out from my heart beating," recalled Keener decades later.[25] Showing no outward signs of nervousness, he fanned Tim Wallach to erase the threat. Keener returned to the mound in the ninth and retired the side in order to send the game to extra innings. The two teams traded runs in the 11th inning, and the Cards took the lead again in the 12th when Willie McGee tripled home Ozzie Smith. With McGee on third and Ken Oberkfell at the dish, Herzog called for another squeeze. Oberkfell, like Ramsey earlier in the game, laid down a superb bunt to score McGee. The successful squeeze was the Cardinals' fifth in six attempts on the season. The insurance run proved to be the decisive tally; Montreal plated one off Sutter in the bottom of the inning but no more. In the visiting manager's office, Herzog called the game "a breathtaking experience."[26]

In the rubber game on June 9, Gary Carter's two-run homer off Bob Forsch provided all the run support Bill Gullickson needed in the Expos' 5–1 victory. Forsch's loss was only his second in nine decisions. Willie McGee finished the series 6-for-15, raising his average to .362. It was becoming increasingly difficult for Herzog to keep him out of the lineup.

The Cardinals next traveled to New York for their first look at the Mets (29–27), the only NL team they had yet to play. The Mets' prized offseason acquisition, 33-year-old outfielder George Foster, was hitting .242 with only seven home runs after signing a franchise-record $10 million contract. Foster paired with Dave Kingman to form a threatening one-two punch in the middle of George Bamberger's lineup—at least when they made contact. The duo had each averaged more than 30 home runs in the previous seven seasons. Kingman entered the series with 15 home runs—on his way to a league-best 37—but was hitting only .209 and had struck out in nearly one out of every three at-bats. The two strikeout-prone sluggers were surrounded by a budding crop of position players like Mookie Wilson, Wally Backman, and Hubie Brooks, but the starting pitching rotation was not on par with the league's legitimate contenders.

The Cards–Mets kicked off the series on June 11 while many folks across the country packed theaters for the premiere of Steven Spielberg's *E.T. the Extra-Terrestrial*, which would eventually become the highest-grossing movie of all-time. Whitey Herzog had most of his regulars in the lineup for the first time in several weeks. The result was a terrific all-around performance in which every spot in the batting order recorded at least one hit in a 7–3 triumph. McGee went 2-for-5 for the fourth consecutive game. Darrell Porter had three hits, including a home run. Even Joaquín Andújar contributed to the offensive attack, going 2-for-3 with a pair of RBIs while tossing another complete game. He walked just one and had allowed only 16 free passes in 102⅓ innings. The eccentric righty was emerging as the de facto ace of the staff.

Joaquín Andújar's whimsical personality grew out of the southeastern Dominican town of San Pedro de Macorís, where he was born and raised by his grandparents. Joaquín's grandfather, like many impoverished Dominicans under Rafael Trujillo's dictatorship, worked in one of the region's numerous sugar mills. As the country went through a series of regime changes in the 1960s, several Dominican ballplayers—including Juan Marichal, Rico Carty, and the Alou brothers—broke out as big-league stars.

Joaquín took to baseball at an early age. Without money to buy gloves and bats, he and his peers made do with what they had. "We used to make a rag ball, or we bought a rubber ball and played in the streets," Andújar later recalled.[27] As he got older and played on organized teams, Andújar developed into a power-hitting center fielder with a strong throwing arm. He displayed a fiery temper as a youngster, once tearing his jersey to shreds after his coach removed him from a game.

Wilfredo Calvino, a former minor-league catcher who scouted for the Cincinnati Reds, observed a teenage Andújar throwing from the outfield and suggested he try his hand at pitching. "I told him that I didn't care, that the only thing I wanted was to go to the United States to make money and help my family and myself," Andújar later reflected.[28] Calvino signed him to a professional contract weeks before his 17th birthday.

Andújar was assigned to the Reds' rookie-level squad in the Gulf Coast League, where the fire-balling righty struck out more than a batter per inning and earned all-star accolades. Andújar's sophomore season in 1971 did not go as well. Pitching for the Reds' Single-A affiliate in Sioux Falls, South Dakota, Andújar struggled with control, walking 7.6 batters per nine innings. "You're not Juan Marichal," manager Dave Pavlesic told the young hurler. "You'd better learn how to pitch."[29]

Andújar spent three seasons bouncing between Double-A Trois-Rivières (Québec) and Triple-A Indianapolis in the Reds system and toiled during off-seasons for a Dominican Winter League team managed by Kittle. The only thing predictable about Andújar was his unpredictability. "Almost every night he pitched—at least one inning—he would walk the first three hitters then turn right around and strike out the next three guys," recalled minor-league teammate Roe Skidmore. "He could rush it up there about 95–96 miles per hour, which, in those days, was really bringing it!"[30] During a game versus Tulsa (the Cardinals' Triple-A affiliate) in 1973, Skidmore recalled playing first base with Andújar on the mound, a runner on third, and two outs. Andújar, known to teammates as "Jack," walked the next man up—Byron Browne. When the count ran full on the next hitter, Skidmore indicated that he was going to play behind the runner. "Andújar goes into his stretch, and the next thing I know, Jack is whirling to throw the ball to first base for the pickoff," recalled Skidmore. "My vision of the ball was totally obscured by the runner. Browne, in a split second, hit the dirt to avoid being smacked in the cabeza. All I could see is some 96 miles per hour cheese heading for my face. My instincts told me it was too late to catch the ball, so I bailed out. The ball headed untouched into the right-field corner and both runners scored. Andújar didn't speak to me for a week. I'm pretty sure he thought it was *my* fault for letting those two runs score!"[31]

During his time with Indianapolis, Andújar butted heads with manager Vern Rapp, an old-school disciplinarian. In 1974, Andújar became incensed after being removed from a game and was suspended for taking out his anger on a water cooler. The Reds ran out of patience with the volatile pitcher the following year and traded him to Houston. He broke camp with the Astros in 1976 and made 25 starts, registering a 9–10 record and 3.60 ERA. Andújar followed that encouraging showing by starting the 1977 season with a 10–5 record, earning a spot on the NL All-Star team. A pulled hamstring prevented his participation in the Midsummer Classic and limited him to only seven second-half appearances.

Andújar was used as a swingman for the next three seasons in Houston, starting 50 games and making 66 relief appearances. He posted an unexceptional 20–27 record but showed glimpses of dominance, including honors as NL Pitcher of the Month in June 1979 and another All-Star Game nod. Andújar's antics and penchant for injury, however, frustrated the Astros. He missed time with another hamstring strain, a roaring case of jock itch, and injuries sustained while swinging for the fences.

Andújar had been banished to the bullpen in 1981 when Houston agreed to trade the 28-year-old righty to the Cardinals for Tony Scott. "He just needed to get away to a place where he was appreciated," observed Don Sutton at the time. "He's a fun-loving kid in a man's body."[32] Before he had a chance to take the mound for St. Louis, the players went on strike.

Post-strike, he won six of seven decisions and earned himself a three-year contract.

"My brother Ken played for Houston, and I asked him what was up with this guy," reflected Bob Forsch years later. "He told me he was a live wire. He was always in the mix. He kept things going in the clubhouse, but in a fun way."[33]

Kittle first saw Andújar pitch as a 16-year-old phenom and knew him better than anyone. "He's got a golden arm. They said he had a million-dollar arm and a 10-cent head. But that's not true. He's a very intelligent person," said Kittle in 1982.[34]

Andújar, a native Spanish speaker, was known for some rather off-the-wall quotes. One of the more memorable: "When I come from the Dominican to the U.S., you could sum it up in one word—you never know."[35] He was without a doubt one of the game's most unique personalities. Teammates took advantage of his well-known fear of snakes by hiding rubber serpents in his locker. He would sometimes wear a warmup jacket on his *left* arm "to be different" and on at least one occasion showered with his uniform on.[36] "He had this persona of being crazy," recalled John Stuper, "but he was one of the nicest people I ever played with in my life."[37]

Though Andújar's antics may have garnered media attention, his fierce competitiveness is what stood out the most to teammates and opponents alike. "Joaquín Andújar was the toughest competitor I have ever been around, ever," said Stuper decades later. "Andújar was a real competitor, never a dull moment," said Expos outfielder Warren Cromartie, looking back. "He had his showboat style and was really tough with his sinker. He added flair to [the Cardinals]."[38]

It was never a dull moment with Joaquín Andújar, who emerged as the ace of the rotation (National Baseball Hall of Fame and Museum, Cooperstown, NY).

Following a loss to the Mets and a rained-out series

finale, the Cards headed home to take on the Expos, who were fresh off a sweep of the hapless Cubs that put them within two games of the Cardinals. Before the first of three, Gene Tenace was reinstated from the disabled list and David Green, who could not crack the lineup despite hitting .325, was sent to Louisville for more regular at-bats. Forsch and Gullickson faced off for the second time in six days to open the series. The Cards had a second-inning scoring opportunity, but a play rarely seen outside of sandlots squashed the threat. With Ozzie Smith on second and one out, Willie McGee flew out to center field. Andre Dawson threw the ball into shortstop Chris Speier, who discretely held on to it instead of returning it to Gullickson. When Smith unsuspectingly took his lead, Speier tagged him for the third out. Herzog said he had not seen the hidden ball trick in 20 years. Expos manager Jim Fanning said, "I can't remember when I've ever seen it. It was nothing that came from the bench. It was never plotted or rehearsed. A play like that just kind of happens."[39]

Smith redeemed himself later in the game with spectacular defensive gems in the sixth and seventh innings that helped Forsch and the Cards maintain a 2–1 advantage. Forsch tired in the eighth and exited after loading the bases with no outs. Bruce Sutter was brought in for the most precarious of situations but calmly fanned Tim Raines and then induced a 1–2–3 inning-ending twin killing off the bat of Terry Francona. Things got interesting again in the ninth when the Expos loaded the bases against Sutter with one out. Warren Cromartie, who had taken Sutter deep the week before in Montreal, rolled into a game-ending 4–6–3 double play. Sutter's pair of late-inning Houdini acts had the clubhouse buzzing afterwards. The next night, McGee hit an 11th-inning, game-winning RBI single to set up a potential sweep. Montreal avoided that outcome by bludgeoning Dave LaPoint and Mark Littell with eight runs in the first three innings of the series finale on June 16. Charlie Lea, who grew up in Memphis rooting for the Cardinals, tossed a complete game for the visitors.

The Mets followed the Expos to the Gateway City for a four-game set that kicked off with a scheduled Friday night twin bill on June 18. Steve Mura started the first game and delivered 6⅔ scoreless frames. The Cards held a 3–0 lead heading to the top of the ninth inning, but the Mets torched Sutter for five runs on four hits and two walks to win, 5–3. A pair of rain delays in the first game caused the second to extend well past midnight. The Redbirds trailed 4–2 in the seventh when Willie McGee came off the bench to deliver a bases-loaded, go-ahead triple off Mets reliever Ed Lynch. At 1:21 a.m. Doug Bair recorded the last out for his second save of the season. McGee's clutch three-bagger made a winner out of John Stuper for the first time in his young career. Dave Kingman's grand slam and

George Foster's eight base hits propelled the Mets to wins in the final two games of the series. In the finale, Sutter yielded two runs in the 10th inning to absorb the loss. Sutter's record fell to 5–5, giving him as many decisions as Forsch and Andújar, a testament to how many close games the closer had pitched.

After such a promising start to the season, the Cardinals had played .500 ball over a stretch of 50 games. The struggles of Sutter were perhaps just as troubling as the extended period of mediocrity. Since recording his 14th save on May 28, he had pitched in nine games and allowed 14 runs in 13⅓ innings for an ERA of 9.45. During that stretch, he had walked eight and struck out only six. "If he doesn't do it, we ain't gonna have a very good season," opined Herzog. "He's the key to the whole thing. And he ain't getting it done."[40] Sutter insisted his arm felt fine, but his signature split-fingered fastball was frequently up in the zone and lacked its devastating break. "Right now, his ball just doesn't have movement," assessed Foster after registering hits in back-to-back games versus Sutter.[41]

The Cards looked to get back on track versus the Phillies, who visited Busch Stadium for a four-game series June 21–24 to conclude the homestand. With four catchers on the active roster and Steve Braun set to return from his sore shoulder, someone had to go. Glenn Brummer was kept as the third catcher and Orlando Sánchez was farmed out. Sánchez, originally acquired as a Rule 5 Draft pick from the Phillies, was hitting .189 (7-for-37) at the time of his demotion to Louisville. He would not see big-league action for the remainder of the season.

The Cards scored five runs in support of Dave LaPoint in the series opener. It could have been six, but Lonnie Smith's attempt to score on a would-be inside-the-park home run was obstructed by LaPoint, who slid into home just ahead of his fleet-footed teammate. With a planned rest day for Sutter, Bair entered in the eighth for the save attempt but promptly coughed up the lead by allowing back-to-back home runs to Bill Robinson and Ozzie Virgil. With the game tied at five per side, Sutter was called to duty after all. He held the Phillies scoreless for two innings, long enough for his offense to plate the winning run.

John Stuper threw on three days' rest the following day and picked up his second win and first complete game. Willie McGee tallied his 15th multi-hit game in 22 starts, raising his average to .357. Pete Rose, the Phillies' first baseman, had one of eight hits allowed by Stuper and moved ahead of Hank Aaron for second place on the all-time hits list—419 behind Ty Cobb. The loss prompted the Phillies to hold a players-only meeting before the following game. They responded with a 7–1 shellacking of Mura behind strong pitching from Mike Krukow. As usual, Ozzie Smith made multiple highlight-reel plays on defense, including a leaping catch and a throw to first from his knees. "Without him, the score might have been 12–1," assessed Rick Hummel of the *St. Louis Post-Dispatch*.[42]

Steve Carlton perpetuated his dominance of the Cardinals in the series finale on June 24 with only two runs and three hits allowed in a complete-game effort. Bob Forsch was lit up for seven earned runs—two of which came on a controversial home run by Gary Matthews that appeared to be foul by several feet. The final score of 10–2 rendered the questionable call moot. The series split left the Cards with a record of 40–30, tied with Montreal and three and a half games ahead of the Phillies, who were three games over .500 following their miserable start.

The Cardinals closed out June with a seven-game road trip, starting with four at Wrigley Field against the last-place Cubbies. Mike Roarke, Bruce Sutter's old pitching coach with the Cubs, flew to Chicago from his home in Rhode Island to work with his former pupil. Sutter's career had taken off under the tutelage of Roarke, who had a short playing career as a backup catcher with the Detroit Tigers in the early 1960s. Roarke had learned the mechanics of Sutter's splitter and noticed flaws with his delivery while watching a nationally televised game earlier in the week. Whitey Herzog and Hub Kittle welcomed the input. Roarke, who had gone into the insurance business in order to spend more time with family, watched Sutter throw a bullpen session and noticed he was overthrowing his splitter.*

Sutter's stumbles were far from the only thing keeping Herzog awake at night. The offense was having trouble putting runs on the board. Darrell Porter and George Hendrick were struggling mightily with batting averages in the .240s. Herzog replaced Hendrick with Dane Iorg in the series opener, but the switch failed to translate into more offense. The Cubs took a 3–0 lead in the fourth inning when Jay Johnstone parked a hanging slider from Joaquín Andújar over the right-field ivy. Fergie Jenkins, meanwhile, held the Cards in check and completed his 264th career game. The loss marked the 33rd time in 71 games the Cardinals had scored three runs or fewer. They had managed to win only seven of those contests. "I don't know what to do about the lineup," said an exasperated Herzog. "It doesn't seem to make any difference what I put out there."[43]

Afterwards, the Cardinals designated Mark Littell for assignment and recalled Jeff Lahti from Louisville. Littell, known as "Country," was 0–1 with a 5.23 ERA in 16 games and had not regained his powerful fastball and hard slider following elbow surgery two years earlier. His ability to lighten the mood with a self-deprecating humor had made him a good

---

*After the 1983 season, Roarke would replace Kittle as pitching coach and remain on Herzog's staff for the remainder of his Cardinals tenure.

fit in the clubhouse. Comments from his confidants after learning of his departure indicated the kind of impact he had. "I think he left a big void on our ball club," said Iorg. "You could vent your frustrations on him if you had any. He was somebody you could always laugh at, always have fun with, and you knew he would never take anything personally."[44]

"Country was a good guy," said Sutter. "I shouldn't say 'was.' It sounds like he's dead or something. He is a good guy, and he *is* fun to have around the clubhouse." In a moment of introspection, he added, "What happened to him is something that, sooner or later, is going to happen to everybody in baseball. To me, Mark Littell is kind of a little preview of what I might have to go through in my career."[45]

The Cardinals and Cubs met again for an afternoon twin bill on Saturday, June 26. Redbird batters managed only 10 hits between the two contests, three of which did not leave the infield. The Cards' pitching was able to overcome the offense's shortcomings, however. In the lid-lifter, Dave LaPoint pitched into the eighth inning before departing with the bases loaded. Sutter, armed with Roarke's advice, wriggled out of the jam and then retired the Cubs in order in the ninth to save the 4–1 victory. In the second game, Jim Kaat made his first start of the season and tossed six innings of one-run ball. The offense scratched out two runs off Cubs starter Lee Smith to take a 2–1 lead. Bair bridged the gap to Sutter, who recorded his second save of the day. Not visible in the box score was more defensive wizardry from Ozzie Smith, who nailed a runner out at the plate on a relay throw and robbed Ryne Sandberg of would-be RBI single.

Though the Cardinals defense and baserunning won many games during the course of the season, June 27 was an exception. The Cubs built a 3–0 lead with the help of errors by Oberkfell and McGee. Still, the Cards had a chance to prevail. In the seventh, McGee came to the plate with the bases loaded and one run already in. He wrapped a single to center field, scoring Oberkfell from third, but Tito Landrum—the runner on second base—got a poor read on the ball and broke late. Lonnie Smith, the man on first, thought Landrum would score easily and kept running until he met up with Landrum at third base. "It resembled rush hour on the Dan Ryan [Expressway], with the Cards double-parked," wrote Bob Logan of the *Chicago Tribune*.[46] Landrum, forced into a rundown between third and home, was tagged out. The Cards' anemic offense was stymied by journeyman pitcher Allen Ripley, who threw six shutout innings. "I don't know if that was his best stuff or not, but he shouldn't have done that to us with what he was throwing," said Darrell Porter, who was mired in a 1-for-17 slump.[47] The Cubs held on to win, 4–2, and the Cards had to settle for a series split.

Steve Carlton's usual brilliance, combined with the Cardinals' hitting woes, translated into a Phillies victory on June 28 at Veterans Stadium. Gary Matthews, who entered the series on a 12-for-24 tear, drove in the game's only run. Carlton's deceptive pickoff move fooled Herr and Lonnie Smith, costing the Cards a pair of precious outs. The baserunning blunders were magnified by the team's absence of power and inability to score. The lineup had managed only five home runs in a span of 40 days. The victory was the eighth in a row for Philadelphia and moved them into a tie with St. Louis for the division lead.

After scoring only 14 runs in seven games, the Cardinal bats finally exploded with a 15–3 throttling of the Phillies on June 29. George Hendrick broke out of an 11-for-68 slump to lead the attack, going 2-for-4 with a grand slam and seven RBIs. Lonnie Smith reached base four times and scored three runs, and Oberkfell and Herr each contributed three hits. Andújar was the beneficiary of the offensive outburst, allowing only one run in seven innings to improve his record to 7–5.

In the final tilt of the series, month, and road trip, the Redbirds racked up 13 hits and drew three walks off Phillies starter Larry Christenson. Of all the baserunners, however, only three came around to score. Bob Forsch was knocked out in the second inning after yielding four runs on six hits and a walk. Philadelphia added another two runs off Jim Kaat and won the game, 6–3. An encouraging sign for St. Louis, despite the defeat, was a terrific game by Porter, who singled three times and threw out a pair of baserunners.

June had not been kind to the Cardinals, whose 12–16 record during the month left the top of the NL East standings tightly bunched:

	W	L	W-L%	GB
Philadelphia Phillies	42	33	.560	--
St. Louis Cardinals	42	34	.558	--
Montreal Expos	40	32	.556	0.5
Pittsburgh Pirates	35	36	.493	5
New York Mets	36	39	.480	6
Chicago Cubs	29	48	.377	14

In the junior circuit, the Brewers managerial change had paid dividends. Under new skipper Harvey Kuenn, Milwaukee caught fire and concluded the month with a 20–7 record to pull within two games of the first-place Red Sox.

8

July

Pitching Carries the Cards

> "[Herzog] was the perfect type of manager for the player I was because he just let you play. He had two rules: show up on time and run hard. And I do that anyways. That's easy."—Willie McGee[1]

The Cardinals opened July with an abbreviated three-game homestand versus the Cubs, whose poor showing during the season's first three months led to speculation that there would be a significant roster shakeup at the All-Star break. Of the 26 major-league teams, only the dreadful Minnesota Twins had a worse record. The Cards outhit their rivals 21–12 in the first two games but lost each by a run, then salvaged a win on Independence Day behind an excellent outing by John Stuper. Battling stifling heat and humidity, in addition to the opposing hitters, the rookie came within one out of a complete game before loading the bases and yielding to Bruce Sutter, who retired Keith Moreland to secure the Redbirds' 7–2 victory. The Cardinal offense was again ignited by Lonnie Smith, who scored four runs and stole his 38th and 39th bases of the season, adding to his league-leading totals in both categories.

The Redbirds hit the road again on July 5, starting with a pair against the last-place Reds (31–47), losers of seven out of eight entering the series. Cincinnati had not had a losing season in 11 years but had entered a transition period. Aging veterans Johnny Bench, Dave Concepción, and Dan Driessen were the last vestiges of the Reds championship teams of 1975 and 1976. Youngsters Eddie Milner, Paul Householder, and Alex Trevino were getting their first extended action.

The Cardinals won both contests, extending the Reds' losing streak to nine, but the sweep came at a cost. Bruce Sutter felt discomfort in the groin area while warming up in the series opener, and the condition worsened when he entered the game. The Cardinals ultimately won in extra innings on Ozzie Smith's game-winning RBI single, but afterwards Sutter was diagnosed with a strained adductor muscle. With the All-Star Game approaching the following week, he would miss the six games leading up to the break as Herzog operated with a nine-man pitching staff. No Cardinals were selected by the fans to start the All-Star Game. Ozzie Smith, the closest to getting voted in, finished second in the shortstop ballot behind Concepción.

The Redbirds next traveled south for a pair versus the Braves, owners of the major league's best record. Andújar was tapped to start the series opener. Before the game, he found out that Tommy Lasorda, the NL All-Star manager, had bypassed him for the Midsummer Classic. Andújar, who was leading the league in innings pitched and second in ERA, was enraged at the slight and referred to Lasorda as a "dumb SOB."[2] The snub hurt the hurler's pocketbook as well as his pride. He had an All-Star clause in his contract worth $50,000.[3]

Andújar carried his frustration on to the field and no-hit the Braves through the first five innings. His counterpart, Rick Camp, was equally locked in. An unfortunate set of circumstances disrupted the duel and resulted in Andújar's first career ejection. He had thrown two pitches inside on Terry Harper, and Camp responded the next inning by throwing a ball several feet over Ken Oberkfell's head. Both benches were warned that any further shenanigans would result in an ejection. Then, with the Braves leading, 2–1, in the seventh, Andújar plunked Bob Horner on the back of the neck. Home-plate umpire Eric Gregg promptly tossed Andújar, and Atlanta held on to win, 3–2.

Braves closer Gene Garber, who entered play on July 8 with six wins, 16 saves, and a 1.57 ERA, was another All-Star snub. He looked to add to his saves total after relieving Rick Mahler in the top of the eighth inning with two runners on base and Atlanta leading, 2–1. The first batter Garber faced, Tom Herr, tripled into the right-center field gap, scoring a pair. The three-bagger was a much-needed bit of good fortune for Herr, whose average had dipped into the .230s after a 4-for-32 slump. Three batters later, Hendrick pulled a ground ball down the left-field line for a double, driving home two more. The comeback made a winner out of John Stuper for the fourth time in five decisions. Bair notched another save in place of Sutter with a big assist from Willie McGee, who reached over the center-field fence to rob Chris Chambliss of a two-run home run to end the game.

Besides McGee's long-ball robbery, another play not visible in the box score was a dazzling stop by Ozzie Smith, who ranged up the middle to rob Dale Murphy of a hit, saving two runs in the process. A measure of Smith's impact is captured in his Defensive Wins Above Replacement (dWAR),

8. July—Pitching Carries the Cards

a statistic calculated by Baseball-Reference.com that aims to quantify a player's defensive value at his position in relation to his peers. Smith led all of major-league baseball in 1982 with a 3.5 dWAR. The Wizard's outstanding glovework and respectable batting average—.268 at the end of play on July 8—earned him a second All-Star Game nod as a reserve. Lonnie Smith was also selected by Lasorda to represent St. Louis.*

The Cardinals ended the first half of the season the same way they started—a trio of games at Houston. In the opener on July 9, Dave LaPoint (4–2) opposed Nolan Ryan (8–8). The Cardinals struck first on George Hendrick's second-inning home run—his 13th of the season. In the top of the sixth, RBIs by McGee and Hernandez provided St. Louis with a 3–1 advantage. LaPoint had trouble getting his changeup over but still managed to limit the Astros to two runs on six hits in 7⅓ innings. Sutter's absence meant a high-leverage opportunity for Jeff Lahti, pitching in just his fourth major-league game. Lahti recorded the final two outs in the eighth and got the first two batters in the ninth before Terry Puhl reached on an error by Hernandez. With left-hand hitting Danny Heap at the plate, Herzog went to southpaw Jim Kaat, who fanned Heap to earn his first save of the season.

In the middle game of the series, Lonnie Smith hit his first homer in nearly two months, a leadoff shot off Joe Niekro. After that, Niekro's knuckleball frustrated the Cardinals for the remainder of the game. Bob Forsch was still on the mound in the bottom of the ninth inning with the game knotted at two. Ray Knight, the Astros' lone All-Star, led off with a single. The defense was expecting a bunt with one-time Cardinal José Cruz at the plate, but manager Bill Virdon let him swing away. With both corner infielders charging, Forsch grooved a fastball that Cruz pounced on for a two-run, walk-off home run. Niekro registered his eighth straight win over St. Louis.

The series finale on Sunday June 11 resulted in the same 4–2 score as the previous night. Houston starter Bob Knepper entered the game with a 2–10 record and 4.99 ERA, but his performance belied his statistics. Hendrick's ninth-inning, two-run home run was the only thing between Knepper and a shutout. "He looked like Rube Waddell, didn't he?" said a perplexed Herzog. "I couldn't believe some of the swings we had."[4] For the 30th time on the season—more than a third of their games—the Redbirds had scored two runs or fewer. Despite the disturbing trend, the Cards—thanks in large part to their April winning streak—entered the All-Star break with a 48–39 record, deadlocked with Philadelphia for first place.

---

*Ozzie Smith would end his career with 15 All-Star Game selections; 1982 would be Lonnie Smith's only All-Star appearance.

The best players from each league met in Montreal on July 13 for Major League Baseball's 53rd All-Star Game. A crowd of 59,057 packed Olympic Stadium to watch the annual midsummer exhibition. Four players in Tommy Lasorda's NL starting lineup represented the host city: outfielders Tim Raines and Andre Dawson, catcher Gary Carter, and starting pitcher Steve Rogers. Three Phillies—third baseman Mike Schmidt, first baseman Pete Rose, and second baseman Manny Trillo—joined Reds shortstop Dave Concepción and Braves outfielder Dale Murphy to round out the starting nine.

Oakland Athletics skipper Billy Martin managed the AL squad, which had lost 18 out of 19 to their NL counterparts. The AL lineup comprised outfielders Rickey Henderson, Fred Lynn, and Reggie Jackson; infielders George Brett, Robin Yount, Bobby Grich, and Cecil Cooper; catcher Carlton Fisk and starting pitcher Dennis Eckersley.

Concepción had a pregame visit with his childhood hero, Luis Aparicio, then went out and took Eckersley deep to give the NL a 2–1 first-inning lead. The senior circuit added two more runs and held on to win, 4–1. The Smiths each made appearances off the bench, but neither got to bat. Ozzie was caught stealing after pinch-running for Concepción and then wowed everyone with a magnificent defensive play to stamp out a two-on, two-out situation in the eighth inning. Lonnie got in the game as a defensive replacement in left field.

Reflecting on the Cardinals' first half, Ozzie Smith said, "We really haven't been consistent in anything we've done, except our pitching. Our offense has been sporadic as heck. We're not moving runners over, getting runners in from third. It's been a total team demise. At the beginning of the year, everybody was into the flow of the offense. Hopefully, we can play that sort of baseball again."[5]

In his midseason predictions, Bill Conlin of *The Sporting News* expressed doubts as to whether the Cardinals had what it took to win the NL East, picking them to finish third behind Philadelphia and Pittsburgh. "Despite blazing team speed and high-average hitters like Keith Hernandez and Lonnie Smith, the Cards probably are a quality starter, a home run hitter, and a backup late reliever short of championship caliber," wrote Conlin.[6]

Following the three-day break, the Cardinals and Reds resumed play at Busch Stadium on July 15. Cincinnati's first-half record of 33–53 had all but dashed any hope of making the postseason and would soon cost manager John McNamara his job. The reeling Reds were last in the league in runs scored. To make matters worse, Tom Seaver was scratched from his scheduled start and returned to the Queen City to have his sore shoulder examined. In the series opener, the Cardinals managed to score three runs on five hits in the first inning off Bruce Berenyi but were then held hitless for the next seven frames. John Stuper, enduring his worst start as a major leaguer, was sent to the showers in the third inning and took the loss in the Cardinals' 7–3 defeat.

A collection of 23,637 fans watched Steve Mura oppose Bob Shirley on July 16. The crowd pushed the Cardinals' home attendance total above one million for the season for the 20th consecutive year, a streak topped only by the Los Angeles Dodgers, who had achieved the mark every year since relocating from Brooklyn in 1958. By the fourth inning, Mura had ceded three runs on seven hits and was replaced by Jeff Lahti, a rookie who pitched with an animated exuberance. The week before, Lahti was so fired up after covering first base for a putout that his around-the-horn throw sailed all the way to the center-field wall, much to the amusement of his teammates. "Lahti bounds around the mound in sprightly fashion as plays are made behind him, and eagerly retrieves the ball," wrote Mike Smith in the *St. Louis Post-Dispatch*. "Once in his possession, he vigorously thumps it in his mitt before composing himself to face the next batter."[7] Lahti kept the Cards within striking distance with only one run allowed in 3⅓ innings. In the seventh, the St. Louis bats finally woke up. Dane Iorg had the key safety, a two-run, pinch-hit single, which gave St. Louis a 6–4 lead. Bruce Sutter pitched two scoreless frames to save the game for Lahti, who recorded his first big-league win.

It had been a disappointing season to that point for Tom Herr, who was batting .235 after being hampered by pneumonia and a pulled leg muscle during the first half. Herzog stuck with the second baseman, installing him at leadoff for a resting Lonnie Smith on July 17. Herr drew a tough assignment in the form of Mario Soto but responded with three hits, indicating that perhaps his physical maladies were behind him.

Like Bruce Sutter, Herr was born and raised in Lancaster, Pennsylvania. In fact, Tom's older brother, Jeff, played American Legion ball with Sutter. Tom played second base and shortstop at Lancaster's Hempfield High School, where, as a senior, he hit .417 and led his team to the Lancaster-Lebanon League Championship.[8] Herr's preferred sport, however, was basketball. The 6-foot guard became Hempfield's all-time leading scorer and was recruited by Duke University as a junior. Then the Blue Devils changed coaches between Herr's junior and senior years, and the new coach rescinded the offer.

Herr graduated from high school in 1974 and was passed over in the June amateur draft. He played with an American Legion team that summer and participated in the state's East-West All-Star Game. Scouts began to take notice, including the Cardinals' Tim Thompson, who signed Herr that August. Herr had already enrolled at the University of Delaware, and even though he was under contract to play for the Cardinals in 1975, he decided to join the basketball team as a walk-on. "I was playing mostly for the conditioning," Herr explained at the time.[9]

Herr learned the art of switch-hitting in his first year with rookie-level Johnson City and then spent two years with the Cardinals' Single-A affiliate in St. Petersburg, Florida, along the way perfecting the fundamentals of second base under the tutelage of George Kissell. "I was like a dry sponge that just soaked everything up my first few years," Herr later recalled. "I was just so fortunate to have great instruction in the Cardinal minor-league system and was smart enough to take stuff in and apply it to my game. I started to develop my baseball muscles because in high school I was an all-around athlete and never really concentrated on baseball. Within my first three years, I went from being a suspect to a prospect."[10]

Second baseman Tom Herr played solid defense and was a threat on the basepaths (National Baseball Hall of Fame and Museum, Cooperstown, NY).

Herr was back at leadoff in the series finale with the Cards poised to take three of four against the Reds. The sweltering heat of July was in full effect, and Busch Stadium's concrete and plastic grass certainly did not help. Herzog offered the struggling Keith Hernandez a day off against lefty Charlie Leibrandt, but the first baseman declined. Hernandez, who had a career batting average of .299 versus righties and .291 against southpaws, preferred facing lefties when he was in a slump because it forced him to stay back on the ball. Leibrandt induced a popup from Hernandez in the first inning on an inside pitch. In his second at-bat, Hernandez got the inside fastball he was looking for, pulling it over the right-field wall for a three-run home run—his fourth of the season. The blast provided St. Louis with a 5–2 advantage. Starter Dave LaPoint labored through four innings and departed in the fifth after the Reds trimmed the lead to 5–4. Jim Kaat threw 2⅓ scoreless innings in relief and was credited with his 282nd career win after St. Louis held on to win, 6–5. St. Louis improved to 40–6 when scoring four or more runs. The series win improved the Cardinals' record to 51–40.

To say that Jim Kaat brought experience to the Cardinals' bullpen would be a huge understatement. He entered the 1982 season having faced 18,540 batters in his 23-year big-league career, which began during the Eisenhower administration. Kaat (pronounced Cot) was born and raised in Zeeland, Michigan, a small town between Grand Rapids and Lake Michigan comprised primarily of Dutch-Americans. His father, John, worked at a turkey hatchery and had a passion for the game of baseball, in particular the lowly Philadelphia Athletics. "He passed that love of baseball on to me, and I took to it like Gaylord Perry to a jar of Vaseline," wrote Kaat in his memoir, *Still Pitching*.[11] From the age of eight, Jim had dreams of being a big-league pitcher. He modeled his throwing motion after Athletics pitcher Bobby Shantz, who like young Jim, was a vertically-challenged lefty. Kaat had success in high school and American Legion ball, but he stood at only 5-foot-8 as a junior and was unlikely to make the grade in the eyes of big-league scouts. He was dismissed by major college programs for the same reason, so he enrolled at Hope College in Holland, just a few miles from Zeeland.

Kaat hit a growth spirt during his freshman year, adding six inches to his burgeoning frame. He pitched in six games as a freshman and allowed a single earned run.[12] Scouts finally began to pay attention. A tryout with the Washington Senators at Comiskey Park led to a contract offer and $4,000 signing bonus. The White Sox then made a much more substantial offer of $25,000, which was an enormous sum compared to the $72 John made each week at the hatchery.[13] However, rules at the time dictated that any player receiving more than $4,000 in bonus money had to remain on the big-league roster for two years. The system was baseball's way of preventing wealthy teams from hoarding young talent. John had observed that many "bonus babies" sat the bench for two years and never reached their full potential. He shrewdly advised his son to take the lesser offer and gain experience in the minor leagues.

Kaat spent most of four seasons moving up the Senators' farm system. Whitey Herzog was a member of the Senators during Kaat's first two years in the organization. "He was a country boy who was wilder than a March hare," Herzog later remembered.[14] Kaat was called up to the majors briefly in 1959 and again in 1960, but the results were unimpressive. In 55 innings, he posted only one win in eight decisions, logged a 6.22 ERA, and walked more batters than he struck out. The Senators stuck with the young southpaw, however. When the franchise relocated to Minnesota in 1961 and changed its name to the Twins, Kaat established himself as a more than capable hurler. He was a member of the Twins' starting rotation for 13 seasons, compiling 189 wins, including a 25-win campaign in 1966. Besides his pitching exploits, Kaat developed a reputation as one of the game's best fielding pitchers—as his 16 consecutive Gold Gloves would attest. Along with Mudcat Grant and Jim Perry, Kaat anchored a Twins staff that competed in the club's first World Series against the Los Angeles Dodgers in 1965. Kaat opposed Sandy Koufax three times in the series. Each hurler picked up a win in the first two matchups. The series ultimately went to a decisive Game Seven, in which Kaat and Koufax again faced off on just two days' rest. Throwing almost entirely fastballs, Koufax prevailed with a three-hitter that the Dodgers won, 2–0. "He was so overpowering, I actually felt sorry for our hitters," recalled Kaat.[15]

During the 1973 season, the Twins' penny-pinching owner, Calvin Griffith, waived Kaat when the team fell out of contention. The experienced southpaw was scooped up by the White Sox and proceeded to post back-to-back 20-win efforts. Kaat spent his next three seasons with the Phillies, compiling a mediocre 26–30 record. At that point in his career, he had developed a quick pitch as a way of keeping hitters off balance. The label "crafty lefty" was certainly apt. The Phillies sold Kaat to the Yankees early in the 1979 campaign. For the first time in his career, he was utilized almost exclusively as a reliever. The following year, Kaat scuffled in his first four outings and was designated for assignment by the Yankees when Rudy May returned from an injury and needed a roster spot. The Cardinals, desperate for relief help, bought Kaat's contract on April 30. He showed he still had plenty of life in his arm with the Redbirds, appearing in 49 games—including 14 starts—while registering a 3.82 ERA. In 1981, he was a reliable arm for Herzog out of the bullpen, posting a 3.40 ERA in 53 innings.

Described by one sportswriter as "Popeye with freckles," the bow-legged, tobacco-chewing hurler had managed to outlast all his peers.[16] Often the first one to arrive at the ballpark, Kaat could often be found pedaling a stationary bicycle hours before game time. A consistent exercise routine and youthful enthusiasm helped him become one of a handful of major leaguers to play in four decades. The fact that he was a lefty—one of the game's most coveted commodities—was perhaps the most important reason for his longevity. Kaat constantly evolved in order to get hitters out. He asked Dave LaPoint to meet him at the park early one day to show him his slide-step change-up and started dropping side-arm to lefties after seeing how Jeff Keener got good movement using a submarine delivery. "Kaat's still around because he's got a good head on his shoulders, and he uses it," assessed Gene Tenace. "He has such a great attitude and he's a big inspiration to all of us."[17] Kaat's career accomplishments would eventually earn him enshrinement in the National Baseball Hall of Fame in 2022.

Southpaw Jim Kaat brought a wealth of experience to the Cardinals bullpen (National Baseball Hall of Fame and Museum, Cooperstown, NY).

What stood out to Jeff Keener four decades later about the 1982 Cardinals was the great team atmosphere and mentorship in the bullpen from Kaat, Bair, Littell, and Sutter. "We had a great blend of focused veterans who kept everything in order," said Keener. "They talked the game all the time at the park. Their focus was win ballgames. It was 'How are going to win this game? Who's coming up next? What am I going to throw this guy?' Those guys would make sure everyone was on task."[18]

Tony Gwynn made his major-league debut with the San Diego Padres on July 19 after hitting .328 for the Triple-A Hawaii Islanders. Gwynn went 2-for-4 with a double and would finish the year with a .289 batting average, the only time in his 20-year career he did not hit over .300. Atlanta, meanwhile, visited St. Louis looking to improve upon a major-league best 54–34 record. The key to beating Atlanta, Herzog assessed, was "to do it before they go to the bullpen."[19] The Braves had a formidable pair of late-inning arms. Gene Garber, who had assumed the role of fireman from Rick Camp earlier in the year, was a side-arming right-hander who entered the series with 16 saves and a 2.05 ERA. The other half of the tandem was rookie Steve

Bedrosian, who had emerged to record five saves and a 1.57 ERA in his first 32 games. Though Sutter's ERA remained a very un–Sutterlike 4.18, the unflappable fireman wasn't losing sleep over it. "I ain't worried about it. To tell you the truth, it doesn't mean a damn thing to me," Sutter told reporters between drags of a cigarette. "I figure as long as I can save games for the starters around here, I'm not going to let my ERA bother me."[20]

Phil Niekro—the one player in the league older than Kaat—found that his knuckleball was not dancing in the series opener and instead relied on his screwball and "fastball," a pitch that moved at the speed of other pitchers' changeups. Niekro's repertoire kept the Redbird hitters off balance in Atlanta's 4–1 victory. The Braves won again the following night despite Willie McGee's first career home run, a grand slam into the left field mezzanine.

Looking to avoid a sweep, the Redbirds jumped out to an early 7–0 lead off starter Bob Walk in the series finale on July 21. Darrell Porter, fresh off a pep talk from his manager, hit a pair of run-scoring doubles. Porter's batting average had dipped into the .220s, and he had only five home runs under his belt. The frequent boos he heard from the home crowd were not helping his confidence. Herzog encouraged him to keep hustling and not get his dauber down.[21] Hernandez, Hendrick, and Porter combined to drive in seven of the Cardinals' eight runs. Provided with a sizeable cushion, Steve Mura pounded the strike zone and needed only 102 pitches to deliver a five-hit shutout, though he received an assist from his home ballpark. The Braves hit several blasts that were hauled in on the warning track. "They would have had a few dingers in Atlanta," assessed Herzog. "But anytime you pitch a shutout, you've pitched well."[22] The win evened Mura's record at 7–7 and lowered his ERA to 3.89. The right-hander out of New Orleans, was a former second round pick by the San Diego Padres. As a member of the Friars in 1981, Mura was a victim of little to no run support, which contributed to a league-high 14 losses.

Having been a role player himself, Herzog understood the importance of having guys on his bench who could be content riding the pine and contributing when needed. One such player was utilityman Mike Ramsey, who sported a Tom Selleck–like mustache and long curly hair that flowed out from beneath his red ballcap. Born in Virginia and raised in Georgia, Ramsey was a homegrown player who offered Herzog the versatility of playing anywhere on the infield.

The slender Ramsey, who stood 6-foot-1 but weighed just a buck-70, got a spot start for Ken Oberkfell on July 24 and contributed two RBIs to help defeat Bob Knepper and the Astros. The following day, Ramsey

8. July—Pitching Carries the Cards

spelled Ozzie Smith at shortstop and faced Don Sutton, a seasoned righty with 250 wins on his résumé. The curly-locked pair faced one another in the bottom of the second inning with runners on first and second and one out. Ramsey, a switch-hitter, owned four professional home runs—all coming from the right side of the plate in the minors. In 421 big-league at-bats, Ramsey had never homered. He claimed he had never even hit a ball over the Busch Stadium wall in batting practice.[23] Ramsey worked an advantageous 3–1 count versus Sutton and got an inside fastball that he managed to yank down the right-field line. "When I hit it, I thought it might go out, but I was out of the box like I was going for a triple," said Ramsey after the game.[24] Like Ozzie Smith's famed home run from the 1985 NLCS, the ball struck the façade over the right-field wall. It was one of two home runs Ramsey hit in his seven-year big-league career. "It was a rare occurrence," remembered Ramsey decades later. "My game was staying in the middle of the field and handling the bat. I could barrel the ball pretty good, but I just didn't play the power game. The home runs were accidents."[25] The blast propelled St. Louis to a three-game sweep of the Astros and allowed the Cards to keep pace with the Phillies.

Unlike Darrell Porter, who had continued to be subjected to boos from the home crowd, Ozzie Smith had become a fan favorite in his short time playing in the Gateway City. "Everything had been great here," said Smith at the time. "I don't think I've gone out of my way to win people over. I'm just doing what I've done consistently for the last four years. I've made up my mind this is the place I want to play."[26] Both players were instrumental in the Cards' 9–4 victory over the Mets on July 27, the penultimate game of the homestand. Porter went 3-for-3 with a home run and pair of walks, raising his batting average to .248 and on-base percentage to .350. Ozzie continued to impress at the plate and marvel in the field. A 2-for-4 day raised his average to .267, and he was equally impactful on defense. With runners on first and third in the eighth inning, Smith converted a double-play by acrobatically leaping over Mike Jorgensen, who came barreling into second base in an attempt to break up the twin-killing.

The Cardinals concluded the homestand with another defeat of the Mets to extend the winning streak to six games. Joaquín Andújar let a four-run lead slip away, but the bullpen avoided further damage, and the Cards won, 7–5. Jeff Keener retired the only batter he faced in the seventh and was credited with his first—and only—career win. Bruce Sutter pitched two scoreless frames to earn his 21st save. The Redbirds hit the road with a 57–42 record and one-game lead over the Phillies. The Cardinals' next

11 games would come against Pittsburgh and Montreal, who were still in striking distance at four and a half and five games back, respectively.

On Thursday, July 29, a crowd of 48,923 packed Olympic Stadium for the first of four between the Cards and Expos. The game went to extra innings tied, 3–3. With Doug Bair on the mound, Andre Dawson led off the bottom of the 10th inning with a shot into the left-center field gap for a sure double. Willie McGee fielded the ball and, instead of making a relay throw to third, threw to second base while Dawson alertly scampered to third. The next two batters were intentionally walked to load the bases. Two batters later, Tim Wallach hit a fly ball that scored the game-winning run.

The next day's contest was also decided in extras. In the bottom of the 11th, a one-out walk to Tim Raines proved to be Bair's undoing. Raines stole second and scored on Dawson's bloop double to secure Montreal's 5–4 victory. For the second consecutive day, Bair suffered a loss and Expos reliever Woodie Fryman got the win.

After two close affairs, the Cardinals left nothing to chance on July 31. The offense battered Ray Burris for seven runs in a 10–1 rout. Hernandez and Hendrick combined to drive in six runs. Steve Mura pitched around nine hits and five walks for a complete-game victory, giving him a perfect 3–0 mark and splendid 1.77 ERA for the month. Mura utilized his outstanding defense during his successful streak, striking out only nine batters in 35⅔ innings.

July concluded with the Braves maintaining a seven-game lead in the NL West, while the Angels held a slim one-game advantage over the Royals in the AL West. In the highly-competitive AL East, a mere half game separated the first-place Brewers and second-place Red Sox. Robin Yount, Milwaukee's young star shortstop, hit .414 and belted eight home runs to win AL Player of the Month honors.

The Cardinals finished July with a 15–10 record and +32 run differential despite a sputtering offense that hit .241. The pitching staff that prognosticators had questioned before the season carried the team with a 3.16 ERA. With two months to play and the dog days of summer in full effect, the NL East was very much up for grabs:

	W	L	W-L%	GB
Philadelphia Phillies	58	42	.580	--
St. Louis Cardinals	58	44	.569	1
Pittsburgh Pirates	53	46	.535	4.5
Montreal Expos	53	47	.530	5
New York Mets	45	56	.446	13.5
Chicago Cubs	40	65	.381	20.5

9

August

Brummer Steals a Game

The National Baseball Hall of Fame held its annual induction ceremony on August 1, enshrining two of the all-time greats—Hank Aaron and Frank Robinson. The pair of sluggers ranked first and fourth on the all-time career home run list, respectively. "For Hank, I'd just like to say I've been chasing him for a long time," said Robinson, who spoke first. "Well I got him today. I'm going into the Hall of Fame before he does." Aaron expressed appreciation for Jackie Robinson, Roy Campanella, and other Black players who paved the way for Frank and him. "They proved to the world that a man's ability is limited only by his lack of opportunity," said Aaron. Travis Jackson and former Commissioner Albert "Happy" Chandler were also inducted.

A few hundred miles north of Cooperstown, the Cards looked to salvage a split versus Montreal. Cy Young Award contenders Steve Rogers and Joaquín Andújar squared off, but neither hurler was at his best. The Cardinals banged out 10 safeties against Rogers and five more against the Expos bullpen, including three each by Tom Herr and Ken Oberkfell. Andújar also surrendered 10 hits and departed in the seventh inning with two runners on and the Cards ahead, 4–2. Jeff Lahti allowed both inherited runners to score and Jim Kaat gave up a go-ahead single to Al Oliver. Woodie Fryman, who threw 7⅔ scoreless innings in the series, closed out the game for Montreal. After the final out was secured, Oliver attempted to give Fryman a high-five, but the old-school reliever left his teammate hanging. "I guess I'm not into that," said Fryman. "A handshake is good enough for me. I'm too old for [high fives]."[1] One can extrapolate how he would feel about bat flips and Gatorade baths. St. Louis dropped three out of four despite outscoring Montreal 22–15 in the series.

The Cardinals returned home to face the Pirates on August 2 for the first of four games. The Bucs were without the services of power-hitting

All-Star Dave Parker, who underwent surgery that day to repair torn ligaments in his thumb. John Stuper's only blemish on the day was a two-run homer by Pirates first baseman Jason Thompson in the top of the eighth. The Cardinals were only able to push one run across against Pittsburgh starter Rick Rhoden, however, and trailed, 2-1, heading into the bottom of the ninth. Lonnie Smith evened the score with an RBI double off Rod Scurry, sending the game to extra innings. The Cards squandered myriad scoring opportunities in the bonus frames, including a bases-loaded, no-out situation in the 16th and stranded a franchise-record 24 runners in the game. Jim Kaat gave a yeoman's effort, pitching five scoreless extra innings before Johnny Ray tripled home two runs in the top of the 17th. "I was just trying to survive," said Ray. "St. Louis is something else. With that humidity nine innings is enough here."[2] Well past midnight, Enrique Romo retired the Cards to secure a victory for the Bucs. Herzog eschewed his usually post-game Budweiser in favor of a stiff drink. "That one," groused the skipper, "was hard to believe."[3]

Having played three extra-inning games in five days, the St. Louis pitching staff needed a fresh arm before the following day's affair. Thus, Jeff Keener was sent to Triple A and replaced on the roster by John Martin. The Cardinals benefited from nine walks by Pirates starter Don Robinson and rebounded from the previous night's enigma with a 4–2 victory. As usual, Bob Forsch pitched to contact and let his defense do the rest, tossing 7⅓ innings of two-run ball without a walk or a strikeout. To that point, Forsch had issued just 33 walks and recorded a mere 43 strikeouts in 157 innings. He acknowledged that the team's stellar glovework was the key to his success. Dan Donovan of the *Pittsburgh Press* called Forsch the "vanilla pudding of starting pitchers."[4]

On August 4, the Mets and Cubs played an afternoon game at Wrigley Field in a battle for fifth place. Mets center fielder Joel Youngblood hit a two-run single off Fergie Jenkins in the third inning. Then, word came down that Youngblood had been traded to Montreal for a player to be named later. He was pulled from the game and made arrangements to meet up with the Expos that night in Philadelphia. He arrived at Veterans Stadium in the third inning and was summarily thrown into action in the sixth. Youngblood then proceeded to single off Steve Carlton in the seventh, becoming the first player in major-league history to record two base hits for two different teams in two cities—and off a pair of future Hall of Famers! While Youngblood was making history, the Cardinals had a tall task, both literally and figuratively. Pirates starter John Candelaria, a 6-foot-7 lefty, was coming off a July in which he posted a 5–0 record and 1.34 ERA to claim the NL Pitcher of the Month award. The Candy Man remained locked in and outdueled Dave LaPoint in Pittsburgh's 5–2 victory.

9. August—Brummer Steals a Game

The Cardinals made another transaction before the series finale on August 5, replacing Tito Landrum with David Green, who was torching American Association pitching with a .341 average, 10 home runs, and 38 RBI.[5] With a number of left-handed opposing pitchers coming up, Herzog hoped Green could light a spark in the Cards' inconsistent offense. Green arrived 45 minutes before first pitch and found his name in the sixth spot on the lineup card. He made an instant impact, contributing a pair of hits. The Cards had built a 7–3 lead after four innings as rain began to fall. When the Pirates came to bat in the top of the fifth, the precipitation intensified as streaks of lightning lit up the downtown St. Louis sky. The umpires kept the game going despite the conditions. Herzog knew a thing or two about the dangers of lightning. "I got struck by lightning playing golf once," said the skipper. "It hit a tree in front of me, went right through me and made my hair stand on end. I felt it for three or four days. If I was a ballplayer out there with metal spikes on, damned right I'd be scared."[6] After the Bucs were retired in the top of the fifth, play was finally halted. Two hours and four minutes later, the game was called, and the Cardinals were awarded a rain-shortened win, much to the dismay of Pirates manager Chuck Tanner. "You're damn right I'm disturbed," said Tanner. "We had to play through all that rain, lightning, and thunder, then it was hardly raining when they called it.… I don't think it's right to stop a game like this with two teams in a pennant race."[7] The Pirates formally protested the game to the league office, but to no avail. The weather-aided victory improved the Cardinals' record to 60–47. Green's two-hit game improved his batting average to .337. The young prospect's potential seemed limitless.

David Green's baseball roots stemmed from his native country of Nicaragua, where his father, Edward "Eduardo" Green, was an outstanding outfielder. Eduardo hailed from Bluefields, a city on Nicaragua's Atlantic coast. Although English was the primary language of the region, the Green household spoke mostly Spanish.

In his early teen years, Green played baseball but showed no signs of having a future in the game. Tito Rondón, a Nicaraguan journalist and broadcaster, saw Green play at the time. "He was a stick of a kid, 14 or so, a terrible player. We were curious because we knew who his dad was," recalled Rondón.[8] At age 15, David served as batboy for an amateur team on which Eduardo coached. Eduardo would throw batting practice to the team, and then David would jump in the cage. "He would throw hard, around 80 miles per hour," recalled Rondón. "David would swing and miss most pitches, and his father would scream at him in English-accented Spanish, 'Hit it … bat like a man, not a girl!'"[9] Eventually, David showed improvement and worked his way on to the team as an outfielder.

In 1977, Green's raw athleticism was on display at the Central American Games in El Salvador, where he represented Nicaragua in track and field and—without much training—set a national record in the long jump. By the following year, his baseball skills had dramatically improved to the point where he possessed legitimate five-tool talent. In the summer of 1979, Green was a member of Nicaragua's national baseball team that competed in the Amateur World Series in Italy. By then, several big-league clubs had scouted Green. The Milwaukee Brewers ultimately signed him for $20,000. Ray Poitevint, the Brewers' scouting director, later said that Green was "without a doubt, the most talented prospect—physically and mentally—that I have been associated with in the 22 years I've been involved in scouting.... David Green has Willie Mays's physical abilities and Pete Rose's mental abilities."[10] Although Green's birth year has always been listed as 1960, Rondón insisted that he subtracted a year when he signed.

Outfielder David Green possessed five-tool talent that made him one of the game's most intriguing young prospects (National Baseball Hall of Fame and Museum, Cooperstown, NY).

Green acquitted himself well during his first two seasons in the minors, quickly becoming the Brewers' consensus top prospect. When Herzog insisted on Green's inclusion in the infamous trade that brought him to St. Louis, Poitevint—who believed Green was the key to Milwaukee's future—was incensed and nearly came to blows with another front office member over the deal. After he was acquired by the Cardinals, Green was sent to the Mexican Winter League to see more breaking balls. He responded by leading the league in hitting. In his first spring training with the Cards, Herzog was cautious about rushing Green and kept him in minor-league camp. Green spent 1981 in Springfield, where he hit .270 with 10 home runs and missed time due to a groin injury. Springfield broadcaster Terry Greene compared Green's defense to that of Andre Dawson. "His range is phenomenal. On top of that, he's got a cannon for an arm. An accurate cannon," said Greene.[11]

Some scouts compared Green to Roberto Clemente. Green once had the opportunity to see Clemente play when the Pirates' star visited Nicaragua for an amateur tournament. "I saw that arm and thought 'Oh, my god,'" remembered Green. "I want to play like Clemente."[12] In 1972, Clemente tragically died in a plane crash while delivering relief aid to Nicaragua after the country was ravaged by an earthquake.

When rosters expanded in September 1981, Green was called up to St. Louis for his first taste of the big leagues.* Unfortunately, Eduardo died of a heart attack in 1980 and never fulfilled his dream of seeing his son play in the majors. Green, only 20 at the time of his debut, recorded only five hits in 34 at-bats and in Herzog's estimation was overawed.[13] By 1982, Green had adopted a new batting stance and appeared better equipped to handle big-league pitching. His pair of opposite-field singles against the Pirates were an encouraging sign.

Montreal visited the Gateway City for a three-game series that commenced on Friday, August 6, with a rematch of Steve Rogers (13–4, 2.31 ERA) versus Joaquín Andújar (8–9, 2.72). Rogers, a Missouri native, entered the game unbeaten on the road in ten decisions while Andújar had never lost to the Expos. Something had to give. Penciling Dane Iorg's name in the lineup was an easy decision for Herzog. The utilityman essentially turned into Ted Williams when he faced the Expos, registering a .453 average (39-for-86) against Montreal since the start of the 1980 season. Iorg had no explanation for his dominance. In a pitchers' meeting before the game, Expo hurlers decided to try throwing Iorg fastballs down the middle because nothing else had worked.[14] That strategy failed too; Iorg doubled twice. Nonetheless, Montreal claimed a series-opening victory by pounding Andújar for 12 hits and four runs. The next night, Lonnie Smith's seventh-inning, two-run triple broke a 5–5 tie, spurring the Cards to a 9–5 win. Forsch held the Expos to only two runs in the rubber game on Sunday, August 8, but the Cardinal bats could only muster a single tally off Expo hurlers David Palmer and Woodie Fryman. The NL East remained tight with the Phillies leading the Cards by one game, the Pirates by three, and the Expos by four. The Mets and Cubs, at 13½ and 17 back, were ostensibly out of the playoff hunt.

---

*Green joined Dennis Martínez, Tony Chévez, and Albert Williams as the only Nicaragua-born players to appear in the big leagues.

As the Cardinals opened up a two-city road trip in New York against the Mets on August 9, Herzog had a good problem on his hands. He had two outstanding young center fielders—McGee and Green—both hitting over .300. With Lonnie Smith and George Hendrick established at the corner outfield spots it meant that on a given day someone deserving of playing time was destined to sit on the bench. Dane Iorg was also worthy of more at-bats but relegated to the pine more often than not. The series opener at Shea Stadium did not get underway until 9:50 p.m. due to rain. Dave LaPoint was pulled after three innings because he had warmed up several times during the delay. Jeff Lahti came on in relief and threw six scoreless innings, his longest outing as a pro. McGee continued to produce, going 3-for-5 with a bases-loaded triple in the Redbirds' 7–2 triumph. His approach was simple: see the ball and hit it. When asked about his penchant for coming through in big moments, the reserved outfielder said, "I'm not that good at discussing baseball. All I can do is play it."[15]

Herzog swapped Green for McGee the following day, and the result was another 7–2 win. Rain wiped out the series finale, which was rescheduled as part of a doubleheader during the Cardinals' next and final trip to Shea in September. Tom Herr, who had entrenched himself as Herzog's leadoff man, reached base seven times in the rain-shortened series. The smooth-fielding second baseman was hitting .340 with a .420 OBP since being moved to the top of the order three weeks earlier. Herr's hot bat allowed Herzog to move Lonnie Smith down to the second spot. With McGee/Green and Oberkfell hitting over .300 in the sixth and seventh spots in the order, the lineup had length and no easy outs.

Watching from the opposing dugout, Mets manager George Bamberger was effusive in his praise of the Redbirds' middle infielders. "It's worth the price of admission just to watch those two guys [Ozzie Smith and Tom Herr] turn the double play," said Bamberger. "Smith can play shortstop as well as anybody I've ever seen."[16] Bamberger failed to mention the other half of the Cardinals' exemplary infield. Ken Oberkfell, who flew under the radar as an unspectacular but solid third baseman, led the NL in fielding percentage at the hot corner. Keith Hernandez, who would capture his fifth of 11 Gold Gloves at season's end, led NL first basemen in putouts, was second in double plays turned, and third in assists. The foursome comprised arguably one of the best defensive infields the game has ever seen.

The second-place Cardinals (63–49) traveled to Pittsburgh for an important five-game series against the third-place Pirates (59–53) beginning August 12. The Bucs had a missed opportunity in the preceding series, losing three of four to the division-leading Phillies. Andújar won the series opener, but the Cards were not so lucky on Friday the 13th. On the same day *Fast Times at Ridgemont High* hit theaters, Pittsburgh won, 7–4, behind a complete game effort by Don Robinson.

John Stuper and John Candelaria faced off on Saturday, August 14. Following the All-Star break, the two hurlers had experienced opposite extremes of success. Stuper was winless in four starts with a 9.00 ERA while Candelaria was undefeated in five decisions with a minuscule 0.99 ERA. With the support of dozens from his nearby hometown and guidance from catcher Gene Tenace, Stuper threw 7⅓ innings of one-run ball. Lonnie Smith's two-run home run—his seventh of the season—helped tag Candelaria with his first loss in nearly six weeks.

The final two games of the quintet came as part of a Sunday doubleheader. The Cardinals' third-place hitter, Keith Hernandez, entered the day with a .277 batting average and .373 OBP. By most standards, he was having a good year offensively, but after topping the .300 mark for three consecutive seasons, he was not happy with his production. The night before the double-dip, Hernandez tried a different routine. He stayed up until 5 a.m. watching an old movie and drinking wine. "When you get into a rut and things aren't going right, you've got to do something different," said Hernandez. "It's a once-a-year thing with me."[17] The result was a 5-for-9 day with five RBIs. It was an exception to George Kissell's old adage that "you can't hoot with the owls and soar with the eagles."[18] The first game was a 12–5 trouncing in which David Green chipped in with his first big-league homer. Lonnie Smith also reached a milestone, joining Lou Brock as the only players in franchise history to reach 50 steals in one season. In the nightcap, Dave LaPoint's eight innings of two-run ball and Hernandez's bat propelled the Cards to a 5–2 win and doubleheader sweep. With six wins in seven games on the road trip, the Cardinals vaulted ahead of the Phillies in the standings and sent the reeling Pirates, seven games back, to the fringes of playoff contention.

The Cardinals' next 18 games came against the NL's three California teams: San Diego, San Francisco, and Los Angeles. All had winning records and were in the mix for the West division crown thanks to a Braves losing skid. Following a much-needed respite on August 16—a day Herzog spent fishing—the Redbirds reassembled near the banks of the Mississippi River to take on the Padres (63–55), who trailed the first-place Dodgers by two and a half games entering the series. Templeton had been a disappointment to that point, producing a subpar .239 batting average and six home runs. Two other ex–Redbirds, Terry Kennedy and Sixto Lezcano were faring much better, both hitting over .290 with 14 home runs apiece for the surprise contenders. Ozzie Smith stole the show in the first game. Besides reaching base in all four of his plate appearances, he doubled home a run, made a diving stop to keep the game tied in the top of the ninth, and scored the winning run in the bottom half on Hernandez's walk-off single. The 3–2 win improved the Cardinals' record to 18 games over .500 for the first time in 11 years. The Cards and Padres split the next two contests, both low-scoring, one-run affairs. From Dick Williams' point of view, the Cardinals were not the most talented team in the NL East but were the toughest to beat. "They're a funny team," remarked the Padres skipper. "Individually, they're not all that impressive. But they play very well as a team."[19]

The August 20 tilt against the Giants was perhaps the Cardinals' most frustrating game of the season. Hernandez and Hendrick combined for five RBIs in the early going, putting the Cards ahead, 7–0. Lonnie Smith's steal of second base with a seven-run lead in the sixth woke up the Giants' bench, admitted manager Frank Robinson after the game.[20] Steve Mura, who threw six scoreless innings to start the game, was pulled by Herzog after allowing three straight singles to start the seventh. Jim Kaat relieved and ceded a double to Dave Bergman and a booming three-run dinger to Jeffrey Leonard. The Cards' commanding lead was abruptly cut to just two. Herzog made three more pitching changes—cycling through Lahti, Martin, and Sutter—before the third out was recorded. When the inning mercifully came to an end, the Giants had tied the score, 7–7. After Darrell Evans tripled and scored the go ahead run off Sutter in the eighth, the Cards rallied to set up an excellent scoring chance in the bottom of the ninth. With one out, Hernandez was on third base and Glenn Brummer—pinch-running for Dane Iorg—was at first. Willie McGee grounded weakly back to Giants closer Greg Minton, who looked Hernandez back and threw to second base. Brummer took out shortstop Joe Pettini on the force play. Hernandez broke for home but then hesitated and got caught in a rundown between third and home. He was tagged out to end the game.

The Cardinals bounced back from the woeful defeat the following night and took an early 6–1 lead against Bill Laskey, thanks in part to three errors by Leonard, an outfielder who was filling in at first base for Reggie Smith. After the third miscue, manager Frank Robinson moved Leonard to left field.* Home runs by Bob Brenly, Joe Morgan, and Leonard off Dave LaPoint cut the deficit to 6–5, and the home team was in danger of blowing a sizeable lead for the second day in a row. In the bottom of the sixth, the ball found Leonard again. He made a futile diving attempt on Lonnie Smith's line drive, but the ball eluded his glove and rolled all the way to the wall. Smith raced around the bases for an inside-the-park home run. The run proved to be the difference in the Redbirds' 7–6 victory. Smith, whose

---

*Leonard had only played first base in 18 games before the three-error game and would not play the position for the remainder of his career.

9. August—Brummer Steals a Game

4-for-5 performance the day before had been overshadowed by the blown lead, recorded three more base knocks and was a double shy of the cycle. At the end of the day the invaluable left fielder was sporting a .314 average, .842 OPS, and maintained the league lead in runs and stolen bases.

The series finale would provide one of the more memorable endings to a game in franchise history. The man responsible was the unlikeliest of heroes.

Glenn Brummer had beat the odds just to be wearing the birds on the bat. He was born in Olney, Illinois, near the Indiana border and was a standout catcher at Effingham High School, 100 miles east of St. Louis. After graduating in 1972, Glenn went to work for his father, Bob, who owned a farm in Fairfield. Bob himself once had a short-lived minor-league career, playing one season for the Class-D Mattoon Indians in 1950. The sports editor at the *Effingham Daily News* heard that Lake Land College was in need of a catcher. The school was located in Mattoon, the same small town where Bob had played two decades earlier. "My dad and I drove up there right before Thanksgiving," Brummer later recalled. "It was either enroll in school or milk cows all my life."[21]

Brummer led Lake Land in batting average during his two years at the school, earning a tryout at Busch Stadium with the Cardinals in 1974. He stepped in the cage to take some hacks in front of Harry "The Hat" Walker, the Cardinals' farm director who was running the tryout. After Brummer had taken five swings, Bob Gibson, the starting pitcher that day, came out to take batting practice. Walker asked if Brummer could get a few more swings. "No, get the kid out of the cage now," said Gibson.[22] Tim McCarver, looking for a laugh, tried to persuade Brummer to stand up to Gibby, but Walker knew that would not go over well and told the youngster to go shag fly balls. Despite the brevity of his audition, the Cardinals offered Brummer a contract, which he gladly signed.

The 6-foot, 200-pound Brummer proved himself a solid defensive backstop and climbed the ranks of the Cardinals' farm system, eventually getting to Triple A, where an injury he suffered on July 16, 1979, jeopardized his career. Brummer attempted to block home plate while taking a throw from the outfield with the baserunner and ball arriving at the same time. He managed to catch the ball and tag the runner out, but the collision caused multiple torn ligaments in his left knee. "That was the most pain I ever felt in my life," said Brummer. "But I thought I could get up and play.... I told [the trainer], 'Give me a couple minutes.'"[23] He underwent surgery and rehabbed his way back in 1980, hitting .257 for Springfield. He split 1981 between St. Louis and Triple A and was trying to make the most of his rare opportunities behind Porter and Tenace on the depth chart in 1982. "He's the best third-string catcher I've ever seen," contended Herzog. "He warms up 97 pitchers every night. Kaat is out here at 3 throwing every day. The rest of these guys are here at 4 and when Brummer's supposed to be hitting, he's catching them. You got to have a '27 Yankees team if you don't have room for that guy."[24]

Though the game would ultimately transform Brummer into a local legend, he was not in the starting lineup when the Cardinals and Giants got underway on August 22. For the third straight day, St. Louis took an early lead. Willie McGee's two-run homer off Atlee Hammaker in the fourth inning made it 3–0. The relentless Giants again battled back in the sixth with four runs off Andújar to take the lead. The Cards were down to their last out in the ninth when Ken Oberkfell doubled home David Green, tying the score and sending the game to extra innings. The Cardinals were playing a man short with Dane Iorg away from the team for the birth of his fifth child. By the 11th inning, Herzog had used every available position player on his bench. When the pitcher's spot came up with a runner on third and one out in the 11th, Jeff Lahti had to hit for himself and grounded out to the pitcher.

Earlier in the game, Steve Braun had pinch-hit for starting catcher Gene Tenace and reached base. The seldom used Brummer pinch-ran and stayed in the game to catch. He had not started a game since June 19 and had not even stepped in the batter's box in over a month. Brummer faced a tough southpaw, Gary Lavelle, to lead off the 10th inning and struck out feebly. "I didn't even see the ball. I was just taking cuts," admitted Brummer.[25]

The game remained tied when Brummer's spot in the order came back around in

Third-string catcher Glenn Brummer's improbable game-winning steal of home on August 22 made him a St. Louis legend (National Baseball Hall of Fame and Museum, Cooperstown, NY).

the 12th. With one out and Lavelle still on the mound, he put wood on the ball and slashed a single to left field. McGee followed with a single, and one out later, Ozzie Smith beat out an infield grounder to load the bases. David Green came up to bat and fell behind in the count, 1–2. Brummer, the runner on third, had crept down the baseline a little further with each pitch and noticed that Lavelle was not looking over. He had stolen home once in college and thought that with Lavelle's high leg kick that he could make it. Brummer looked at third base coach Chuck Hiller and said, "Chuck, I think I can make it."[26] Hiller didn't exactly say no. He didn't exactly say yes, either.[27]

As Lavelle began to deliver his next pitch, Brummer made a mad dash for home. Green, a right-handed hitter, did not see Brummer barreling down the line but took the pitch, which he perceived to be outside. Brummer slid in under the tag of catcher Milt May as home-plate umpire Dave Pallone, who moved up the third-base line to get a better look, signaled that Brummer was safe. Robinson was outraged and argued the fact that Pallone did not make a call on the pitch. "If he had let that ball cross home plate, it was strike three," Brummer said years later. "Looking at the instant replay, it was right down the middle."[28]

Mike Shannon's call of the play on KMOX radio would be one of the most replayed of his 50-year career as a broadcaster. "Two down, sacks jammed. Lavelle at the belt.... Brummer's stealing home ... he is saa-aafe! And the Cardinals win. Brummer stole home! The dugout comes out and they congratulate him. You wouldn't believe it!"[29]

"I had no idea what would have happened if I had been out," said Brummer in retrospect. "I might have been on a bus to Louisville."[30] The stolen base would be one of four in Brummer's five-year major-league career in 12 attempts. "The only problem after that was, I couldn't put him in to run anymore because he was always trying to steal bases," said Herzog years later.[31]

With the win, the Cardinals gained a game on Philadelphia and Montreal, both of whom had lost. Brummer's heroics also boosted the confidence of an already determined club. "If there was one game that convinced me and the rest of the guys that this was going to be our year, it came on August 22," Ozzie Smith later wrote in his memoir.[32]

The Cardinals concluded the nine-game homestand with three versus the Dodgers (69–56). Tommy Lasorda's bunch held a one-game lead over Atlanta, though both teams were even in the loss column. In the opener on August 23—a nationally televised Monday night affair—the Cards forged out to an early 4–0 lead against Jerry Reuss and then tacked on seven more runs off the Dodgers bullpen. Gene Tenace and Willie McGee each recorded three hits and combined for six RBIs. Tenace's performance raised his batting average to .346 to go with hefty 1.169 OPS, while McGee boosted his average to .336. Bob Forsch was the beneficiary of the offensive explosion and picked up his team-leading 13th win.

The Dodgers' superior starting pitching and Ken Landreaux's bat carried Los Angeles to victory in the other two games of the series. Landreaux had been mired in a 3-for-31 slump but went 5-for-9 with four extra base hits to lead the Dodgers' offensive charge. Bob Welch and Fernando Valenzuela each flummoxed the Redbird bats with complete-game victories. Valenzuela helped his own cause, clubbing his first career home run. Tenace accomplished a personal milestone in a losing effort, hitting his 200th career round-tripper.

The year 1982 was Gene Tenace's 14th season in the major leagues. The Cards' second-string catcher brought a hard-nosed approach and valuable experience to Herzog's bench. Tenace had been a starting catcher for eight seasons after bursting on the scene in the 1972 World Series. Half-Irish and half–Italian, he was born Fiore Gino Tennaci. His Italian grandfather Americanized the name to Gene Tenace, pronouncing the last name like tennis. Gene grew up in Lucasville, Ohio, and by high school had developed into an outstanding football and baseball player. He earned all-state honors as a shortstop and played on an American Legion team that included two other future big leaguers—Al Oliver and Larry Hisle. After graduation in 1965 he was selected by the Kansas City Athletics in the 20th round of baseball's first amateur draft. The stocky 6-foot, 190-pounder bounced around between the infield and outfield during his first few years in the minors before being converted to catcher.

Owner Charlie Finley had moved the Athletics to Oakland by the time Tenace made his big-league debut in 1969. He stuck in the majors for good in 1971, serving as Dave Duncan's backup for the 101-win A's, who fell to Baltimore in the ALCS. Tenace filled the same capacity in 1972 and was used sparingly during the season's first four months. By late August, he was hitting only .189, but when Duncan missed time fulfilling obligations with the Marine Corps Reserve, Tenace got his chance. He hit in all four games during Duncan's absence and remained the starter through the remainder of the season and into the playoffs. Tenace went 1-for-17 in the ALCS as Oakland topped Detroit to advance to the Fall Classic. Despite Tenace's lackluster results, he was seeing the ball well and making hard contact.

The A's, without Reggie Jackson due to a hamstring injury, were heavy underdogs in the World Series against Cincinnati's Big Red Machine. The series started at Riverfront Stadium, only an hour from Lucasville. Tenace experienced a strange sensation in Game One which he later described to author Jason Turbow. As Tenace knelt in the on-deck circle before his first plate appearance, he noticed everything had gone silent, as if someone had flipped a switch and turned off the cacophony of the crowd.[33] The man hitting in front of him—George Hendrick—drew a two-out walk. Tenace stepped in against the hard-throwing Gary Nolan and noticed that the first delivery appeared to be floating to the plate. He thought that perhaps Nolan was hurt. The next pitch appeared to be just as slow, and Tenace yanked it foul. The third pitch looked just as enticing. This time, he kept the ball fair and hit it on a line over the left-field wall. "I didn't even feel the ball hit my bat," Tenace recalled. "It looked like a batting practice fastball."[34]

Tenace noticed that his hearing seemed normal when he was in the field, but when he came to plate a second time, the stadium again went silent. Just as before, Nolan's pitch looked like a beachball coming toward him. Tenace pounced, and parked a homer into the second deck, becoming the first player in major-league history to homer in his first two World Series at-bats. Years later, Tenace would hear Michael Jordan describe being in the zone and realize he had experienced the same phenomenon.[35] Tenace's three RBIs accounted for all of Oakland's runs in the Game One victory. He launched two more round-trippers in the series and claimed Most Valuable Player honors as the A's shocked the Reds to win the franchise's first title.

Tenace split his time between first base and catcher in 1973–74, earning two more World Series rings for the three-peat A's. He took advantage of the players' newly-granted free agency following the 1976 season, signing a six-year, $1.85 million pact with the San Diego Padres to serve as the club's starting catcher. Owner Ray Kroc's desire to field a winner did not come to fruition, however, and Tenace endured three losing seasons during his four years in San Diego.

Between 1973 and 1980, Tenace averaged 21 home runs and over 100 walks per season. The balding backstop was acquired by Herzog to serve as the second-stringer behind Darrell Porter. Nonetheless, Tenace said at the time he was "tickled to death to be out of San Diego" and have a chance to play for a contender.[36] He embraced the role of a bench player and mentor. "I'm kind of outspoken," said Tenace. "That's just the way I am. If you can't swallow a little pride and walk up to one of the kids and offer to help him out, you don't belong here. I know I would always appreciate when one of the veterans would come up to me and help out. Sal Bando had a lot to do with my getting started out in Oakland. We're all in this for one thing, and that's to win."[37]

Tenace was flourishing in a reserve role and credited Herzog's strong communication skills with playing a part in his success. The skipper would let the bench players know a day or two in advance if they would be starting and what he was thinking. "He shows the individual players respect," said Tenace. "and that makes you want to bust your butt for the man."[38]

When Tenace's former team, the Athletics, visited Milwaukee's County Stadium on August 27, the chance of seeing history created a buzz in the ballpark. Oakland's base-stealing extraordinaire, Rickey Henderson, entered the day with 118 steals—tied with Lou Brock for the single-season record. Brock was on hand to offer congratulations if, and when, Henderson eclipsed his record. Brewers starter George "Doc" Medich, recently acquired in a trade with Texas, retired Henderson to lead off the game but walked him on four pitches with two outs in the top of the third. "We knew he was going on the first pitch, and I knew Ted [Simmons] was going to call for a pitchout," recalled Medich, who tried everything in his bag of tricks to keep the speedster close—alternating throws over to first and holding the ball. Finally, Medich delivered a pitchout to Simmons. Sure enough, Henderson took off in a flash. "Ted made a good throw and he was out by three feet, but they called him safe," said Medich, looking back. "I think the umpires just wanted to get it over—they wanted the circus to stop. Robin [Yount] brought the ball back and said, 'He was out by three feet.' There was no replay back then, so it was what it was. We did win the game though."[39] For good measure, Henderson stole three more bases that day and would the season with 130, a record that may never be broken. "I'm glad it's over," said Henderson after the game with a bottle of champagne in hand. "Now I can relax more. The whole experience has been a lot of hard work and troubled my mind. When I broke the record, the next three came easy."[40]

While Henderson was making history in Milwaukee, the Cardinals opened up a three-game series with the Padres at Jack Murphy Stadium. Joaquín Andújar outdueled Tim Lollar in the Friday night opener. Following an unusual Saturday off-day, the two teams split a Sunday afternoon doubleheader. Bruce Sutter notched two more saves in the series, pushing his season total to 29. After his ERA had ballooned to 4.96 on June 20, Sutter had been dominant in his next 26 outings, sporting a 0.73 ERA while holding opposing hitters to a paltry .194 batting average.

The Cards next traveled up the coast to Los Angeles for a three-game set with the unenviable task of facing Valenzuela for the second time in a week. When Herzog was asked what his strategy was for beating the young prodigy, he said, "I'm going to take a bleeping gun, go out where he warms up, and shoot him in the foot."⁴¹ Assault and battery were not needed to overcome Valenzuela, however. The Redbird offense managed to push across three runs against the young sensation, which was two more than John Stuper allowed in his 7⅔ innings. The Cards won, 3–2. "There were probably only two or three people who thought I had a chance to win," said Stuper afterwards. "You can't say it was just another game, but the difference was confidence. I had faith in God and myself."⁴²

Burt Hooton and the Dodgers cruised to a 4–1 victory over Steve Mura and the Redbirds on August 31, the day of the waiver trade deadline. Several pitchers were moved, including ex–Cardinal John Denny to the Phillies, Tommy John and John Curtis to the Angels, and Sparky Lyle to the White Sox. The Cardinals did not make any deals but had conversations with Houston about acquiring 37-year-old Don Sutton, whose age and salary—$700,000 a year through 1984—made him expendable for the fifth-place Astros. Sutton had a career record of 254–192 at the time and would have provided a boost to the St. Louis rotation, but the asking price was too high. Rick Hummel of the *St. Louis Post-Dispatch* speculated that the Astros likely asked for David Green, whom the Cardinals considered untouchable.⁴³ Instead, Houston sent Sutton to Milwaukee for minor leaguers Frank DiPino, Kevin Bass, and Mike Madden. Although Sutton was shipped to the American League, the Cardinals had not seen the last of him in 1982.

10

September

Andújar Shines, Cardinals Clinch

With a two-and-a-half-game division lead at the start of September, the Cardinals were tasked with fending off their NL East foes through 31 more games. Though they were inactive in the trade market, the Redbirds received reinforcements in the form of five minor-league callups when rosters expanded. Rejoining the team were outfielders Gene Roof and Tito Landrum and pitcher Jeff Keener. The club also added infield prospect Kelly Paris and pitcher Eric Rasmussen. The front office made a bid for 41-year-old Luis Tiant, who had been pitching in the Mexican League, but he chose to sign with the Angels.

Rasmussen's return to St. Louis was a homecoming of sorts. The 6-foot-3 right-hander and Racine, Wisconsin, native had been drafted by the Cardinals in 1973 out of Louisiana State University-New Orleans after leading the nation year that year with a 0.90 ERA.[1] Rasmussen's given first name was Harold, and he was known as Harry when he debuted with the Cardinals in 1975. He later legally changed his name to Eric, which was more befitting of his Danish ancestry.

Rasmussen accumulated a 24–39 record in parts of four seasons with St. Louis before he was traded to the Padres for George Hendrick. He won 12 games for the Friars in 1978 but suffered from a lack of run support his next two seasons, during which he lost 20 of his 30 decisions. He was released by San Diego in the spring of 1980 and, when no big-league offers came, signed with a team in the Mexican League.

After experiencing the luxuries of big-league life, the Mexican League was quite a shock. "The travel was terrible," described Rasmussen. "Bus trips of 20 to 24 hours were common. And some of the hotels were fleabags. One towel to last you for three days, and that towel smelled like the guy who had used it last. You ended up drying off with the bedsheets."[2]

Many American players returned home after a few weeks because

10. September—Andújar Shines, Cardinals Clinch

of the shoddy conditions, but Rasmussen stuck it out for the entire 1981 season. He then pitched winter ball in Venezuela, where he won eight of ten decisions—including a no-hitter. He received an invitation to spring training with the Cardinals in 1982 on a conditional contract, meaning he had to make the team or be sent back to the Mexican League.[3] He was cut on the last day of camp, so he returned to Mexico, posting a 10–8 record and 2.26 ERA for Leones de Yucatán. During the season, Rasmussen made sure Joe McDonald kept him in mind. "Twice a month he'd write me," said McDonald. "Very touching letters. I'd never had a ballplayer do that. He'd say things like, 'Pitched a two-hitter last night. Don't forget me.'"[4] When the Mexican League season ended in early August, McDonald offered Rasmussen a spot on the Louisville Redbirds' roster. He jumped at the chance and pitched his way back to St. Louis.

The September callups contributed to the Cardinals' playoff push immediately. The Dodgers held a 5–4 lead in the top of the ninth inning of the series finale at Chávez Ravine on September 1. Tom Herr led off the inning with a single and moved up 90 feet on a sacrifice bunt by Mike Ramsey. Tito Landrum, who had entered the game in the eighth inning as part of a double switch, singled to score Herr, tying the score, 5–5. The game went to extras, and in the 13th inning, Kelly Paris made his major-league debut as a pinch-hitter for Doug Bair. Paris, a native Californian in his eighth season of professional baseball, had earned a long-awaited promotion by hitting .328 with 11 home runs and 20 stolen bases for Louisville. He legged out an infield chopper for his first career hit. After Herr sacrificed Paris to second, Ramsey struck out and George Hendrick was intentionally walked, bringing up Ozzie Smith. The Wizard's ground ball up the middle was knocked down by second baseman Steve Sax, but Chuck Hiller aggressively waved home Paris, who crossed the plate safely with the go-ahead run. Rasmussen and Jim Kaat closed the door in the bottom of the inning to seal the Cardinals' 76th win of the season.

The Cards concluded the California jaunt at San Francisco's Candlestick Park, known for its swirling winds and blustery temperatures. "Until I played at Candlestick, I never realized how great Willie Mays must have been," said Ozzie Smith. "My God, what would he have done in a real ballpark?"[5] Fly balls that would typically be routine outs turned into outfield adventures at the ballpark by the bay. As Art Spander of the *San Francisco Examiner* wrote, "Candlestick Park isn't so much a stadium as a test of will. The guy who built it may not have disliked mankind, but he definitely disliked baseball."[6]

Candlestick's notorious gusts came into effect in the series opener on September 3. Each of the Giants' three runs came on innings with misplayed fly balls the outfield trio of Lonnie Smith, Tito Landrum, and

Willie McGee. The latter two contributed to the Giants' tying and winning runs.

The next day, Lonnie Smith, described by Dan McGrath of the *San Francisco Chronicle* as "a disrupter in the Rickey Henderson mold," nearly ran the Cardinals to victory.[7] Smith went 3-for-3, walked, scored three runs, and tied Davey Lopes' National League single-game record with five stolen bases. McGee contributed his third home run of the season, and St. Louis was well-positioned for victory with a 4–2 lead heading to the bottom of the ninth. Bair, who relieved Dave LaPoint in the seventh, started the inning but was pulled after allowing a one-out single to Jeffrey Leonard. Kaat was summoned for the lefty-lefty matchup against 38-year-old Joe Morgan, a two-time MVP who was winding down his career. Kaat got ahead with two quick strikes, but Morgan managed to push a single to left field. With two on, two out, and the powerful Jack Clark coming up, Herzog brought in Bruce Sutter. "Whitey asked me if I wanted to walk Clark, but Reggie Smith was due up and he's a tough hitter, too," said Sutter after the game.[8] Clark connected on Sutter's first pitch and sent it 425 feet into the left-center field seats for a walk-off home run.

The Giants completed a three-game sweep the following afternoon behind the pitching of righty Fred Breining, who twirled his first career complete game while surrendering only one run. The San Francisco native said after the game that the wind aided his forkball by slowing it down and giving it more movement. John Stuper, who walked nine and took the loss, clearly did not find the elements as beneficial. While the Cardinals dropped all three contests at San Francisco, Philadelphia swept Houston to pull even with St. Louis in the win column. The NL East was still very much up for grabs:

	W	L	W-L%	GB
St. Louis Cardinals	76	59	.563	--
Philadelphia Phillies	76	60	.559	0.5
Montreal Expos	73	63	.537	3.5
Pittsburgh Pirates	72	64	.529	4.5
New York Mets	60	77	.438	17
Chicago Cubs	53	81	.396	22.5

The Cards returned home on September 6 with 27 games remaining on the schedule—all against NL East opponents—starting with Montreal. St. Louis was outscored 7–6 in the three-game set but managed to take two of three, thanks to a pair of 1–0 shutouts authored by Joaquín Andújar and Bob Forsch. The former improved his career record against Montreal to 11-1. Against the rest of the league he was ten games under .500. During the series, word came that Ken Boyer had died of lung cancer. Forsch admitted to having his former manager on his mind when he tossed his 91-pitch complete game gem the following day. "I was thinking before the game that it would be nice to do well," said Forsch. "Besides being a great player, Boyer was a great guy, a great individual."[9]

Boyer's number 14 would eventually be retired by the Cardinals, though he would continue to be overlooked for the National Baseball Hall of Fame. The 1964 National League MVP had a lifetime batting average of .287 and accumulated 282 home runs during his 15-year playing career. Boyer's JAWS score, a system developed by sabermetrician Jay Jaffe as a way of measuring a player's Hall of Fame credentials, is 14th all-time at the hot corner, a position woefully underrepresented in Cooperstown.*

In the Redbirds' 2–1 loss to the Mets on September 10—a game that featured an unlikely inside-the-park home run by Dave Kingman—Ozzie Smith aggravated a leg injury and showed up to Busch Stadium the following day on crutches. He was kneed in the thigh by Bob Brenly while turning a double play in San Francisco and then exacerbated the injury diving for a ball against the Mets. The Wizard would be out of action for the next 14 games. The Birds were dealt another blow on September 11 when Andújar was struck on the knee by a comeback line drive, forcing him out of the game after five innings. X-rays of the injured limb were negative. The offense came out of hibernation to soften the blow of the injuries. Hendrick broke a 34-day homerless streak in the bottom of the second inning with a three-run jack—his team-leading 17th of the season—to lead the Cards to victory.

Before the Sunday afternoon finale on the following day, the Cardinals honored Butch Yatkeman, who was retiring after 59 years with the organization. The diminutive Yatkeman got his start with the Cards as a batboy in 1923 before his promotion to equipment manager in 1931 and had been a part of all 12 of the franchise's pennant-winning teams. Facing erstwhile Cardinal Pete Falcone, who came into the game with a 7–9 record and 4.18 ERA, the offense mustered only one run on three hits. It marked the fifth time in seven games the Redbird offense had produced only one tally. Struggling righty Steve Mura took the loss after allowing four runs and failing to make it out of the fourth inning for the third consecutive start.

On the morning of September 13, Glenn Burke appeared on NBC's *Today* show with Bryant Gumbel and became the first major-league player

---

*Graig Nettles is the only Hall of Fame eligible third baseman with a higher JAWS score not to be enshrined.

to come out as gay. The interview coincided with an *Inside Sports* article in which Burke, who had last played professionally in 1980 after stints with the Dodgers and A's, detailed his double life in baseball. To that point, the speedy outfielder was best known as the inventor of the high-five when he extended his hand to congratulate Dusty Baker after a home run in 1977. Though Burke kept his sexuality to himself during his playing career, he refused the cover of a girlfriend and came up with excuses as to why he would not hang out with teammates on the road. Dodgers GM Al Campanis attempted to quell rumors of Burke's sexuality by bribing him to get married and even offered to pay for a honeymoon. Burke told him, "Al, I don't think I'll be getting married no time soon."[10] Burke was traded to Oakland shortly thereafter. A knee injury and the realization that some in the league had figured out his secret led him to walk away from the game. "I had finally gotten to the point where it was more important to be myself than a baseball player," he said at the time.[11] Though he had hoped his coming out would pave the way for other players to do the same, it would be another 17 years before another major leaguer, Billy Bean, followed his lead. Burke's public acknowledgment went largely uncovered by most media outlets and was essentially swept under the rug by Major League Baseball.

───

Later that day, the Cardinals began an eight-game road trip with an all-important series in Philadelphia. Bob Forsch pitched valiantly in the opener, but he was no match for the brilliance of Steve Carlton, who tossed a 12-strikeout shutout. Keith Hernandez, one of the few players maintaining a hot bat through the Cardinals' offensive drought, accounted for two of the team's three hits, raising his average above .300. Carlton contributed one of the Phillies' two runs with a solo home run—one of 13 he would hit in his career. As Richie Ashburn wrote, Lefty "did everything but sweep out the stadium."[12] The win was Carlton's 20th of the season, the sixth time he had reached the plateau in his storied career. After starting the season 0–4, he had won 20 of his last 25 decisions, completed 16 games, and proved he was still the game's most dominant ace.

On September 14, the world was shocked by the death of Princess Grace of Monaco—the royal moniker of Oscar-winning actress and *Philadelphia Story* star Grace Kelly—following a car accident the day before. The Cardinals, looking to write a different type of Philadelphia story, flipped the script on the Phillies in the second game of the series at the Vet. Darrell Porter produced the Cardinals' only two runs when he deposited a Mike Krukow changeup over the right-field fence in the top of the fourth inning. John Stuper shut out the Phillies through seven but loaded the bases in the bottom of the eighth with one out and one of the game's most dangerous hitters—Mike Schmidt—due up. It was Bruce Sutter time. Schmidt had doubled in both of his at-bats against the Cardinal relief ace earlier in the season. With the bases packed, Sutter had no choice but to attack the strike zone. He used his splitter to get ahead with two swinging strikes, but then Schmidt battled back to even the count. The next pitch induced a weak comebacker to Sutter, who threw home to start a 1–2–3 double-play. The Redbird fireman pitched a scoreless ninth to preserve the 2–0 shutout and record his 32nd save. Following the game, Schmidt discussed his eighth-inning at-bat against Sutter: "I'd have been better off striking out. I've hit into a pitcher-to-home-to-first double play maybe once in 10 years. I've had a pretty good average against him, but it didn't mean diddly-squat tonight."[13]

In the rubber game on September 15—with the division lead on the line—there was palpable excitement in Veterans Stadium with news that the NBA's 76ers had signed Moses Malone. The Cards made sure the fans had nothing else to celebrate that day with an 8–0 blowout—the most runs St. Louis had scored in 20 games. Lonnie Smith turned in a four-hit performance, and Hendrick racked up four RBIs. Andújar, showing no lingering effects from the line drive that knocked him out of his previous outing, extended his scoreless streak to 23 innings. The complete-game victory pushed his season innings total to 246, which was 52 more than any season in his 12-year professional career. Though the Phillies trailed the Cardinals by only a game and a half, the mood in the home clubhouse after the game "bordered on funereal," reported the *St. Louis Post-Dispatch*.[14] The vibe was certainly more positive in Montreal after five consecutive wins positioned the Expos only two games off the pace.

From Philadelphia, the Cardinals made the short commute to New York for a five-game series with the Mets. Because of two rain outs earlier in the year, the NL East foes had to play five games in three days, including back-to-back doubleheaders on September 17–18. Herzog dug deep into his roster to cover innings. Eric Rasmussen got the starting assignment for the first game and limited New York to two runs in seven innings before passing the torch to Sutter in the eighth. The game went to extra innings, the last thing either team needed with so much baseball left to play. Willie McGee broke out of a 0-for-24 slump with an RBI double in the top of the 10th inning to put the Cardinals ahead. Sutter retired all nine men he faced to close it out and save the bullpen from further usage. Herzog stuck with the same lineup in the nightcap, and the Cards cruised to a 7–1 victory behind adequate pitching by Steve Mura and 3⅓ scoreless innings by Doug Bair, who earned his seventh save.

Bair had experienced a career renaissance after arriving in St. Louis.

He originally came up in the Pirates' minor-league system as a starter but stalled at Triple A. After being converted to a reliever, he was traded to Oakland and then Cincinnati, where he became one of Sparky Anderson's more dependable relievers. Bair saved 28 games and posted a sub-two ERA in 1978 but then experienced shoulder trouble and ineffectiveness over the next two seasons while being relegated to a long-relief role. Bair's ERA was close to six in 1981 when the Cardinals acquired him, hoping that a change of scenery would do him some good. Hub Kittle suggested a tweak in his mechanics, and Bair's confidence grew as Herzog turned to him in high-leverage situations. By 1982, Bair had become Herzog's trusted setup man and a more than capable fill-in for Sutter when he faltered or was nursing an injury.

The starting lineup in the Saturday lid-lifter included rarely-utilized Julio González, who recorded his first hit in three months, and rookie Kelly Paris—making his second big-league start. David Green, batting second in the order, hit a colossal 425-foot home run off Pete Falcone to get St. Louis on the board in the top of the fourth. It would be all the run support Forsch needed; he pitched 7⅓ scoreless frames to pick up his team-leading 15th win. In the second game, starting pitcher Walt Terrell made his major-league debut for the Mets. The Cardinals welcomed him to The Show with six runs—one on a Darrell Porter solo home run and another on Gene Roof's first base hit of the season. Jim Kaat and Jeff Lahti combined for nine innings of two-run ball in the Redbirds' nightcap victory. Timely hitting and exceptional pitching continued for St. Louis in the series finale on September 19. The offense manufactured three runs while the Cards' pitching combo of Stuper and Bair yielded only one.

In completing a resounding sweep of the Mets on their home turf, the Cardinals won five games in just over 46 hours and increased their stronghold on the division. The unheralded Mike Ramsey, filling in at shortstop for Ozzie Smith, played all 46 innings of the series, reached base seven times, and converted all 37 defensive chances. "You can't replace a guy like Ozzie Smith; he's too unique of a talent," said Ramsey in retrospect. "I was just trying to give my A game. I knew that my teammates, manager and coaches believed in me, and that gave me confidence."[15] The Redbirds headed home with a suddenly commanding four-and-a-half-game lead over Philadelphia and a magic number of only 10 with 13 games to play. The Expos and Pirates both had quickly fallen six and a half games off the pace and were for all intents and purposes out of the race. Sutter was not taking anything for granted: "Was today the last game? When they tell we're in the playoffs, then I'll talk."[16]

The Cardinals' dominance in the Big Apple had taken the wind out of the sails of the Phillies, who opened the Cards' final homestand on

10. September—Andújar Shines, Cardinals Clinch

September 20. "Mentally that hurt us," admitted Phillies first baseman Pete Rose. "I don't think any of us thought they could go into New York and win back-to-back doubleheaders."[17] With Carlton scheduled to pitch the second of a brief two-game set, there was added importance for the Cardinals to take the first game—a matchup of Joaquín Andújar versus John Denny. Andújar continued his mastery of the Phillies, extending his scoreless-inning streak to 29⅔ before the Phillies pushed across a run in the top of the seventh. The Cards held on for a 4–1 victory and Andújar improved his season record against Philadelphia to 4–0. "With Big Lefty going tomorrow, we needed this one," said a relieved Herzog in his office after the game. "I'll tell you what, I like our chances much better than I like theirs."[18]

In the seven days following Carlton's shutout that catapulted the Phillies ahead of the Cardinals for the NL East lead on September 13, St. Louis had won eight in a row—a stretch during which they allowed a total of seven runs. "We just don't have that type of staff that can go out and throw shutouts and hold the other team to one run," said Tom Herr. "On paper, it just doesn't look that way, but they've gone out and done it. They've made believers out of me, and they should have made believers out of everybody else."[19]

While the Cardinals were sprinting toward the finish line, the Phillies were limping, losing seven of nine to fall five and a half games behind. Carlton took the mound at Busch Stadium on September 21 with a better shot at the Cy Young Award than the playoffs. Pitching for the third time in nine days, the 37-year-old workhorse added to his sterling résumé, logging 167 pitches in a 14-strikeout, complete-game effort. With Carlton on the mound, there was no room for error by the Cardinals, and two defensive miscues led to four unearned runs. Carlton snapped the Cards' winning streak just as he had done when the club had won 12 in a row in April, improving his lifetime record against St. Louis to 35–10. He would finish the season with a league-best 23 wins and capture his fourth NL Cy Young Award.

On September 22, Dave LaPoint made his first start in 18 days in the first of two games versus Pittsburgh. Herzog had avoided using the lefty against the right-hand heavy lineups of the Phillies and Mets. "I hadn't done anything to contribute to the [eight-game winning] streak," said LaPoint. "All day long, I was thinking, 'here's my chance to do something.'"[20] He showed no signs of rust from the long layoff, tossing eight frames of one-run ball. For seven innings, Rick Rhoden was equally sharp for the Pirates, allowing only a solo home run to Ken Oberkfell—just one of two he would hit all season. With the game tied at one apiece in the eighth, LaPoint was lifted for pinch-hitter Steve Braun.

Although he had not started a game since April, Braun managed to stay sharp and productive when called upon. For the first six years of his career, he had been a semi-regular third baseman and outfielder with the Minnesota Twins, hitting .284 with a .376 on-base percentage while averaging more than 400 at-bats per season. After he was acquired by Kansas City during Herzog's tenure as manager, Braun became a pinch-hitting specialist.

Bullpen coach and batting practice pitcher Dave Ricketts helped Braun prepare by simulating relief pitchers he might face late in the game. Braun also braced for duty by practicing the art of meditation. "Brauny would go down in the runway and meditate," recalled Herzog decades later. "He'd take a god dang nap and picture what the guy was going to throw him. He was a good breaking ball hitter, he didn't strike out, and even when he didn't get a hit, he'd always seem to go 3-and-2 in the count and put the ball in play."[21]

"I take great pride in my pinch-hitting ability," Braun said during his tenure in St. Louis. "If Whitey wants me to play in the outfield, I'm ready. But I know what my role is. I find it very satisfying to do a job successfully that most guys don't want to do."[22] For two consecutive seasons, Braun had signed a minor-league contract and made the club because of his ability to give a tough at-bat late in games.

The left-hand hitting Braun, who possessed an excellent batting eye, came to the plate against the righty Rhoden and boosted his average to .304 with his 11th pinch-hit of the season—a double down the right-field line. The next man up, Tom Herr, singled home pinch-runner Tito Landrum for the go-ahead run. Sutter held the Pirates in check in the ninth to record his 35th save. The 2–1 victory improved the Cardinals' record to 88–64. Their streak of allowing two runs or fewer had reached 11 games, a period during which they posted an incredible 1.00 ERA. At the time, only 11 other teams in the live-ball era had matched the feat, and only the 1920 Giants, 1968 Indians, and 1968 Dodgers had a longer stretch of pitching supremacy.

Following an extra-inning loss to the Pirates on September 23, the Cardinals hosted the Cubs for the final home series of the season. Though admittedly not 100 percent, Ozzie Smith returned to the lineup and showed no visible effects of the thigh hematoma that had kept him off the field for 14 games. Stuper and Andújar tossed complete-game gems to defeat the Cubs in the first two contests. Andújar's win was his fifth in a row, a stretch during which he posted a 0.47 ERA and held opposing hitters to a .164 batting average. "He's probably pitched better this year than anybody thought he could," assessed Herzog. "He's been outstanding. The key is that he's a complete pitcher now—his control is good, he pitches in and out, and he

10. September—Andújar Shines, Cardinals Clinch 153

keeps the ball down."²³ Cubs manager Lee Elia did not mince words about his own club. "We have a lot of guys who I hope aren't back. You get tired of looking at garbage in your own backyard," said the skipper.²⁴

Elia was surely not speaking about Fergie Jenkins, who pitched the Cubs to a 6–1 victory on Fan Appreciation Day for his 277th career win. A crowd of 46,789 boosted the Cardinals' home attendance total to 2,111,906, breaking the previous mark set in Busch Stadium's inaugural season of 1966. The Cards passed the two million mark for just the third time in franchise history.*

Cubs first baseman Bill Buckner, who saw the Cardinals 18 times over the course of the season, gave the Redbirds their due in a backhanded way. "The Cardinals get the ugliest base hits I've ever seen," said Buckner, who would finish fifth in the NL batting race. "They're not the kind of team that impresses you. They have no great pitchers, but they have good pitching. No great hitters, but they get the job done. Keith Hernandez is a good hitter, for example, but he's no Mike Schmidt."²⁵

With a magic number of two and six games to play, the Cardinals' NL East title was all but certain. The NL West, on the other hand, was still very much up for grabs. At the start of September, it had appeared to be a two-team race between the Braves and Dodgers. By September 18, the Los Angeles had pulled ahead of Atlanta by three and a half games after winning 10 of 12. Then, the Dodgers lost six of seven, allowing both the Braves and Giants—who had reeled off 18 wins in 22 games starting with their sweep of the Cardinals—to pull within a game of the division lead with seven to play.

⸺

Olympic Stadium had been the site of the Cardinals' two previous managerial firings, recalling less fruitful times in the organization's recent past. Now, the Redbirds strode into Montreal with a chance to clinch the division against the team prognosticators had favored when the season began. LaPoint opposed Bill Gullickson in first game, which was delayed until 9:05 p.m. local time due to rain.† Meanwhile, the Cubs took an early lead over the Phillies. Armed with knowledge they had a chance to clinch the division with a win, the Cardinals came out swinging. Ken Oberkfell got things going with a one-out double and scored two batters later on Dane Iorg's single. After Darrell Porter drew a two-out walk, Willie McGee hit a sinking line drive into left-center field that Andre Dawson attempted to backhand. The ball skipped under his glove and rolled to the

---

*Since 1982, the Cardinals have drawn more than two million fans in every season except for 1994 and 1995.
†Olympic Stadium's roof was not installed until 1987.

wall as McGee sped around the bases for an inside-the-park home run. Before the Expos even got to bat, the Cards held a 4–0 advantage. As the game progressed, the scoreboard flashed a final score: Cubs 8, Phillies 1. St. Louis did not score again for the final eight innings, but no additional runs were necessary. LaPoint, aware of the potential to clinch with a win, was locked in. "I saw that Philadelphia was losing, and I knew I could be the one to win the pennant," said the rookie. "After a while, I couldn't see anything out there but Darrell's glove."[26] LaPoint and Bair combined to limit the Expos to two runs through 7⅓ innings, and Bruce Sutter retired all five men he faced, including future Hall of Famers Tim Raines, Dawson, and Gary Carter. After the final out, Sutter was mobbed by his elated teammates. The celebration continued in the clubhouse, where players doused each other with champaign and beer.

The game was a microcosm of the season, as Keith Hernandez pointed out. "It was an appropriate clincher. Two rookies [LaPoint and McGee] won it for us, and Mr. Sutter saved it for us," noted the first baseman.[27] McGee, always humble, deflected acclaim to his teammates. "The credit goes to everybody else in this room," he said during the celebration. "They went out of the way to make me feel welcome. That helped me relax and concentrate on playing to the best of my ability and helping the team."[28]

As he was leaving the stadium, Al Oliver, the 1982 NL batting champion, walked by the entrance of the visitor's clubhouse and heard the cacophony of celebration. "That was supposed to be us. We had the talent but were inconsistent all year," lamented Oliver, whose team lost 15 of 20 games before the All-Star break. "They supposedly didn't have as much talent, but they kept plugging away at the same solid pace."[29]

With the fates of both teams sealed, the Cards and Expos reconvened on September 28 to complete the series. Herzog used the opportunity to rest Herr and the Smiths—all dealing with nagging lower extremity injuries. Warren Cromartie delivered a walk-off double against Jeff Lahti in the 10th inning to give Montreal a 5–4 victory. Steve Rogers pitched a complete game to notch his 18th win. Oliver recorded his 200th hit of the season, joining Nap Lajoie as the only players in major-league history with 100 RBIs and 200 hits in a season in both leagues.

"These games are like the last days of spring training," said Herzog. "Nobody remembers your record." The skipper scoffed at the importance of going into the playoffs with momentum. "Momentum never matters. Momentum starts at that time when the playoffs open. I've had teams that had to bust their butts the last week to get into the playoffs and I've had teams that didn't have to do anything the last week, and it doesn't make any difference how you approach it."[30]

The Cardinals dropped both games at Pittsburgh on September 29–30

10. September—Andújar Shines, Cardinals Clinch   155

as bench players subbed in for the regulars as if it were a spring training game. Rick Hummel noted that the only things missing were seagulls and pitchers running in the outfield.[31] At the completion of play on September 30, the Braves had moved atop the NL West and held a one-game lead over both the Dodgers and Giants with three games remaining. Meanwhile, on television screens across the country, viewers were introduced to Sam "Mayday" Malone, a fictional ex–Red Sox reliever who operated a Boston bar called *Cheers*.

The Cardinals concluded the regular-season schedule with two meaningless games versus the Cubs at Wrigley Field. Andújar started the first game on a limited pitch count and was pulled after four innings. Forsch got in some work in relief. The Cards played sloppy defense, committing four errors that led to five unearned runs. Porter hit a pair of opposite field home runs off Fergie Jenkins, but that was not enough to overcome the defensive lapses. The Cards' 8–4 loss was their fourth consecutive defeat, their longest losing streak of the season.

While Major League Baseball concluded its final weekend of regular season action, newspaper front pages across the country described a bizarre series of deaths in the Chicago metropolitan area. The link between the victims was cyanide-laced Tylenol capsules. Investigators hypothesized that someone methodically removed Acetaminophen from the capsules, replaced it with the deadly substance, and put the bottles back in the supply chain. Police officers cruised streets and visited train stations with loudspeakers warning people about the possibility of lethal pills in their medicine cabinets. Seven people died, and there were subsequently a number of copycat crimes. No suspect was ever charged or convicted.

The season finale on October 3 provided some levity to the news that weekend. Keith Hernandez entered the game hitting .299 and went 1-for-4 on the day to just miss the .300 mark. Lonnie Smith finished with a team-best .307 average but fell short in his bid to become the first player since Ty Cobb to steal 70 bases and drive in 70 runs, ending with 68 and 69 in the two categories, respectively. Ken Oberkfell went for 3-for-5, ending the season on an eight-game hitting streak during which he hit .548 (17-for-31). Julio González, who had 17 hits in the first 161 games of the season, recorded four base knocks and broke a 4–4 tie in the top of the 14th inning with his first home run of the year.

The Cardinals finished the regular season with a record of 92–70, compiling an identical 46–35 record both at home and on the road. They became the first team in the two-division era to win a division title despite hitting the fewest home runs. Only four other teams in major-league history—the 1906 White Sox, 1924 Senators, 1959 White Sox, and 1965 Dodgers—finished first in the standings but last in homers.

The Cardinals' 200 stolen bases were second only to the Athletics' 232. Rickey Henderson's record setting season accounted for 130 of Oakland's total. Lonnie Smith's 68 steals were good for second in the NL, 10 behind Tim Raines. Six other Cardinals (Ozzie, McGee, Herr, Hernandez, Oberkfell, and Green) reached double digits.

The Redbirds' top two starters—Forsch and Andújar—finished the season tied for the team lead with 15 wins. Mura was credited with 12, and Stuper and LaPoint each racked up nine. Andújar's 2.47 ERA tied Joe Niekro for the second-best mark in the NL, trailing only Steve Rogers' 2.40. Bruce Sutter, who won nine games himself, led all of baseball with 36 saves.

The Braves entered the final day of the season with a one-game lead over the Dodgers. Atlanta lost in San Diego, opening up the door for the Dodgers to force a tiebreaker with a win over the Giants. Braves players gathered in the clubhouse to watch the conclusion of the Dodgers–Giants game in San Francisco. Joe Morgan played the part of spoiler, hitting a three-run home run in the seventh inning to break a 2–2 propelling the Giants to victory and sealing the division for Atlanta. The Braves had spent 129 days in first place thanks to an April surge but had gone 28–33 from August to October—just good enough to outlast their NL West foes.

The AL East also came down to the final game of the season. The Orioles beat the Brewers in the first three games of a season-ending four-game series in Baltimore, setting up a decisive game 162. A storybook ending was still possible for longtime Orioles manager Earl Weaver, who announced he was bowing out after the season. A matchup of Jim Palmer versus Don Sutton had the makings of a pitcher's duel, but the Brewers' explosive offense proved too much for Palmer to handle. Milwaukee peppered four home runs in a 10–2 rout of the Orioles to clinch the organization's first division title. The Kansas City Royals had entered the last month of the season leading the AL West but went 11–16 in September, allowing the California Angels to claim the division crown—Gene Mauch's first in 23 years of managing.

Neither the Cardinals nor the Braves had played playoff baseball since the 1960s. The Redbirds' postseason drought was at 14 years; Atlanta's was 13. The two teams had shown to be evenly matched during the regular season. The Braves won seven of the 12 games, but five of the contests were decided by one run. One area where the Braves possessed a clear advantage was in power, hitting a league-best 146 home runs compared to the Cardinals' 67. However, slugging third baseman Bob Horner—who accounted for 32 of the Braves' bombs—was nursing a hyperextended elbow that kept him out of action for most of the season's final two weeks.

The Braves had endured a topsy turvy route to the NL West crown, jumping out to a 13–0 start and then enduring a brutal 2–19 stretch from July 30 to August 18 that included five walk-off losses to division rivals. Outfielder Dale Murphy (.281, 36 HR, 109 RBI) was at the center of Atlanta's record-setting start and division crown. The humble Portland, Oregon, native played a graceful outfield, had a cannon for an arm, and possessed underrated speed on the basepaths. His breakout season would earn him the first of two consecutive Most Valuable Player Awards. First baseman Chris Chambliss (.270, 20 HR, 86 RBI) and right fielder Claudell Washington (.266, 16 HR, 80 RBI) also enjoyed productive seasons for the Braves.

Joe Torre and Bob Gibson, in their first seasons as Braves manager and pitching coach, respectively, cobbled together an inconsistent staff anchored by 43-year-old Phil Niekro (17–4, 3.61 ERA). The venerable knuckleballer posted a 10–1 record in the second half. Rick Mahler and Bob Walk had pitched well early on, while Pascual Pérez and Tommy Boggs had stabilized the rotation down the stretch. The Braves' exceptional relief tandem of Gene Garber and Steve Bedrosian each sported sub-2.50 earned run averages while combining for 41 saves and 257 innings pitched. For the Cardinals, the keys to winning the series were getting to Atlanta's starting pitching and avoiding the long ball. In Torre's estimation, keeping Lonnie Smith off the bases was paramount.

The Cardinals enjoyed an off day on Monday, October 4. Herzog spent the day charting his opponent based on reports from scout Marty Keough, who had followed the Braves during their final seven games. On October 5, the Redbirds held a late-morning workout at Busch Stadium, the site of the NLCS Game One.

A confident Bedrosian predicted that the Braves would run the table. "Okay, I'm cocky right now," said the 24 year old. "But we're going to sweep the Cardinals, and then it's on to the World Series, and we'll sweep that, too."[32] Bedrosian's sanguine words served as bulletin board material for the Cardinals. "It wasn't that Bedrosian said anything different from what everybody believed, but you don't say something like that out loud," Ozzie Smith later wrote. "And when they came town, I think everybody had fire in his eyes and his heart."[33]

Tim Tucker of the *Atlanta Constitution* offered a more unbiased opinion, predicting that the Braves would win in five games.[34] Bob Gibson's competitive nature outweighed any nostalgia he held for his old team: "I just want to beat the blazes out of the them."[35]

Final Regular Season Standings

National League East Division

	W	L	W-L%	GB
St. Louis Cardinals	92	70	.568	--
Philadelphia Phillies	89	73	.549	3
Montreal Expos	86	76	.531	6
Pittsburgh Pirates	84	78	.519	8
Chicago Cubs	73	89	.451	19
New York Mets	65	97	.401	27

National League West Division

	W	L	W-L%	GB
Atlanta Braves	89	73	.549	--
Los Angeles Dodgers	88	74	.543	1
San Francisco Giants	87	75	.537	2
San Diego Padres	81	81	.500	8
Houston Astros	77	85	.475	12
Cincinnati Reds	61	101	.377	28

American League East Division

	W	L	W-L%	GB
Milwaukee Brewers	95	67	.586	--
Baltimore Orioles	94	68	.580	1
Boston Red Sox	89	73	.548	6
Detroit Tigers	83	79	.512	12
New York Yankees	79	83	.488	16
Cleveland Indians	78	84	.481	17
Toronto Blue Jays	78	84	.481	17

American League West Division

	W	L	W-L%	GB
California Angels	93	69	.574	--
Kansas City Royals	90	72	.556	3
Chicago White Sox	87	75	.537	6
Seattle Mariners	76	86	.469	17
Oakland Athletics	68	94	.420	25
Texas Rangers	64	98	.395	29
Minnesota Twins	60	102	.370	33

11

League Championship Series

The best-of-five NLCS kicked off in mid-afternoon on October 6 in the shadow of the Gateway Arch. Parking lots around the stadium doubled the usual charge to five bucks. Fans dressed in red filed into Busch Stadium past vendors hocking paper visors designed to look like a yellow bird beak. Box-seat tickets sold for $17 and a 12-ounce beer cost $1.35—a nickel more than the regular-season price.

The game was broadcast nationally on ABC with a three-man booth of Al Michaels, Howard Cosell, and Tommy Lasorda. During pregame introductions, players emerged from their respective dugouts and jogged to the baselines as deep-voiced public address announcer Joel Meyers called out each name. The Cardinals wore their white home jerseys adorned with a black arm band in remembrance of Ken Boyer. The visitors donned baby blue V-neck pullovers with Atlanta written in cursive across the chest. Joe Torre and Bob Gibson received standing ovations, but the loudest cheers were reserved for "Bruuuuce" Sutter, Ozzie Smith, and Whitey Herzog.

Joaquín Andújar was tapped to start Game One opposite Phil Niekro, who allowed only three earned runs in 21 innings versus St. Louis during the regular season. Phil and his younger brother, Joe, grew up in Ohio and learned to throw the knuckleball from their father. Phil signed with the Braves in 1958 after attending a tryout camp and had been in the organization ever since. He made his big-league debut in '64 when the Braves still called Milwaukee home and had 19 years of big-league experience, racking up a 257–220 record along the way.*

Few pitchers in baseball history have mastered the art of the knuckleball, a deceptive pitch thrown using the fingertips. An effective knuckleball floats to the plate with no spin and unpredictable movement, and Phil Niekro's was known to break as much as two feet in either direction. He

---

*Phil Niekro pitched until he was 48 and ended his 24-year Hall of Fame career with a 318–274 record.

occasionally mixed in a fastball which, compared to the fluttering knuckleball, appeared deceptively quick. "He's not unhittable," said Keith Hernandez, "but you have to be a disciplined hitter. You have to relax and wait until the last possible second before you pull the trigger."[1]

As Game One got underway, Niekro struggled to control his signature pitch. He worked out of a bases-loaded jam in the first inning and pitched around a two-out Lonnie Smith triple in the third. By the fourth, he had settled into a groove—bad news for the Cardinals. Then, with the Braves leading, 1–0, in the bottom of the fifth, rain began to pelt the Busch Stadium AstroTurf. Home-plate umpire Billy Williams quickly halted play—two outs before the game became an official contest. After a delay of two hours, 29 minutes and no signs of the rain letting up, NL president Charles "Chub" Feeney postponed the game, erasing it from the record books. As a result, there would be no off days in the series. Niekro would likely pitch only once—much to the Cardinals' good fortune.

In Torre's opinion, the game was delayed prematurely but he expressed understanding with Williams' decision not to have the game decided by Mother Nature. "I have no animosity or bitterness about it," said Torre. "I understand it's a playoff game and they don't want a team to win by completing only five innings just ahead of a downpour. But, on the other hand, at the moment the game was delayed, it wasn't raining very hard at all, and we could have easily finished the inning. In the regular season, you never see time called with so little rain falling."[2]

As if someone hit the reset button on the Atari console, Game One restarted the next night. Fans deprived of a complete game the day before returned to Busch Stadium to witness Bob Forsch make his long-awaited playoff debut. Atlanta's starter, Pascual Pérez, was a 25-year-old Dominican right-hander who had entered the 1982 season with an unimpressive 2–8 record in parts of two seasons with the Pirates. To that point in his career, he was perhaps better known for his driving than his pitching. In late July, Pérez was performing well in the minors and earned a promotion to help bolster the Braves' struggling rotation. He had a decent first four starts, but the Braves were in the midst of a miserable stretch, losing 19 of 21 between July 30 and August 18. Atlanta had squandered a record-breaking start and trailed the NL West-leading Dodgers by four games.

Pérez was the scheduled starter on August 19 for a home date versus the Expos. He had just received his Georgia driver's license and attempted his first solo commute to Fulton County Stadium. Instead of taking I-85 to the ballpark for a quick 20 minute drive, he got on I-285, which circles the Atlanta metropolitan area. Pérez proceeded to drive 150 aimless miles around the city until he was nearly out of gas. Finally, he stopped at a gas station, only to realize he did not have his wallet. An attendant recognized him and gave him $10 worth of fuel and directions to the park. By the time Pérez arrived at the stadium, the national anthem was in progress and Niekro had already warmed up to start in place of his missing teammate. A Braves victory that night started a six-game winning streak. The next day, Pérez's teammates decorated his locker with maps of Atlanta, and he was given a warmup jacket with the number I-285 on the back. "That lightened the mood," said Torre. "That made the players laugh and relax. And that turned us back around. I really believe that."³ Pérez, who possessed excellent control—17 walks in 79⅓ innings—had recorded three of his four wins in the final two weeks of the season, a strong-enough finish to earn Torre's trust.

Both Pérez and Forsch breezed through the first two innings by pounding the strike zone and letting their respective defenses make plays. The first baserunner came with one out in the top of the third inning when Braves catcher Bruce Benedict bounced a high chopper to Ken Oberkfell, who got an in-between hop and booted the ball for an error. Forsch pitched around the miscue and stranded two men on base. In the bottom half of the inning, Willie McGee recorded the Cardinals' first hit, a smash down the right-field line. Claudell Washington slipped and fell on the wet turf and was just getting to the ball as McGee arrived on third base with his head down. The Cardinal rookie did not see third-base coach Chuck Hiller frantically waving him home, nor did he realize the frenzied crowd and St. Louis dugout were all urging him to run toward home for what would have been an easy inside-the-park home run. By the time McGee realized what was happening, Washington had retrieved the ball and heaved it back toward the infield. "[McGee] could have gotten five bases on that," lamented Herzog. "Instead he got three. That's why he's so exciting."⁴ The next man up, Ozzie Smith, atoned for his roommate's blunder with a sacrifice fly to put St. Louis ahead, 1–0. The Cardinals had gone 63–17 when scoring first during the regular season, so the odds were already in their favor.

There was no additional scoring until the Redbirds came to the bat in the bottom of the sixth. Lonnie Smith led off with a check-swing groundball to first base. Chris Chambliss threw to Pérez, who could not handle the throw, allowing Smith to reach safely on a generously-scored single. Keith Hernandez and George Hendrick followed with consecutive singles of their own, the latter plating Smith. Looking to limit further damage, Torre turned to Steve Bedrosian. The Braves' braggadocious reliever walked Darrell Porter to load the bases, then ceded run-scoring singles to McGee and Ozzie Smith. A sacrifice fly off the bat of Forsch made it 5–0. The Cards scored a sixth run when Bedrosian failed to cover first base on Oberkfell's ground to Chambliss.

Lonnie Smith's eighth-inning sacrifice fly tacked on another run for the Cardinals, who cruised to a decisive 7–0 victory. Forsch, who accounted for two of his team's 13 base hits, needed only 103 pitches to author a brilliant three-hitter. He went to three-ball counts only twice and kept Braves hitters off balance all night by moving his pitches up, down, in, and out. "It was a masterpiece," said Hernandez, "as good as I've ever seen him throw."[5]

Rain forced another postponement the following night, pushing Game Two to October 9.

Niekro returned to the mound, matching up against John Stuper. The game got under way after Toni Tennille—half of the duo Captain and Tennille—belted out the national anthem. Stuper appeared as cool as a cucumber in the first inning, retiring Claudell Washington on a fly ball before striking out Rafael Ramírez and Dale Murphy to retire the side in order. In the bottom of the first, Niekro's knuckleball was dancing too much, allowing Tom Herr to walk on four pitches. Oberkfell followed with a fielder's choice and went to third on Lonnie Smith's single to right field. The next man up, Hernandez, hit a sinking line drive directly to the shortstop. Smith was running on the pitch and would have been doubled up easily, but Ramírez dropped the ball and only had a play at first. With runners on second and third and two outs, Porter skipped out of the way of a knuckleball at his feet. Benedict deflected the ball into the Cardinals' dugout, allowing Oberkfell to score from third for the game's first run.

The score remained 1–0 at the start of the third inning when a defensive miscue by the Cardinals allowed Atlanta to get on the board. With Benedict at second and two out, Ramírez singled to center field. The ball got by McGee and rolled all the way to the wall, allowing both Benedict and Ramírez to score on the error. Suddenly, the momentum had turned.

Atlanta tacked on another run in the fifth on a Niekro sacrifice fly, extending the lead to 3–1. The Cardinals got a run back in the bottom of the sixth, but aggressive baserunning by Porter proved costly. The Redbird catcher drove home Hernandez with a drive into the right-field corner but was thrown out trying to stretch a double into a triple. Later in the inning, the Cards wasted a two-on, two-out scoring opportunity when Steve Braun, pinch-hitting for Stuper, grounded out.

Bair, who had just become a father for the first time the day before, entered the game for St. Louis in the top of the seventh. Jerry Royster laced his first pitch into left field for a leadoff single and then advanced to second on Glenn Hubbard's sacrifice. After Benedict walked, Torre pulled back Niekro for pinch-hitter Biff Pocoroba, who had taken Bair deep to win a game earlier in the year. Pocoroba hacked at Bair's first offering and bounced an easy two hopper to Herr for the second out. With runners at second and third and first base open, Herzog elected to intentionally walk the left-hand hitting Claudell Washington to get to Ramírez, a righty swinger. The strategy paid off; Bair induced a routine fly ball to McGee for the third out.

St. Louis went down in order in the seventh, and Herzog stuck with Bair to start the eighth with the heart of the Braves order due up. Murphy scorched the first pitch he saw to left for a leadoff single and then stole second with Chambliss at the dish. With the count already at 3–0 and first base unoccupied, Herzog called for an intentional ball four to Chambliss. That created a two-on, none-out situation with the dangerous but sore-elbowed Bob Horner coming up. Herzog turned to Bruce Sutter to get out of the mess. Sutter's first two pitches were out of the zone, but his next three were devastating splitters that Horner flailed at helplessly. With one out and Royster in the batter's box, Murphy attempted to steal third. His right foot hit the bag just before Oberkfell's glove tagged his knee, but third-base umpire Dutch Rennert saw it differently and called Murphy out. Sutter then induced a weak comebacker from Royster to extinguish the threat.

Gene Garber retired the Cardinals without incident in the bottom half of the seventh and returned to the mound to work the eighth still clinging to a 3–2 lead. Porter coaxed a one-out walk and then advanced to third on George Hendrick's sharp single up the middle. McGee, who had thrice struck out feebly against Niekro, came to the plate. Batting left-handed against the righty Garber, McGee lunged for a pitch that was a foot outside, but his lumber made just enough contact to send a high chopper over the pitcher's mound. Ramírez ranged far to his left and fielded the ball on the first-base side of second base, where he tagged out Hendrick. McGee streaked down the first-base line and easily reached on a fielder's choice. Porter scored on the play to tie the game, 3–3.

Sutter held serve in the top of the ninth inning, setting up a walk-off opportunity in the bottom half. David Green, who had replaced Lonnie Smith as part of a double switch, led off with a single. Herr then executed a sacrifice bunt, moving Green into scoring position. The next man up, Oberkfell, was 6-for-10 with a home run in his career versus Garber. With first base open and Dane Iorg on deck, Torre rolled the dice and elected to pitch to the Cardinal third baseman. From the stretch, Garber twisted his body and whipped his sidearm delivery toward the plate. Oberkfell got a fastball down the middle and put the barrel on the ball, drilling a line drive to right-center field that sailed just beyond the outstretched glove of defensive replacement Brett Butler. Green raced home with the winning run as the Redbirds erupted from the dugout and swarmed Oberkfell in celebration.

An exuberant Gussie Busch visited the Cardinals' clubhouse after the game. "I'm so happy, I can't see straight," crowed the 83-year-old owner. "Marvelous! Wonderful! You guys did a hell of a job."[6]

Herzog, who repeatedly said the Braves were the toughest team he played during the regular season, cautioned that the series was far from over. "Heck, anybody thinks this thing's over's crazy," said the skipper. "They're not gonna quit. They only gotta win two games and we're all tied up."[7]

The series shifted to Atlanta the following night—Sunday, October 10. Braves owner Ted Turner donned his lucky green jacket in hopes of spurring his team to victory. Andújar got the start for St. Louis while the Braves' hopes hung on righty Rick Camp, who had lost his last six decisions to close out the season.

Each starter managed a scoreless first inning, but Camp's pitches—in the words of Lonnie Smith—"didn't have any zip."[8] Camp concurred with Smith's assessment. "From the time I started warming up in the bullpen I knew I didn't have anything on the ball," said the Atlanta starter.[9] Though Camp escaped the first inning unscathed, he was not so fortunate in the top of the second. Hernandez singled to lead off the inning. Then, Porter walked, Hendrick singled, McGee tripled, and Ozzie singled. Just like that, the Cards had built a 4–0 lead and sent Camp to the showers. Pascual Pérez come on in relief and prevented any further scoring until the top of the fifth. Herr led off with a double and scored on another single by Hernandez, making it 5–0.

Andújar held the Braves off the scoreboard through the first six frames. As usual, his defense had a lot to with it, turning three twin killings and making several deft plays. Hendrick snagged a potentially run-scoring liner off the bat of Horner, and Hernandez fielded a ground ball that caromed off the leg of Andújar, diving to the first-base bag ahead of Chambliss. Andújar got into hot water in the seventh inning, ceding a pair of runs on four singles. With two outs and the lead trimmed to three, Herzog brought in Sutter to attempt a seven-out save. The fireman squelched the rally by inducing a fly out off the bat of Benedict.

The Cardinals wasted excellent scoring opportunities in the seventh and eighth, stranding the bases loaded in both frames. McGee took matters into his own hands in the ninth, tacking on an insurance run with a solo homer off Garber. Sutter pitched a flawless ninth to secure the 6–2 victory and series sweep for St. Louis. After the final out, the Cardinals mobbed each other on the field and then decamped to the locker room, where they popped corks on bottles of champagne and let loose in celebration. Dave LaPoint estimated that he had seven bottles poured down his back and into his pants pockets within minutes.[10]

"This is what baseball is all about," said Braun, heading to his first Fall Classic in 12 major-league seasons. "Everybody on the roster really contributed. The word is 'chemistry.' There has been a certain kind of chemistry on this club that I've never seen before anywhere in all the years I've been playing. Everybody knows his job. They're a relaxed bunch of guys. We were all so confident. I never doubted our chances against Atlanta."[11]

Rookie Jeff Lahti likewise noted the contributions of the whole roster in achieving a World Series berth. "Just think about how much help we got from everyone up and down the line. Look at Kelly Paris. He won a game for us in Los Angeles. And Tito Landrum. And Glenn Brummer, and so many others."[12] The good fortune of being part of a pennant winner as a rookie was not lost on John Stuper, who noted that many great players like Ernie Banks never got the opportunity to play on the game's grandest stage.

Porter, a .231 hitter during the regular season, finished the series 5-for-9 with five walks and threw out two of three attempted base stealers to earn series Most Valuable Player honors. McGee (4-for-13, HR, five RBIs), and Sutter (retired all 12 batters he faced) would have also been reasonable choices for the accolade.

The Cardinals' game-changing speed, impervious defense, timely hitting, adequate starting pitching, and Sutter's splitter proved to be more than the Braves could handle. St. Louis hurlers limited Atlanta to only 15 hits in the series, only one of which went for extra bases. The Braves' power-hitting triumvirate of Murphy, Horner, and Chambliss was held to just four hits in 32 at-bats. "They outplayed us, and it hurts, but I like the Cardinals," said Niekro in the aftermath of Game Three. "They're a low-key bunch of guys; they don't have any real superstars. They're just a real good team and we'll all be pulling for them."[13]

———

While the NLCS was decided in only three games, the ALCS went down to a pivotal fifth game. The series between the California Angels and Milwaukee Brewers—neither of whom had ever appeared in a World Series—featured the game's two most potent offenses.

With an average age of 32, the Angels were baseball's oldest squad. The experienced lineup boasted four former MVPs: Reggie Jackson, Don Baylor, Rod Carew, and Fred Lynn. Jackson, who had signed a lucrative four-year contract before the season, tied for the AL lead with 39 home runs. Doug DeCinces, acquired from Baltimore in a lopsided trade for Dan Ford, hit 30 home runs and posted a career-best OPS of .916. Perhaps overshadowed by their more decorated teammates were Bobby Grich and Brian Downing, who quietly posted all-star caliber numbers for Gene Mauch's 93-win club. The Angels' pitching staff was anchored by 18-game winner Geoff Zahn and had received a boost with the trade deadline acquisition of Tommy John. The Angels pitched to contact and were the junior circuit's best team at run prevention. No member of California's pitching staff struck out more than 86 batters.

If there was one team who could outslug the Halos, it was the Brewers—baseball's winningest team in 1982. The Brew Crew led the majors with 216 home runs and 891 runs scored—an average of 5.47 runs per game. They catapulted to the top of the AL East after a mid-season managerial switch from Buck Rodgers to Harvey Kuenn. With the more laid-back Kuenn at the helm, Milwaukee went 72–43 and charged to the division lead. "When he took over, he just said 'Relax.' The other manager put pressure on some of the people," explained outfielder Cecil Cooper. "Harvey just said, 'I have confidence in you as a team. Go out and play baseball.'"[14] Slugging center fielder Gorman Thomas, perhaps speaking from personal experience, equated the change to someone opening the door of a smoky poker room and allowing stale air out and fresh air in.[15]

Kuenn, a former shortstop and outfielder, had a superb 15-year playing career, which included the Rookie of the Year Award, a batting title, eight All-Star appearances, and a career .303 batting average. The Milwaukee native had served as the Brewers' hitting coach since 1971 and earned the respect of his players. Kuenn overcame myriad health maladies, including quadruple bypass surgery, kidney problems, complications from Crohn's disease, and poor lower extremity circulation that resulted in the amputation of his right leg. With Kuenn in charge of the Brewers' prodigious offense, the team acquired the nickname "Harvey's Wallbangers."

At the top of Milwaukee's lineup was 25-year-old third baseman Paul Molitor, who hit .302 in the regular season and led the league in runs scored. Hitting second was five-tool shortstop Robin Yount, whose outstanding defense, .331 batting average, 29 home runs, and 114 RBIs would earn him the AL Most Valuable Player Award. His 10.6 WAR and .957 OPS led all of baseball. Perennial .300 hitter Cecil Cooper occupied the number three hole. Yount, Cooper, and Molitor each topped the 200-hit mark and finished first, second, and third in the AL in hits.*

The Brew Crew's powerful middle of the order—Cooper, Thomas, Ted

---

*It was the first time three players from the same team led the league in hits since Ty Cobb, San Crawford, and Bobby Veach did it for the Tigers in 1915.

Simmons, and Ben Oglivie—averaged 32 home runs and 108 RBIs during the regular season. Even ninth-place hitter Jim Gantner (.295 batting average) was a tough out. No wonder Goose Gossage called the Brewers lineup the best he had ever faced.[16]

The ALCS started in Anaheim, where Baylor paced the Angels with five RBIs in support of John for a Game One victory. In Game Two, Bruce Kison outdueled Pete Vuckovich to give the Halos a commanding advantage. In the 13 years since Major League Baseball adopted a divisional format with a best-of-five League Championship Series, no team had come back from a 2–0 deficit. The series then shifted to Milwaukee for the next three games. The Brewer offense provided Don Sutton with an early lead in Game Three, a contest Milwaukee held on to win, 5–3. Prior to Game Four, word came that a wildfire was quickly spreading in Orange County, California—a result of 90-degree temperatures and hard-blowing Santa Ana winds.[17] The blaze destroyed numerous homes in close proximity to where several Angels players lived. With the raging fire back home weighing on their minds, the Angels committed three errors, allowed six runs, and were no-hit by Milwaukee starter Moose Haas through five innings.

"Finally, we get a phone call in the dugout that everybody's okay, the fire went in a different direction," said Fred Lynn looking back.[18] With that burden lifted, the Halos mounted a late-inning rally but fell short. "The bottom line is that we lost that game and gave them a little momentum," said Lynn.[19] In the decisive Game Five, Mauch elected to ride the hot hand of Kison on short rest rather than start Ken Forsch. Kison outdueled Vuckovich early as the Angels built a 3–2 lead. In the seventh inning, a based-loaded single by Cooper put the Brewers ahead 4–3. Pete Ladd, subbing for injured Brewers closer Rollie Fingers, saved it in the ninth. Amazingly, Milwaukee advanced despite their big thumpers—Cooper, Thomas, Oglivie, and Simmons—hitting a combined .130 for the series. Lynn hit .611 (11-for-18) to win series MVP honors despite being on the losing end.

With the World Series set to begin only two days later, neither the Brewers nor the Cardinals had much time to relish in their LCS successes. The NL had home-field advantage in even number years, so the Cardinals would host the first two games of the best-of-seven series.

Once the Cardinals clinched the pennant, plans for revelry in St. Louis sprang to action. Caterers got to work peeling shrimp, shucking oysters, and carving ice sculptures. On the night of October 11, the Cardinals and Commissioner Bowie Kuhn hosted a party at the visitor's center beneath the Gateway Arch. Some of the game's biggest personalities—Bob Uecker, Tommy Lasorda, and Sparky Anderson—joined legions of reporters and photographers to partake in a smorgasbord of food and Anheuser-Busch beverages. A few blocks away at Kiener Plaza, thousands of fans gathered at a public event to celebrate the Cardinals. The congregation waved pennants as a cover band provided music, including a rendition of the Redbirds' adopted theme song, Kool & the Gang's "Celebration." The Cardinals and their fans hoped to hear the song four more times.

12

Game One

Brewers Pounce

Major League Baseball's 79th World Series was the first between Midwestern franchises since the Tigers defeated the Cardinals in 1968. The American League held a 45–33 advantage in previous Fall Classics, though the Redbirds had won eight of their 12 Series appearances. St. Louis and Milwaukee's strong ties to the beer industry provided fodder for scribes and headlines writers, who coined such puns as Sudsway Series, Six-pack Series, and World Beeries.

Milwaukee ball teams with the nickname "Brewers" dated back to the 19th century. In fact, the Milwaukee Brewers were one of eight charter members of the AL when the circuit was formed in 1900. After its inaugural season, the AL achieved major-league status on par with the National League. At the same time, the Brewers relocated to St. Louis and became the Browns. After hosting a minor-league iteration of the Brewers, Milwaukee acquired the Boston Braves in 1953 and served as the home of such stars as Henry Aaron, Eddie Mathews, and Warren Spahn. The Braves deserted Milwaukee for Atlanta in 1965, and Wisconsin regained a major-league team in five years later when car salesman Bud Selig bought the Seattle Pilots, moved the club to Milwaukee, and reestablished the "Brewers" name. It would be eight years until the Brewers posted their first winning record. Their fortunes began to turn with the hiring of GM Harry Dalton, who molded a talented roster through astute free-agent signings and homegrown talent. The trade with St. Louis for Pete Vuckovich, Ted Simmons, and Rollie Fingers provided the final pieces Milwaukee needed to contend for the AL pennant.

For the first time in World Series history, the team with the most home runs squared off against the team with the fewest. Milwaukee out-homered St. Louis by an astonishing 149 during the regular season and had four players smash 29 or more. George Hendrick led St. Louis with

19 round-trippers, and Darrell Porter was the only other Redbird to reach double figures. The Cardinals outran the Brewers nearly as much as they were outslugged. In contrast to the Cardinals' 200 stolen bases, Milwaukee swiped just 84—nearly half of which belonged to Paul Molitor.

In the 1980s, rudimentary statistics such as errors and fielding percentage were the primary means of quantifying defense. The Brewers were considered a strong defensive club and committed only one error more than the Cardinals in 1982. The range and glovework of the St. Louis infield, however, reigned supreme. In the 21st century, Sean Smith—founder of Baseball Reference—has attempted to measure defense in the game's past using Total Zone, a defensive metric that uses retrospective play-by-play data to calculate a player's defensive value. The Cardinals' starting infield in 1982 combined for a TZ of 56, whereas the Brewers infield posted a TZ of 17. Ozzie Smith alone had a TZ rating of 21.

In terms of pitching, St. Louis's regular-season ERA of 3.37 was more than a half-run better than the Brewers' 3.98, though it is hardly an apples-to-apples comparison. Milwaukee hurlers—backed by baseball's most prolific offense—had a greater margin for error than every other team in the game so perhaps at times pitched to the score. The AL pitchers also had the disadvantage of facing designated hitters everyday instead of weak-hitting opposing pitchers.

At full strength, the St. Louis and Milwaukee bullpens—led by Bruce Sutter and Rollie Fingers, respectively—may have been fairly even. But Fingers' right arm was far from full strength. The handle-bar mustachioed righty had been an integral part of the Brewers' success after being traded by Herzog. In 1981, he post a Bob Gibson–like 1.04 ERA, led the AL in saves, and won *both* the AL MVP and Cy Young Awards. Though not as spectacular in 1982, Fingers posted a solid 2.80 ERA and recorded 29 saves before sustaining an injury on September 2. At that time, the Brewers were sitting pretty—four and a half games up on Boston for the AL East lead—and had just landed Sutton at the trade deadline. Cleveland was in town for a doubleheader, and Fingers—known to teammates as "Buzzard"—entered the first game looking for his 30th save. "I threw three or four pitches and it was fine. Then on one pitch, I felt a burning sensation in my elbow," Fingers said looking back. "I threw a couple more pitches, and I could hardly get the ball to the plate. I called timeout and called for Harvey Kuenn to come out. I told Harvey, 'I don't think I can pitch right now.'"[1]

Fingers' teammate, George "Doc" Medich, who held a medical degree from the University of Pittsburgh, immediately understood the gravity of the situation. "Buzzard comes off the field holding his arm. I followed him into the clubhouse," recalled Medich. "The flexor wad had detached and was about three inches down his forearm. It was a season ending injury. I said 'Oh, geezus.' I was not only thinking about the rest of the season but this guy's career."[2] Being a player and not the team doctor, Medich did not want to say too much, but his medical acumen told him this was the type of injury that required a surgical solution.*

The team doctor had a different opinion. "The doctor looked at me and said to take a couple weeks off and it should be okay," said Fingers years later. "They kept me on hoping that I was going to be able to pitch. I told them, 'guys, there's no way I can pitch.' They should have just taken me off the list and added another guy."[3] Based on the team physician's prognosis, the Brewers held out hope Fingers could recover and kept him on the World Series roster.

Besides Fingers' infirm throwing arm, two of Milwaukee's offensive stars—Oglivie (bruised ribs) and Thomas (knee contusion)—sustained injuries during the ALCS that left them potentially compromised for the Series. Thomas had played through excruciating pain during Game Five and afterwards joked about asking Kuenn to let him use his wooden leg.[4] Unlike their counterparts, the Cardinals entered the series in relatively good health.

Because there was no interleague play and a limited number of televised games at the time, the World Series provided some degree of mystery and intrigue. Many St. Louis fans—and even players themselves—had never seen Milwaukee play, and vice versa. Advanced scouts provided advice on defensive positioning and how to pitch to opposing hitters, though this was not always accurate, as the Cardinals would quickly discover. Herzog possessed some familiarity with Milwaukee from his years managing in Kansas City, and Ted Simmons had played with Keith Hernandez, Ken Oberkfell, George Hendrick, among others. Simmons knew, for example, that the key to getting Hernandez out was pitching him with hard stuff up and in and avoid anything off-speed over the plate.[5]

The Series provided the Cardinals with the franchise's first-ever designated hitter, which had been adopted by the AL in 1973. Major League Baseball instituted the DH in the World Series during even numbered years starting in 1976. Having an extra position player in the lineup was certain to provide an upgrade to the St. Louis offense. The ten pitchers on the Cardinals' World Series roster combined to hit .123 with 135 strikeouts in 358 regular season at-bats. "Worst hitters I've ever seen," lamented Herzog.[6]

During the pre-game festivities before Game One, a team of Gussie Busch's Clydesdales pulled him and his beer wagon around the perimeter of the playing field. One of the horses made a deposit of feces near the first

---

*Fingers ultimately did require surgery and missed the entire 1983 season.

Milwaukee Brewers manager Harvey Kuenn shares a laugh with Whitey Herzog before the start of the World Series (National Baseball Hall of Fame and Museum, Cooperstown, NY).

base coaching box, perhaps the first indicator of what was to come when the game commenced. Lou Rawls sang the national anthem, and Busch—decked out in a red sports coat and cowboy hat—threw out the ceremonial first pitch. The Goodyear Blimp hovered in the sky, providing aerial views of Busch Stadium to those tuning in at home.

The Brewers' frontline starters—Pete Vuckovich and Don Sutton—had pitched the final two games of the ALCS, so Kuenn turned to southpaw Mike Caldwell, a former 22-game winner and fierce competitor known for throwing tantrums after defeat and staring down any opponent who dared to hit a home run off him. He was sarcastically nicknamed "Mr. Warmth." With a lefty on the mound for Milwaukee, Herzog penciled in Gene Tenace at DH and elected to start David Green in center field rather than Willie McGee.

Bob Forsch received the starting assignment for St. Louis. With his right cheek bulging from chewing tobacco, the righty kicked off the series by retiring Molitor before allowing a solidly-struck single to Yount and a walk to Cooper on four pitches. After a brief mound visit by Hub Kittle and Darrell Porter, Forsch fanned Simmons to bring up Ben Oglivie with two outs. Oglivie, a tall and slender left-handed swinger, was born in Panama and attended high school in the Bronx. He was known to study philosophy and could allegedly complete the *New York Times* crossword puzzle in a matter of minutes.[7] On the baseball diamond, he was a true five-tool talent who blasted 41 home runs in 1980, tying Reggie Jackson for the league lead. Standing in his customary upright batting stance, Oglivie got a 2–2 pitch he could handle and blistered a line drive that short-hopped Keith Hernandez and bounded into right field, scoring Yount and advancing Cooper to third. The play was a difficult chance for Hernandez, who was charged with an error, but one the four-time Gold Glover was accustomed to making. Gorman Thomas followed with a run-scoring infield single, and then the uncharacteristically wild Forsch plunked DH Roy Howell to load the bases. The Brewers were a bloop or a blast away from breaking the game open. Jeff Lahti loosened post-haste in the Cardinal bullpen, but Forsch retired Charlie Moore to escape further damage.

Caldwell, who had a reputation for pinpoint control, worked briskly and cruised through the first three innings. His only blemish was a two-out, second-inning double by Darrell Porter, who was left stranded. The Brewers added to their lead in the middle innings. Molitor's broken-bat single in the fourth plated Milwaukee's third run, and Simmons' solo homer an inning later made it 4–0. While Caldwell continued to flummox the St. Louis lineup, the Milwaukee onslaught continued. In the sixth inning, consecutive two-out singles by Jim Gantner and Molitor set the table for Yount, who hit a perfectly-placed bloop double down the right-field line to score both runners, giving the Brewers a 6–0 advantage. The stunned partisan crowd was silent as Herzog pulled Forsch and brought in Jim Kaat to get the final out of the inning.*

As the innings wore on, the Cardinals were unable to mount any sort of comeback. One by one, Redbird batters pounded Caldwell's sinker into the ground, each ball finding the glove of a Brewer infielder. St. Louis did not record another tally in the hit column until Porter led off the eighth inning with a single. One batter later, Oberkfell reached safely, giving the Cardinals their best scoring opportunity of the night. Caldwell summarily stamped out the rally by extinguishing Ozzie Smith and Tom Herr to end the inning.

The Brewers battered Dave LaPoint and Lahti for four more runs in the ninth, extending their lead to 10–0. Milwaukee banged out a total of 17 hits, including a record-setting five by Molitor—whose bat was sent to Cooperstown. Caldwell went the distance, needing only 102 pitches to secure the three-hitter. The blowout was the widest margin of victory in a World Series opener since the "Go-Go" White Sox defeated the Dodgers,

---

*Kaat became the second oldest player in the World Series, ranking only behind Jack Quinn, who was 47 when he pitched for the Philadelphia A's in the 1930 Fall Classic.

11–0, in 1959. "We got a good old-fashioned butt-kicking," sighed Herzog. "I'm glad we didn't have a doubleheader."[8]

After the game, Hernandez intimated that Caldwell may have been throwing spitballs. "Nope—nothing but natural sinkers tonight and I've got the blister to prove it," responded Caldwell between swigs of Miller Lite. "Actually, I look at it as a compliment. If the ball drops so much that they're accusing me of throwing a spitter, I've got pretty good stuff."[9]

Saliva jive or not, Caldwell's gem and the 17-hit barrage proved the Brewers were more than just Wallbangers. "There is a great misunderstanding that we are a one-way club … that we only have power," said Molitor after the shellacking. "But that isn't true. We can adjust to playing on artificial turf. We can run. We can be aggressive."[10] The Cardinals clearly had their hands full.

13

Game Two

Sutton Versus Stuper, Part One

A Cardinals' loss in Game Two with the next three games slated for Milwaukee would have spelled disaster. Avoiding that scenario would largely rest on the right arm of John Stuper, who finished the regular season with a 9–7 record and 3.36 ERA. Opposing the rookie was Don Sutton, a veteran of three World Series—all losses—during his time with the Dodgers. In contrast to the youthful appearing Stuper, the 37-year-old Sutton had gray curly hair flowing from beneath his cap. Sutton proved to be a vital trade deadline acquisition for Milwaukee, posting a 4–1 record in seven starts. He had not fared well at Busch Stadium during his career, however, compiling a middling 7–14 record. Kuenn rolled out the same barrels that had appeared unstoppable in Game One. With a righty on the mound, Herzog installed the left-hand hitting Dane Iorg at DH and replaced David Green with Willie McGee in center field.

A mass of 53,723 patrons flowed through the turnstiles hoping to see the home team avenge the previous night's drubbing. The game got underway following a ceremonial first pitch by Lou Brock. In the first inning, a defensive adjustment by the Cardinals was evident. After underestimating Milwaukee's speed in Game One, the infielders positioned closer to home with Paul Molitor at the plate to start the game. Stuper retired the stud third baseman on the first pitch of the game, but a free pass to Robin Yount and hit-and-run single by Cecil Cooper followed. With runners on the corners and one out, cleanup man Ted Simmons stepped to the plate. He smoked a one-hopper to Keith Hernandez, who fielded it cleanly and started a 3–6–3 double play to end the threat. Three fly ball outs made for an uneventful bottom of the first for Sutton.

Stuper struck out Ben Oglivie to start the second inning but then walked Gorman Thomas on four pitches. A fielder's choice and wild pitch placed Roy Howell on second base with two outs and Charlie Moore at the plate. Moore worked the count full and then sent a belt-high fastball into the left-center field gap to put Milwaukee on the board. Staked with an early 1–0 lead, Sutton replicated his first inning by dispatching the Cardinals in order on 11 pitches in the home half of the second.

The Brew Crew's potent offense kept the pressure on Stuper in the third. Molitor singled, stole second, advanced to third on Stuper's second wild pitch, and scored on Yount's ground out to second. With two outs and the bases empty, Simmons jolted a fastball over the right-field wall, making it 3–0 Brewers. Oglivie followed with a single, and the restless crowd let loose with a chorus of boos. Stuper retired Thomas for the third out, but St. Louis clearly needed something positive to shift the momentum. To that point in the series, the Brewers were averaging a run per inning while the Cardinals had mustered three hits and zero runs.

"They really beat us badly in the first game, then got up on us in the second game. I think some of us may have thought, 'are we good enough to be here?' But you just play hard, keep trying, and that's what we did," said Iorg looking back.[1]

Iorg provided a lift in the bottom of the third with a leadoff single to right field—the Cards' first hit of the game. McGee took Iorg's spot on first base with a fielder's choice, easily stole second base, and then came around to score on Tom Herr's two-out, ground-rule double to the right-center field gap. Ken Oberkfell then scalded a line drive to right field to score Herr. St. Louis had cut the deficit to 3–2 and relieved the palpable tension within Busch Stadium.

After a scoreless fourth inning, Yount—the first shortstop to ever lead the AL in slugging percentage—narrowly missed a home run to lead off the fifth. The ball struck the top of the left-field wall and Yount settled for a double. Whitey Herzog, hoping to keep it a one-run game, had a quick hook of Stuper and brought in Jim Kaat to face the lefty-hitting Cooper, whose regular season batting average against righties was nearly 50 points higher than southpaws. Cooper won the matchup, lacing an RBI single to score Yount. After Kaat retired the next two, Herzog brought in the righty Doug Bair to face Thomas, who went down swinging to end the inning.

In the bottom of the fifth, Sutton disposed of the bottom third of the Cardinals' lineup—Iorg, McGee, and Ozzie Smith—on eight pitches. Bair just as easily retired the Brewers' seven through nine hitters in the top of the sixth. With Milwaukee still ahead, 4–2, in the bottom of the sixth, Oberkfell started a rally with a one-out single and moved up 90 feet on a steal of second base. Sutton induced a fly out from Hernandez and got ahead of Hendrick, 0–2, but then threw four straight balls to put the tying run aboard. Cheers from the crowd grew louder as the notoriously streaky Darrell Porter stepped to the plate. Crouched in the left-hand batter's box,

13. Game Two—Sutton Versus Stuper, Part One

he got a breaking pitch to his liking and hit a frozen rope into the left-field corner for a rare opposite-field double. Oberkfell and Hendrick both scored to tie the game. Sutton fanned Lonnie Smith for the third out, but the score was even with a well-rested Bruce Sutter lurking.

Bair returned to the mound in the top of the seventh and retired Molitor and Yount in succession before yielding a double to Cooper. Herzog, unwilling to risk falling behind without utilizing his best pitcher, strolled to the mound and motioned with his right hand for Sutter. With the DH in play, Herzog did not have to worry about the pitcher's spot in the batting order, allowing him to use Sutter for an extended outing. The crowd chanted "Bruce, Bruce, Bruce," as the bearded reliever jogged in from the bullpen down the first-base line. Herzog deferred to Sutter on whether to pitch to Simmons or issue an intentional walk and take his chances with Oglivie with two runners on and two out. Simmons was 5-for-25 in his career against Sutter but had taken him deep once. Sutter elected to take his chances with Oglivie, a career American Leaguer who had never faced him. "It was only logical to pitch to someone who didn't know me," Sutter later explained.[2] The strategy paid off. Oglivie hit a bouncing ball to the right of second base. Ozzie Smith, ranging far to his left, cut in front of Herr and threw a laser to first base, beating Oglivie by a step for the third out.

Kuenn played the percentages and brought in lefty Bob McClure to face Iorg leading off the bottom of the seventh. McClure possessed a deceiving herky-jerky pitching motion that held lefty hitters to a .186 average during the regular season. Herzog countered by pinch-hitting David Green. McClure struck out him out and then did the same to McGee. After Ozzie Smith's two-out single to center, the Redbirds continued to push the envelope against the mediocre throwing arm of Simmons. Despite McClure's excellent pickoff move and a pitchout, Smith stole second as Simmons' throw sailed high. Herr then walked to make it first and second with two outs. With Oberkfell due up, Herzog again went to his bench, sending up Gene Tenace, who lifted a routine fly ball that landed in the glove of Thomas to end the inning.

Sutter allowed an infield hit in the eighth but otherwise set the Brewers down quietly. In the home half of the inning, a walk by Hernandez, fielder's choice by Hendrick, and single by Porter put runners on first and second with one out. Kuenn went to his bullpen again, replacing McClure with right-hander Pete Ladd, who pitched only 18 innings during the regular season but allowed a staggering five home runs in his limited duty. Ladd was 6-foot-3 with red curly hair, a thick mustache, unibrow, and size 15 shoes, attributes that earned him the nicknames "Big Foot" and "Sasquatch." His intimidating presence was befitting of his offseason job as a probation and parole officer at a prison in Portland, Maine. Ladd had gained the trust of his manager during the ALCS by retiring all 10 men he faced, half of them on strikeouts. Kuenn still held on to a belief that Fingers was potentially available and said after the game that he preferred to use him only in a save situation.[3]

The first man Ladd faced—Lonnie Smith—worked the count full. Simmons set up on the outside edge of the plate and did not have to move his mitt when Ladd delivered his next pitch, but in home-plate umpire Bill Haller's estimation the ball was outside. Simmons turned in disbelief and argued the call to no avail. "It was a strike if I've ever thrown one," said Ladd after the game.[4] Smith's assessment was more diplomatic: "I was pretty surprised. But the umpires are never wrong."[5] With the bases full of Cardinals and still only one out, Herzog called on eagle-eyed Steve Braun to pinch-hit. Ladd, who was admittedly rattled by the questionable call to Smith, issued four straight balls, none of which were even remotely close to the strike zone. Hendrick jogged home with the go-ahead run as organist Ernie Hays played "Here Comes the King," an Anheuser-Busch advertising jingle and Busch Stadium staple. After McGee lined out to Yount for the second out, Ozzie Smith smashed a one-hop liner that was destined for right field, but the ball struck the back foot of Braun for the third out. "Some of us are born to run, and some of us are born to hit—and walk," said Braun later.[6]

Sutter, now pitching with a 5–4 lead, returned to the mound for the top of the ninth. With the top of the Milwaukee order due up, the last three outs would not come easy. Molitor pushed a bunt to the right side on Sutter's first pitch. Hernandez went to field the ball but briefly took a peek at the streaking Molitor, and the ball ricocheted off his glove. The official scorer ruled it a base hit. Kuenn then called a hit-and-run on the first pitch to Yount, who swung through a high delivery. Porter's throw bounced in front of second base, but the sure-handed Herr fielded the ball cleanly and applied the tag before Molitor could reach the bag. Sutter subsequently retired Yount and Cooper to end the game and even the series. Whitey's Rugburners had avoided the difficult position of being down two games and proved they could compete with the Wallbangers.

In the Cardinal clubhouse after the game, a mock interview program referred to as the "John Cosell Show" was staged, featuring Stuper as host with Dave LaPoint, Jeff Lahti, Glenn Brummer, and Mike Ramsey serving as correspondents. The bit had become a routine following wins. Using a beer bottle as a microphone, Braun served as a guest interviewee. "Steve Braun, the Golden Eyeball," said LaPoint. "Tell us, Steve, how come you can eyeball a fastball at 90 miles an hour, but you can't get your lousy feet out of the way of a ground ball?"[7]

14

Game Three

The Humble Hero

> *"I don't know anybody who ever played a better World Series game."*—Whitey Herzog[1]

Game Three was a long time coming for the Dairy State. Milwaukee had not hosted a World Series game since the Braves lost to the Yankees in 1958. The Brewers' faithful were so fired up for the event that 25,000 of them packed the County Stadium parking lot for a tailgate party on October 14—an off day before the Series resumed. Management finally had to turn off the parking lot lights just to get folks to go home.[2]

Each team trotted out their best starting pitcher for Game Three—Pete Vuckovich for the Brewers and Joaquín Andújar for the Cards—a pair of hurlers who wore their emotions on their nylon sleeves. Vuckovich, listed at 6-foot-4 and 220 pounds, had a menacing appearance. He sported a Fu Manchu and looked more like someone you might encounter at a motorcycle rally than a major-league baseball diamond. His various mound quirks and mannerisms included crossing his eyes when looking in for the catcher's sign and making twitch-like movements with his head while holding runners on base. There was a calculated method to his theatrics, however. His persona would later lend itself to the role of "Clu Haywood" in the 1989 film *Major League*.

Vuckovich utilized an excellent slider to amass a regular-season record of 18–6 and 3.34 ERA, statistics that would earn him the AL Cy Young Award, but he had struggled in his final two outings. He tended to work the edges of the plate and went deep into counts, leading to heavy traffic on the basepaths and high pitch counts. Following an 11-inning, 163-pitch effort on September 20, Vuckovich lost his last two regular-season starts versus Baltimore, allowing 10 runs in 11 innings.[3] Andújar, on the other hand, had been dominant down the stretch. In his final eight regular-season starts, he won all six decisions and posted a 0.96 ERA before winning his NLCS outing.

Just a few hours before game time, Harvey Kuenn was still wearing his orange bathrobe and signing autographs at Cesar's Inn, the tavern and boarding house that he and his wife, Audrey, operated in West Milwaukee. The Kuenns lived in an apartment attached to the establishment. Audrey finally stepped in: "If you don't get to the ballpark soon, I'm going to have to make out the lineup—*again*."[4]

The game-time temperature was a brisk 54 degrees at County Stadium, where a cool breeze blew in off the shores of Lake Michigan just a few miles east. Whitey Herzog went back to Dane Iorg at DH with a righty on the mound and stuck with Willie McGee in center field. Some wondered if the natural grass of the Brewers' home park would neutralize the Cardinals' speed. That had not been the case during the regular season, when St. Louis posted a better winning percentage on grass (.643 in 42 games) than artificial turf (.562 in 110 games).

The Redbirds, decked out in their road powder blue uniforms, went quietly in the first inning. The Brewers, in home whites with blue pinstripes, also went three up, three down in the first, though Paul Molitor made a loud out on a ball that McGee hauled in with a leaping catch just in front of the 402-foot mark on the center-field wall.

George Hendrick led off the second inning with a high hopper down the third-base line. Molitor fielded the ball, but his throw pulled Cecil Cooper off first base, resulting in an infield single. Third-base umpire Jim Evans appeared to call the ball foul before signaling fair, drawing an argument from Kuenn, who gave the men in blue an earful. Replays showed that the play was ruled correctly. Hendrick advanced as far as third base but was stranded.

Both starters remained locked in and had posted nothing but zeroes through four innings. In the top of the fifth, Lonnie Smith hit a frozen rope into the left-center field gap. As if someone left a banana peel on the field, Smith slipped rounding first base and cost himself a chance for a triple, instead settling for a one-out double. Iorg followed with a slow ground ball to the right side. The ball kicked off the heel of Cooper's glove, allowing Iorg to reach first base safely on what was ruled an error. The switch-hitting McGee, batting left-handed, stepped into the batter's box with runners on the corners and a chance to put the Cards on the board. The scouting report the Brewers received on McGee indicated he was a slap hitter who was susceptible to off-speed pitches. Vuckovich followed this guidance and threw a first-pitch slider. The ball came in belt-high to McGee, who leaned back on his left foot, hips hinged at 45 degrees, and put a swing on it. The ball hit the barrel and was redirected deep into right field. Charlie Moore drifted back to the wall but watched helplessly as the ball landed five rows deep in the right-field stands. The unassuming McGee put his head down and circled the bases as if it was just another day at the office. For the first time in the series, the Cardinals scored first and held a 3–0 lead.

Andújar set down the Brewers in order in the bottom half of the fifth, and both teams went three up, three down in the sixth. Jim Gantner recorded his—and the Brewers'—second hit of the game in the top of the sixth, but he was erased on a beautifully turned 4–6–3 double play. Gantner attempted to break up the twin killing with a hard slide into second base, but Ozzie Smith simultaneously jumped in the air and delivered a perfect throw to Hernandez.

In the top of the seventh, Lonnie Smith came to the plate with one out and turned around a Vuckovich pitch that struck the right-center field fence on one hop. This time, Smith managed to stay on his feet and sped around the bases, diving head-first into third just as Gantner's relay throw arrived. The ball struck Smith and bounced into the third-base dugout, allowing him to score the Cardinals' fourth run. Later in the inning, McGee came up with two outs and the bases empty. Vuckovich's first offering was a purpose pitch—a high fastball that whizzed under McGee's chin. The rookie stepped back into the box but stood noticeably further back from the plate. Vuckovich went back to the scouting report and delivered a straight changeup on his next pitch. McGee's quick hands delivered a short but powerful stroke, the barrel of the bat sending the ball soaring into the Milwaukee night sky. Like his first home run, it flew over the head of Moore in right field. This one, however, was a no doubter. After hitting only four home runs during the regular season, McGee had hit two in one game and three in the postseason. Asked by a reporter after the game if he was trying to hit homers, McGee said, "No, sir, I'm a line drive hitter, and I just be tryin' to make contact."[5]

McGee joined Charlie Keller and Tony Kubek—who happened to be broadcasting the game for NBC—as the only rookies to ever hit two homers in a World Series game. "I'd like to know what Willie McGee eats for breakfast," said Vuckovich to reporters in the post-game scrum. "I don't know if it's Wheaties or what, but gosh dang, he just jumped all over me."[6]

With a five-run lead and Andújar cruising, the Cardinals were seemingly in the driver's seat. Darrell Porter said he had never seen the hurler pitch better.[7] Then, in the bottom of the seventh, Simmons struck a one-hop smash back up the middle that struck the right leg of Andújar just below the knee. Andújar dropped to the ground as if he were shot. Play was halted as trainers Gene Gieselmann and Bob Bauman joined team physician Dr. Stan London to check on the fallen ace. Andújar screamed in pain with the slightest movement of his knee. He was clearly in no shape to continue pitching, or even walk. John Stuper and Gene Roof came out and carried him off the field. "Tell my mommy I'm okay," Andújar told teammates as he was escorted to an ambulance and hauled off to nearby Mount Sinai Hospital.[8]

It would be up to the St. Louis relief corps to record the final eight outs. Jim Kaat, pitching for the third time in as many games, was the first man out of the pen. He struck out Ben Oglivie and then ceded a single to Gorman Thomas. With two on and two out, Kuenn pinch-hit Don Money, and Herzog countered by calling on Doug Bair. Money worked the count full and then watched ball four to load the bases. Herzog wasted no time in making his third pitching change of the inning, signaling for his stopper. Charlie Moore swung at Bruce Sutter's first pitch and sent a pop fly into foul territory near the Cardinals' dugout along the third-base line. With his feet on the edge of the dugout steps, Ken Oberkfell reached over and made the rally-killing catch.

With two outs in the bottom of the eighth and St. Louis still ahead by five, Sutter issued a two-out walk to Robin Yount. The Brewers had been shutout just once all season, and Cooper ensured there would not be a second. The Brewers first baseman blasted a home run to right field, cutting the Cardinals' lead to 5–2.

With Vuckovich still in the game, Hendrick led off the top of the ninth inning and reached on catcher's interference, the fifth time that had happened in World Series history. The interference call accounted for the Brewers' third error of the contest. Porter attempted to sacrifice Hendrick to second, but his bunt was popped in the air and caught by Cooper, who made a diving catch in foul territory. With two outs and Hendrick still on first, Iorg hit a deep drive over the head of Moore in right field. A fan reached over the wall and interfered with the ball. Hendrick would have scored easily on the play, but the umpires ruled that he had to return to third base. Herzog and third-base coach Chuck Hiller pleaded their case, but the play stood as called. With runners on second and third and two outs, McGee came to the plate. Kuenn would not be burned by the rookie for a third time and intentionally walked him to get to Ozzie Smith. Vuckovich, running on fumes, walked Smith to force in a run. Bob McClure relieved and recorded the third out.

Sutter returned to the mound for the bottom of the ninth looking to nail down an all-important road victory. Oglivie led off with a groundball down the first-base line that Keith Hernandez could not handle, continuing a series trend of shaky defense by both sides. The next man up, Thomas, hit a deep drive to right-center field. Just as the ball was about to travel over the yellow line atop the 10-foot tall fence, McGee made a

14. Game Three—The Humble Hero

perfectly-timed leap and pulled in a spectacular backhanded snag. "That moment still seems like it was slow motion to me," said McGee four decades later. "Luckily, I had time to set up, gauge it and then make the jump."[9] Two batters later, McGee fittingly made a running catch for the third out to seal the win.

McGee's amazing performance attracted swarms of media attention, much to the chagrin of the shy rookie. The humble hero was much more at ease hitting in front of 50,000 spectators than facing dozens of reporters with microphones. With an anguished look on his face, he politely answered every question that came his way, including queries about an unflattering nickname that Howard Cosell had used on-air during the NLCS. After the movie *E.T.* had hit theaters earlier in the year, some opposing players took to calling McGee "E.T." because a perceived resemblance to the dark-skinned film character. Then, Cosell used the racially-tinged moniker during a telecast despite McGee's objections. "I appreciate people calling me by my name," said McGee at his locker. "People say things

Willie McGee capped off his thrilling Game Three performance with a home run–robbing catch (National Baseball Hall of Fame and Museum, Cooperstown, NY).

and I really don't like it."[10] A less unpleasant topic that came up in the scrum was how in the world George Steinbrenner let such a talent get away. Asked if he had any words for the Yankees' mercurial owner, McGee graciously said, "I thank him for the opportunity. It prepared me well for this situation."[11]

The Cardinals received reassuring reports from Andújar's hospital visit. His x-rays showed no fractures, meaning he could potentially be available for Game Seven—if necessary. Asked what he would do if Andújar could not pitch, Herzog said he'd "pray for three or four days of rain."[12]

15

Game Four
Seventh-Inning Debacle

Up two games to one, the Cardinals had turned the tide in their favor. At worst, they would be guaranteed at least one more home game. If things went their way, they could take the next two games and win it all. Sunshine and blue skies covered County Stadium for Game Four, an afternoon affair on October 16. Looking to continue the trend of exceptional rookie performances, the Cardinals trotted out Dave LaPoint, undefeated during the season in both afternoon and road games. Toeing the rubber for Milwaukee was Moose Haas, a 6-foot tall righty who never attained the size his father thought he would when he bestowed the name of the largest species of deer to his infant son. Haas (11–8, 4.47 ERA) had lost his spot in the Brewers' starting rotation after the trade deadline acquisition of Don Sutton but earned a pivotal win in Game Four of the ALCS.

Tom Herr led off the game and struck out on three pitches. Ken Oberkfell followed with a sharply-hit ground ball down the first-base line for a one-out double. After Keith Hernandez fanned, cleanup man George Hendrick—wearing an old-style shell helmet without ear flaps—came to the plate. From his closed batting stance, Hendrick put wood on the ball and hit a high chopper over the pitcher's mound. Robin Yount charged and tried to field the short hop, but the ball caromed off his glove and into the outfield, allowing Oberkfell to race home. Darrell Porter singled to keep the line moving, but Haas induced a groundout off the bat of Lonnie Smith to end the threat.

LaPoint worked a quick bottom of the first, providing minimal rest for Haas. The Cardinal offense put more traffic on the bases in the second. With one out, McGee singled, Ozzie Smith walked, and both runners advanced 90 feet when Haas spiked a pitch off the chest protector of Ted Simmons. In a prime RBI opportunity, Herr came through with a deep fly to center field. Gorman Thomas initially broke in, but the ball carried further than he anticipated, forcing him to backpedal to the edge of the warning track. He made the catch, but then his gimpy right knee gave out when he stepped on the dirt surface of the track, sending him to the ground. McGee scored easily and Smith—thanks to Thomas's stumble—scampered all the way home from second base for a rare two-run sacrifice fly.

For the second consecutive game, the Cards had jumped out to a 3–0 lead. And they were not done. Though Haas averaged less than two walks per nine innings during the season, he issued his second free pass of the inning with four straight balls to Oberkfell. The home crowd grew restless and the Brewer bullpen began to stir as Hernandez stepped in. Haas, seemingly out of sorts, paid Oberkfell no attention as he got a walking lead and stole second easily. Even though Haas had thrown seven straight pitches out of the zone, Hernandez swung at a 3–0 pitch and hit a solidly-struck grounder directly at second baseman Jim Gantner. The typically reliable infielder backed up to the edge of the outfield grass and the ball skipped between his legs and rolled into right field. Oberkfell scored on the error, extending the Cardinals' lead to four runs. On his 37th pitch of the inning, Haas retired Hendrick for the third out.

Ben Oglivie's two-out triple in the bottom of the second briefly gave the stunned crowd something to cheer about, but he was stranded when LaPoint fanned Don Money to end the inning. Porter helped save a run during the at-bat with blocks of two balls in the dirt. Haas settled in with a much needed 1-2-3 third inning and faced the minimum in the fourth by picking Ozzie Smith off first base following a bunt single. LaPoint worked out of a two-on, one-out situation in the fourth with an assist from County Stadium's ample foul territory, which provided just enough room for Porter to catch Thomas's foul popup.

The Cardinals' lead remained 4–0 in the home half of the fifth when the bottom of the Brewer batting order ignited a rally. Money led off with a double that glanced off the glove of a leaping McGee, and Charlie Moore followed with a bloop single to center. With runners on the corners, no outs, and Jim Gantner coming up, Porter and Smith jogged to the mound with words of encouragement for the young southpaw. The Cardinals would gladly trade a run for the double play. LaPoint got ahead of Gantner, 1–2, before inducing a soft ground ball up the middle. Smith fielded the ball with his foot on second base and then made an off-balance throw to first to complete the twin killing. Money's run put Milwaukee on the board, but LaPoint had quelled the rally, then retired the scalding-hot bat of Molitor for the third out.

The Cards reclaimed a four-run advantage in the top of the sixth on back-to-back doubles by Lonnie Smith and Dane Iorg. Kuenn sauntered to

15. Game Four—Seventh-Inning Debacle

the mound and signaled to the bullpen for righty Jim Slaton, who worked around a two-out error by Yount to keep the score 5–1.

LaPoint pitched a scoreless sixth and returned to the mound after the seventh-inning stretch. The struggling Thomas made the first out with a foul pop to Porter amidst a serenade of boos. Oglivie then hit a chopper to Hernandez, who displayed cat-like reflexes in adjusting to a bad hop. He fielded the ball cleanly and threw belt-high to LaPoint covering first, but the ball bounced in and out of his glove, allowing Oglivie to reach safely. Money followed the error with a duck snort that fell in front of Hendrick in right field. With runners on first and second, Moore popped out to Ozzie Smith for out number two. LaPoint needed one out to end the inning, and the Cardinals were seven outs from taking a commanding 3–1 series lead. Then, Gantner—who had hit into a double play with two runners on earlier in the game—hit a flare off the end of the bat that sailed into the right-center field gap, allowing Oglivie to score and Gantner and Money to cruise into second and third, respectively.

With the lead trimmed to 5–2 and the vaunted top of the order coming up, Herzog went to his bullpen and called on Doug Bair to get the crucial third out. As the crowd of 56,560 grew louder with each pitch, Molitor coaxed a walk to load the bases. When Bair fell behind Yount, 2–1, Porter and Hub Kittle jogged to the mound, providing Bair with a brief reprieve. Bair's next pitch sailed up and in to Yount, who started to offer but checked his swing. The ball made contact with the bat and was redirected to right field for an excuse-me single. Two runs scored on the play amidst deafening cheers from the crowd. Clinging to a one-run lead with the potential go-ahead run on first and the left-hand hitting Cooper coming up, Herzog went to his pen again. Instead of going to Sutter, however, he asked Jim Kaat to get the final out.

Cooper, from his crouched stance, pushed a grounder to the left of Oberkfell, who got a glove on the ball but could not make the play, allowing Molitor to score the tying run. With Simmons at the plate, Kaat let loose a 1–1 wild pitch that allowed Yount and Copper to each move up 90 feet. The game was quickly spiraling out of control. Herzog came out of the dugout and made a rare mid-batter pitching change, calling on Jeff Lahti, who inherited a 2–1 count. With first base open, Herzog decided to intentionally walk Simmons, loading the bases for Thomas. Lahti got ahead in the count, but a 1–2 pitch caught much of the plate. Thomas drilled it to center field for the first solidly-struck ball of the inning. Two more runs scored, making it 7–5 Milwaukee. Following an intentional walk to Oglivie, the inning mercifully came to a close when Money flew out to Lonnie Smith. By the time the calamitous frame was over, the Brewers had sent 12 men to the plate and scored six runs on five hits, three walks, and an error. The game—and the momentum—had swung 180 degrees in Milwaukee's favor.

Slaton and Bob McClure held the Cardinal bats in check to secure the win. Herzog received criticism for not using Sutter when he had the lead in the seventh, but the skipper stood by his decision. With the series knotted at two games apiece, the trophy was still very much up for grabs.

16

Game Five

Cards Pushed to the Brink

With the National Football League idle because of a players' strike, Major League Baseball had the undivided attention of American sports fans for Game Five on the afternoon of Sunday, October 17. The hearty County Stadium crowd—many of whom spent hours before the game tailgating—were bundled up in coats and stocking caps. The temperature was in the upper 40s, though the wind chill made it feel even colder. R&B singer and Milwaukee native Al Jarreau performed "The Star-Spangled Banner." Viewers of the pregame show on NBC saw advertisements for the Ford LTD sedan, Atari video game console, and Timex wristwatches.

After watching his team hit only .197 through the first four games, Whitey Herzog adjusted his lineup against lefty Mike Caldwell. Rather than Gene Tenace, who was mired in a 3-for-47 slump, David Green got the start in left and Lonnie Smith shifted to DH. Bob Forsch, looking to bounce back from his Game One struggles, took the ball for the Redbirds.

Leadoff man Lonnie Smith went up hacking against Caldwell and lined the first pitch of the game back up the middle. The ball struck Caldwell's glove and rolled to Molitor, who had no play. Smith then stole second base as Green, hitting second, went down swinging. With Keith Hernandez at the plate, Smith tried to swipe third, but Simmons delivered a perfect throw to nab him. Hernandez, hitless in his first 15 series at-bats, hit a frozen rope to right field for a two-out single but was forced at second base on George Hendrick's grounder to third to end the inning.

Just as they had done in Game One, the Brewers jumped out to an early lead on Forsch in their half of the first. After a pair of one-out singles by Robin Yount and Cecil Cooper, Forsch's pickoff attempt at second base sailed over the head of Ozzie Smith and into center field, allowing both runners to advance. The error proved costly when Simmons bounced a high chopper to first that scored Yount for the game's first run. Ben Oglivie hit a well-struck fly ball to center field, but Willie McGee hauled it in for the third out.

The Cardinals still trailed, 1–0, at the start of the third. Following hard-hit outs by Ozzie and Lonnie Smith, Green hit a blooper to right field that eluded the dive of Charlie Moore. Green hustled all the way to third base as Moore got back on his feet and chased after the ball. Hernandez followed with a line drive to the left-center field gap. Like Moore, Gorman Thomas made a valiant diving effort but came up short. Green scored the tying run while Hernandez cruised into second base with an RBI double.

The Brewers' table setters continued to torment Forsch in the bottom of the third. Molitor drew a one-out walk and advanced to third on Yount's double to left field. Cooper followed by pulling a ground ball to first base that took a wicked hop on Hernandez, who quickly adjusted and made the play for the second out. Molitor scored, but Hernandez's slick fielding kept Yount at third. Forsch retired Simmons on a routine fly ball to keep it a one-run game.

Caldwell, wearing a five o'clock shadow and soiled hat that was closer to Padres brown than Brewers blue, remained locked in. Through five innings, Mr. Warmth had worked around seven hits, an error, and a walk with only one run allowed.

Moore started the bottom of the fifth with a double over the outstretched glove of Oberkfell and advanced to third on Gantner's groundout. Molitor stepped to the plate amongst cheers of "Here we go Brewers, here we go!" Steve Mura and John Martin, neither of whom had pitched in the series, hastily loosened in the bullpen. Herzog stuck with Forsch, even as he yielded an RBI single to Molitor and infield hit to Yount. Herzog's faith in his seasoned righty paid off. Forsch induced a fly out off the bat of Cooper and then, after walking Simmons to load the bases, struck out Oglivie. Ultimately, neither Mura nor Martin would appear in the series. "John and I were both out in the bullpen the whole time freezing," recalled Mura years later. Bruce [Sutter] would say, 'Sorry guys, you're not getting into this game either.' But I could have been in San Diego."[1]

Following a scoreless sixth, the Brewers carried a 3–1 lead into the seventh. The Smiths got going things going for the Cards—Ozzie with a walk and Lonnie with a single. Caldwell was one out away from escaping unscathed after retiring Green on a fly ball and inducing a fielder's choice off the bat of Hernandez. With runners on the corners and two out, Hendrick drilled a single up the middle to score Ozzie and pull the Cards to within one. The next man up, Porter, nearly tied the game, but Cooper—a two-time Gold Glove winner—made a fantastic diving stop and threw to Caldwell covering first for the third out.

Forsch returned to the mound in the bottom of the seventh as Sutter

16. Game Five—Cards Pushed to the Brink   191

began to stir. Forsch disposed of Gantner and Molitor in succession, but then Yount blasted Forsch's 109th pitch of the game to the opposite field over the 375-foot mark in left. The homer was Yount's fourth hit of the game and second four-hit performance of the series—a first in World Series history. The accomplishment occurred as his wife was hospitalized awaiting the birth of their third child. Yount was living up to the "MVP, MVP, MVP" chants he heard during each at-bat. Forsch retired Cooper to end the inning, but Milwaukee held a 4–2 lead and were six outs from victory.

The Cards failed to score in the top of the eighth, and Herzog tasked Sutter with keeping the deficit at two runs in the bottom half. The bearded stopper ran into trouble, however, and the bottom third of the Brewers' batting order again wreaked havoc. Moore and Gantner each delivered two-out RBI singles that padded the Brewers' lead. The crowd roared with approval, waving foam fingers and souvenir pennants in the air. "It's like New Year's Eve!" proclaimed Dick Enberg on the NBC broadcast.[2]

Caldwell looked to go the distance, but the Cardinals did not go down without a fight in the ninth. With one out, Green and Hernandez produced back-to-back doubles. Hendrick then singled home Hernandez, cutting Milwaukee's lead to 6–4. Viewers waiting to watch Ponch and Jon on *CHiPs* would have to wait a little longer. With Caldwell at 128 pitches and clearly running on fumes, Kuenn ambled to the mound and signaled for southpaw Bob McClure to face the left-hand hitting Porter.[3] The County Stadium crowd grew eerily quiet as McGee came to the plate representing the go-ahead run. The silence was quickly replaced by boisterous cheers when McGee whiffed on three pitches. One out from defeat, Herzog pinch-hit Gene Tenace for Oberkfell, despite the latter's three-hit game and .438 average in the series. "I know Obie had three hits, but I wanted to take a crack at a home run, and I figured Tenace was a better shot at it," explained Herzog.[4] Tenace smoked the first pitch he saw but the ball fell in the glove of Oglivie in medium-depth left field to end the game.

The Brewers needed just one more win, but it would have to come on the Cardinals' home turf. As the team bus pulled away from County Stadium, the raucous Brewer faithful pounded on the Cardinals' team bus and taunted the players. Ozzie Smith calmly said, "Don't they realize we're going to win the next two games?"[5]

On the flight back to St. Louis, Sutter—sensing the team needed to relax—declared there would be a party at Forsch's house that night. "I couldn't believe it," recalled Forsch. "I'd just lost two of the biggest games of my life. I said, 'Bruce, this is a bad idea.'"[6] Unbeknownst to Herzog, the majority of the team gathered with their wives at the Forsch residence and had a great time. With an open date and optional workout the next day, there would be time to recover from the effects of the night's festivities.

17

Game Six

Sutton Versus Stuper, Part Two

Fittingly, the man who wore the number six on his jersey threw out the first pitch before Game Six. Stan Musial, seated next to Gussie Busch in the owner's box, tossed a ball to retiring clubhouse manager Butch Yatkeman. Though the temperature was 70 degrees at the outset, the forecast for the night was ominous. Heavy rain and sleet were approaching with warnings of possible tornadoes.

In a rematch of Game Two, Don Sutton squared off against John Stuper—the first rookie to start two games in a World Series since Dick Hughes did so for the Cardinals in 1967. The contrast in experience was not lost on Stuper, a former journalism major, who shared his own lede with reporters. "I'd have to write something to the effect, 'Don Sutton versus John Stuper looks like a mismatch of huge proportions but come out and watch the game. Stranger things have happened.'"[1]

Relishing in the role of underdog, Stuper got off to a promising start. He retired the dynamic trio of Molitor-Yount-Cooper in order in the first, then navigated around a pair of baserunners in the second with the help of an inning-ending double play.

Sutton retired the first five Cardinals he faced before DH Dane Iorg struck an opposite-field double that fell beyond the reach of Ben Oglivie. Willie McGee followed with a routine ground ball to Robin Yount, but the ball went through his legs for a run-scoring error. The miscue proved even more costly when the next man up, Tom Herr—only 1-for-19 in the series—doubled off the right-field wall to drive in McGee and put the Cards ahead by two.

Sutton did not have much time to rest between innings. Stuper, working quickly and efficiently, benefited from another twin killing and needed only nine pitches to retire the side in the third. In the home half, the Cardinals' speed again came into play. Lonnie Smith hit a slow grounder to

17. Game Six—Sutton Versus Stuper, Part Two

Jim Gantner, who looked up for a split second to see who was covering first, causing the ball to clank off his glove for Milwaukee's second error. Smith subsequently stole second and advanced to third on Keith Hernandez's ground out. With two outs and George Hendrick at the plate, Sutton worked from the windup as opposed to pitching from the stretch. On the second pitch of the at-bat, Smith broke for home as Sutton started his windup. The pitch was high and inside. Simmons reached up and caught the ball, then put the tag down on Smith as he dove headfirst across the plate. Home-plate umpire Jim Evans called Smith out, though replays clearly showed that Smith's hand beat the tag.

Stuper mixed fastballs, curves, and sliders to induce weak contact, retiring the Brewers' 3-4-5 hitters in order in the top of the fourth. In the bottom half, Hendrick led off with a single and Darrell Porter followed with a two-run blast over the right-field wall. Iorg then tripled into the right-field corner and scored on Herr's perfectly-executed squeeze bunt, expanding the Cardinals' lead to 5-0.

Rain began to fall as the Brewers came to the plate in the fifth. The game was three outs from becoming official, but Commissioner Bowie Kuhn indicated he was willing to delay the game as long as necessary in order to get in a complete nine innings. Stuper, seemingly unfazed by the moment or the precipitation, breezed through Oglivie, Thomas, and Money.

The Cardinals' battering of Sutton continued in the fifth. Lonnie Smith led off with a single and moved up to second base on a check-swing ground out by Ken Oberkfell. Hernandez then attempted to bunt for a hit on the first pitch he saw but missed the ball. Sutton responded with a brushback fastball that sailed up and in on the Cardinal first baseman. As a steady rain pelted the turf, Hernandez fell behind and fouled off several tough two-strike offerings before getting one he could handle. He tattooed a Sutton delivery deep into right field. The ball sailed through the rain drops and over the wagon gate. After hitting only 27 home runs in their home park all season, the Cards had two in the most important game of the season and held a commanding 7-0 advantage. Kuenn replaced Sutton with Jim Slaton, but before the reliever could throw his first pitch, the umpires halted play. Following a delay of 25 minutes, Slaton dispatched Hendrick and Porter in short order.

In the top of the sixth, Stuper picked up where he left off and retired the Brewers in order on nine pitches. With his team down seven, Kuenn turned to Doc Medich to pitch the home half of the sixth. Medich, a starter working out of the bullpen, had the potential of working multiple innings. The aptly-nicknamed hurler planned to retire at the end of the season to focus on an orthopedic surgery residency. "I hadn't pitched in 17 days," remembered Medich. "[Pitching coach] Pat Dobson came to me and said, 'Do you want to pitch a couple of innings?' I always wanted to pitch in the World Series—this was my only chance to do it. I went out and felt strong, but then it started to rain."[2]

Iorg greeted Medich with a leadoff double, his third extra base knock of the game. As the rain intensified, the ball became slippery. A wild pitch allowed Iorg to take third, and McGee drove him home with a single to right field. After Tom Herr singled, Medich uncorked another errant pitch that sailed several feet behind Ozzie Smith, allowing McGee and Herr to each advance 90 feet. "I had never done that in my whole career," said Medich, looking back. "The ball just slipped out of my hand."[3] The runners stood pat on Smith's ground out to first base. Up stepped David Green, who had replaced Lonnie Smith because of a jammed finger earlier in the game. With a 2–2 count on Green, the steady rain turned into a deluge, and play was stopped for a second time.

It took two hours for the rain to subside and play to resume. During the delay, the temperature had dropped 23 degrees since the first pitch, and the majority of fans had departed for warmer and drier environs. Green resumed his at-bat with a 2–2 count and watched two balls from Medich to load the bases. Oberkfell followed with a ground ball to Cooper, who threw home for the force out. Hernandez and Hendrick kept the line moving with consecutive two-out singles to drive in another three runs. By the time the inning was over, St. Louis had sent 10 men to the plate and scored six runs on four hits, a walk, and an error. Medich rebounded with a scoreless seventh and threw his last pitch as a major leaguer. Perhaps most importantly for the Cardinals, a 13–0 lead all but assured Bruce Sutter could be saved for the decisive Game Seven.

Stuper kept loose during the long rain delay by applying heat packs and receiving multiple rubdowns from Gene Gieselmann. The extended period of rest did little to disrupt Stuper's rhythm. He returned to the mound and picked up where he left off. Until a one-out error by Oberkfell in the eighth, Stuper had set down 15 straight batters. Herzog stuck with his rookie into the ninth inning despite the lopsided score, but he did use the opportunity to get Glenn Brummer into the game. Coach Dave Ricketts was sitting in the bullpen and he said, "Brummer, you're going into the game," Brummer recalled years later. "I said, 'Are you sure?'"[4] For the third-string catcher from a small town in Illinois, the cameo made for a memorable moment and left Julio González as the only position player who had not seen action.

Milwaukee's only tally came in the ninth inning. Gantner and Molitor started the frame with consecutive base hits, doubling the Brewers' total for the game. Gantner then scored on a wild pitch that Brummer admitted should have been a passed ball. It would be the only blemish on Stuper's outstanding stat line. By outpitching a future Hall of Famer and staving off elimination, Stuper had cemented his place in Cardinals' lore. The two teams had played a combined 344 games during the regular season and playoffs. The World Series title would come down to a winner-take-all Game Seven.

18

Game Seven

For All the Marbles

> "Not everybody gets to play in the seventh game of the World Series, and not many people get to think they're going to win it. And I thought I was."—Ted Simmons[1]

As if Mother Nature was declaring the end of the baseball season, the temperature at the start of Game Seven was 44 degrees and dropping. A rematch of Game Three pitted Pete Vuckovich versus Joaquín Andújar, who would attempt to pitch through his knee contusion in the biggest game of his life. Dave LaPoint warmed up alongside Andújar in case he was unable to go. "The biggest problem was you couldn't ask him anything," said LaPoint. "You'd say, 'Joaquín, how you feeling? And he'd answer, 'Me one tough Dominican.'"[2]

Andújar was able to go and brimmed with confidence as first pitch approached. He advised traveling secretary C.J. Cherre that he had "better get the champagne ready."[3] In the dugout, he told his teammates, "You get me one run, we world champs."[4]

As the Cardinals took the field, Ozzie Smith executed his signature backflip, which he reserved for Opening Days, All-Star Games, Fan Appreciation Day, and—in this case—the final game of 1982. Paul Molitor and Robin Yount loosened in the on-deck circle while Andújar threw his warmup pitches to Darrell Porter. On Andújar's final toss, he flicked the ball in the air, rocked back, windmilled his arm, and fired the ball as hard as he could. He picked up the routine from fellow Dominican Juan Marichal as a way of psyching himself up. "We may need a big jar of mustard before this day's over with all the hot dogs we've seen so far," said Joe Garagiola on the NBC broadcast.[5]

If Andújar had pain in his injured limb, it was not reflected in his pitching. He broke Molitor's bat on the first pitch of the game, resulting in a lazy fly ball to George Hendrick. Yount and Cecil Cooper followed with meager ground balls that Ken Oberkfell gobbled up for easy outs. Andújar continued to pound the strike zone and just as easily disposed of the opposition in the second and third. Brewer hitters were consistently late on his fastball. Nine batters came to bat, and nine made outs.

Vuckovich, on the other hand, allowed traffic on the basepaths early and often. He pitched around a Keith Hernandez infield single in the first, then found himself in a bigger pickle in the second. With one out, Dane Iorg recorded his eighth hit in 15 series at-bats. Later in the inning, a walk to Tom Herr and AstroTurf–aided infield single by Ozzie Smith loaded the bases. Vuckovich escaped the jam by retiring Lonnie Smith on a can of corn to right field. The scowling hurler, none too pleased with Lee Weyer's strike zone, gave the umpire a piece of his mind as he walked off the field.

The Cardinals created another golden scoring opportunity in the third. With one out, Hernandez drew a walk and then advanced to second on Hendrick's single through the left side. Porter followed with a deep blast to right field that would have been a home run in many ballparks— but not at Busch Stadium. The ball landed in Charlie Moore's glove, though both runners advanced. Iorg—as hot as any hitter on the planet not named Molitor or Yount—came to bat with an opportunity to put the Cardinals on the board. He made solid contact, but his sharply-hit roller was handled by Gantner for the third out. The Cardinals were making Vuckovich work but had stranded six runners through three innings and nothing to show for it on the scoreboard.

Molitor recorded Milwaukee's first hit of the game when he pushed a ground ball by Herr for a leadoff single in the top of the fourth. After Yount reached on a fielder's choice, Cooper yanked an Andújar delivery into right field. Yount attempted to go from first to third, but Hendrick fired a perfect one-hop throw to Oberkfell, who applied the tag to Yount's cranium before he could reach third base. Ted Simmons popped out to Porter in foul territory to end the inning.

Consecutive singles by Willie McGee and Herr to start the bottom of the fourth put runners on first and third with no outs. Ozzie Smith, choking up on the bat, produced a weak pop fly to Gantner for the first out. The next man up, Lonnie Smith, pulled a grounder to the left side. Yount, who was playing even with the bag in hopes of turning a double play, could not reach the ball. Molitor fielded it deep in the hole, but there was no play on any of the Redbird speedsters, and McGee scored easily. Vuckovich subsequently retired Oberkfell and Hernandez, but St. Louis had finally broken through with the game's first run.

The Cardinals' 1–0 lead did not last long. Ben Oglivie, who had struggled throughout the postseason, turned around Andújar's first pitch in the top of the fifth, depositing it over the right-field wall for a game-tying solo home run. Andújar rolled through the next three hitters on four pitches. Vuckovich pitched around another hit by Iorg in the bottom half of the frame, and the score remained even.

Gantner, hitting ninth in Harney Kuenn's batting order, registered his fourth double of the series with a shot into the right-center field gap to start the top of the sixth. The Brewers then gave the Cards a taste of their own medicine. Molitor attempted to sacrifice Gantner to second with a bunt to the third-base side of the mound. Andújar fielded the ball, spun, and made an off-balance throw to first. The ball glanced off Molitor and rolled toward the Cardinals' bullpen down the right-field line as Gantner scored the go-ahead run and Molitor advanced to second. Not only did the Brewers possess a 2–1 lead, they had a runner in scoring position, no outs, and the AL MVP coming to the plate. At minimum, Youant was looking to hit the ball to the right side to move Molitor to third. He accomplished just that, pushing a bouncing ball toward the hole between Hernandez and Herr. Both infielders converged on the ball with Herr making the play. Andújar, perhaps having lost focus following his defensive lapse moments earlier, failed to cover first and Yount reached safely. With the inning and game in danger of unraveling, Jim Kaat and Doug Bair quickly warmed up in the bullpen as Hub Kittle visited his longtime pupil. Following the brief breather and Kittle's sage advice, Andújar induced a fly ball off the bat of Cooper. The ball traveled deep enough into left field for Molitor to score without a play. Andújar prevented further damage, but the Brewers now held a 3–1 lead and were 12 outs away from victory.

As he warmed up Vuckovich in the bottom of the sixth, Simmons experienced an overwhelming feeling that would stick with him decades later: "I never felt anything like it as a professional baseball player, or anywhere else I've walked this earth. That very moment in that very game, at that very time, I thought I was going to win the World Series and was convinced of it."[6]

The Cardinals sought to create a different reality. With one out, Ozzie Smith slapped a single to left field and then moved to third on Lonnie Smith's double down the third-base line. With two in scoring position and a pair of left-hand hitters—Oberkfell and Hernandez—due up, Kuenn summoned Bob McClure from the pen. As he had done throughout the series, Herzog countered by lifting Oberkfell for pinch-hitter Gene Tenace, who drew a walk to load the bases. Mike Ramsey was inserted as a pinch-runner for Tenace and represented the potential go-ahead run. "I was just thinking, 'I don't want to mess things up for us,'" recalled Ramsey.[7] Hernandez, who was celebrating his 29th birthday, stepped in the box to face McClure, who was no stranger. The two had grown up in the same neighborhood and played youth baseball with one another. McClure hoped to induce a double-play ball off the bat of his old friend but fell behind in the count, 3–1, and needed to throw a strike. Hernandez peppered an inside fastball that split the center and right fielders. The two Smiths scored and Ramsey slid safely into third base on the game-tying single.

Hendrick, the Cardinals' RBI leader three years running, had a chance to put his team ahead. Kuenn had a righty, Moose Haas, loose in the bullpen but with the lefty Porter on deck he chose to stick with McClure. Hendrick fell behind in the count, 1–2, but McClure caught too much of the plate with his next offering. Hendrick, who stood as far from the plate as any hitter in the league, got his arms extended and laced a line drive to the opposite field, scoring Ramsey. After Porter grounded into a fielder's choice, runners were on the corners with two outs. A series of chess moved ensued. David Green was announced as the pinch-hitter for Iorg, then Kuenn went to the righty Haas to face Green. Herzog then countered by pinch-hitting for his pinch-hitter—lefty-hitting Steve Braun for Green. Braun grounded to Gantner for the third out, but the Cardinals had turned the table and held a 4–3 lead.

Andújar set down Gorman Thomas and Roy Howell to start the top of the seventh—the former coming on his first strikeout of the game. Charlie Moore then singled, bringing Gantner to the plate. Meanwhile, Bruce Sutter tossed warmup pitches in the bullpen—ready if needed. With Molitor and Yount lurking, retiring Gantner was imperative. The Brewers' second sacker swung at Andújar's first pitch and tapped softly back to the mound. Andújar tossed the ball to Hernandez for the third out. As Andújar was walking off the field, Gantner called him a "hot dog."[8] Those were fighting words to Andújar, who threw down his glove and attempted to go after Gantner. Lee Weyer, looking like an offensive lineman in stature and technique, restrained the comparatively smaller Andújar. Kittle came out and ushered his pitcher into the Cardinals' dugout before the situation escalated further.

After the skirmish, Herzog signaled to his bullpen that Sutter would be coming in for the eighth. Haas expeditiously set down the bottom third of the Cardinal batting order in the home half of the seventh. With six outs to go, it was Sutter's ballgame. The fireman navigated the top of the Milwaukee order with ease in the eighth, sandwiching a strikeout of Yount between a pair of groundouts.

With Haas still on the mound, the Redbirds looked to pad the lead for Sutter in the bottom of the eighth. Lonnie Smith started the inning favorably with a ground-rule double. Ramsey, who had stayed in the game to play third base after pinch-running earlier, then came to bat for the first time in the series. He attempted to sacrifice Smith to third but was called out on strikes after three unsuccessful attempts. Hernandez was then intentionally walked to get to Hendrick, whose fly ball to center accounted for the second out. With Porter and Braun coming up, Kuenn went to southpaw and Game Five starter Mike Caldwell, who was pitching on just two days' rest.

After Caldwell completed his warmup pitches, Porter adjusted his glasses and dug in the batter's box. The man who had battled back from addiction and endured two years of Busch Stadium jeers looked to add to his team's lead. With the crowd now urging him on, the newly-venerated backstop pulled a line drive over Gantner and into right field for a base hit. Smith raced home safely from second as Charlie Moore's throw sailed halfway down the first-base line. With Hernandez on third and Porter on first, Braun stepped in. The proficient utilityman fell behind in the count but then got a pitch he could handle and delivered a solid smash to center field, scoring Hernandez and giving St. Louis a 6–3 lead. With two insurance runs on the board, the delirious crowd roared with approval. Still, Sutter had three outs to get against the game's most potent offense.

Simmons, Oglivie, and Thomas were due up in the ninth. Though each hitter had endured postseason struggles, their collective accomplishments spoke for themselves—601 career home runs to that point. The first man up, Simmons, hit a dribbler back to Sutter, who made an easy toss to Hernandez for the first out. Oglivie followed with a slow bouncer to Herr, who calmly threw to first. It came down to Thomas—who tied Reggie Jackson for the AL home run crown—against the NL saves leader. Hernandez, who had been playing first base since early childhood, later described feeling so nervous when Thomas came up that a knot in his stomach prohibited him from even bending over to get into fielding position. "I've never had that feeling in my life," he said. "I was out there at first base thinking, 'don't hit the ball to me.'"[9]

Thomas worked the full count and then fouled off several tough pitches. On the 10th pitch of the at-bat, Sutter did not use his bread and butter—the splitter. Instead, he threw a fastball at the top of the zone. Thomas put forth a mighty hack but came up empty. "Bruce, being that split-fingered guy, you would think that would be the pitch he would use in that instance," recalled Ozzie Smith four decades later. "But boy, he threw a fastball that looked like it was 100 miles an hour. Bruce couldn't break a pane of glass with his 85 mile an hour fastball."[10]

Sutter raised his fist in the air. Porter launched his mask, then ran and jumped into Sutter's arms. The Cardinals were world champions for the ninth time in franchise history. Players piled on one another as thousands of fans overcame the police and poured on to the field. The players

Darryl Porter and Bruce Sutter embrace each other immediately following the final out of Game Seven (National Baseball Hall of Fame and Museum, Cooperstown, NY).

quickly dispersed to the clubhouse with one exception. George Hendrick ran through the right-field wagon gate, changed into civilian attire, and listened to the celebration on his drive home.[11] Sans their right fielder, the group of men who had competed together for six months wearing nylon jerseys with two Cardinals perched atop a baseball bat let loose, bedraggling one another with champagne—except for Porter, who celebrated with sparkling grape juice.

"Every young boy that plays baseball dreams of playing in the World Series," reflected Dane Iorg more than 40 years later. "You think about all the time you played baseball in Little League, high school, and college. You almost have to pinch yourself. It's just a great feeling. We had a bunch of good guys who got along well. It was incredible to play on the best team in the world and win the World Series. It's even more than you'd even hope for."[12]

As fireworks lit the downtown St. Louis sky, Bowie Kuhn presented the World Series trophy to Gussie Busch and Whitey Herzog. Just as he had done in the NLCS, Darrell Porter earned series MVP honors after hitting .286 with a pair of doubles, a home run, and five RBIs. Bob Costas, a young NBC broadcaster, interviewed Porter, who exclaimed in his southern drawl, "It's just so wonderful, I can't believe it!"[13] Though Porter performed solidly, several other Cardinals would have been equally deserving of the award. Hendrick (.321, five RBIs), Hernandez (.259, eight RBIs), Iorg (.529, five extra-base hits), Lonnie Smith (.321, four doubles), and McGee (.240, two home runs, five RBIs) all had similar contributions. Arguably, no other player outshone Andújar, who turned in a 1.35 ERA in his two winning starts.

Though the series was tightly contested, the Cardinals bested the Brewers in every facet of the game. Milwaukee had bludgeoned opponents by a total of 206 runs during the regular season but were outscored by St. Louis in the series, 39–33. The Cards accumulated 23 extra-base hits versus Milwaukee's 19. On the basepaths, Redbird runners stole seven; the Brewers swiped just one. Cardinal pitchers posted a series ERA of nearly a run less than the Brewer hurlers and held Simmons, Oglivie, Thomas, and the DH duo of Howell/Money to a combined .160 average. "That's the only thing about a speed-versus-power World Series, power can stop; can be stopped," observed Sparky Anderson.[14] There were many highlight reel defensive plays in the seven games but also more lapses than anyone would have anticipated. The two teams committed a collective 18 errors, and there could have been more if not for generous official scoring. More than one sportswriter pointed out that the 1982 Fall Classic was one of the uglier series they could remember. For the Cardinals and their fans, however, the series was a thing of beauty, and the season was one they will never forget.

Epilogue

The Cardinals were well-positioned to contend for another World Series trophy in 1983. Gene Tenace, Steve Mura, and Julio González were the only players subtracted from the roster, and Tenace was the only one of the three to appear in the postseason. Despite the continuity, the team went—in Herzog's words—from penthouse to the outhouse.[1]

The 1983 Cardinals posted better offensive numbers than the previous year's championship team, including a higher average (.270), more home runs (83), and a higher stolen base total (207). However, Herzog observed that Lonnie Smith's defense dropped off and Keith Hernandez was "dogging it," particularly on the bases.[2] While some of the team's struggles were intangible, the faltering of the pitching staff was clear statistically. Bob Forsch (10–12, 4.28 ERA) and Joaquín Andújar (6–16, 4.16) fell off considerably, perhaps a side effect of heavy workloads each shouldered the year before. Opposing hitters even found a way to solve Bruce Sutter, who compiled a pedestrian 4.23 ERA.

Despite several cogs taking steps back, St. Louis was eight games over .500 and in first place on June 1. Nonetheless, Herzog recognized the need for reinforcements on the pitching staff. He also had concerns about how Hernandez's effort and attitude were affecting the clubhouse. "A couple of my coaches even told me, 'You'd better get rid of that guy. He's poisoning the whole ball club,'" Herzog recalled.[3]

The Redbirds were having some challenges between the white lines of the baseball diamond, but white lines of a different sort may have contributed to the team's backslide. By the early 1980s, cocaine use had become pervasive in the upper echelons of society, including professional sports, and the Cardinals clubhouse was not immune. Hernandez later estimated that 40 percent of major leaguers were using cocaine in 1980.[4] Several big leaguers, including young stars Tim Raines and Alan Wiggins, entered treatment for chemical dependency in 1982. Then, in early 1983, the Cardinals' front office was informed by the FBI that two members of the team were seen using cocaine at a party. Herzog addressed the club and asked the guilty parties to come forward privately, but none did.[5]

One player's cocaine use reached a tipping point in June. Lonnie Smith had first experimented with the drug while playing winter ball in Venezuela. His use escalated until it consumed his every thought. "After 1982 I started getting the stuff in the mail through the winter, and in 1983 I was involved pretty bad," said Smith, looking back. "I wasn't eating or sleeping. I got down to 160 pounds, and I had a 28-inch waistline, which is the size I was in junior high school. I was very weak. I was constantly sweating and constantly nervous. Everything was crashing down on me. I would go three days without sleeping, then try to go out and play."[6] After experiencing a frightening near-fatal overdose, Smith walked into Herzog's office and admitted he needed help. He was placed on the disabled list and entered treatment.

On June 15, 1983, Hernandez was traded to the Mets in exchange for pitchers Neil Allen and Rick Ownbey. Fans were outraged by the transaction, reminding Herzog of sentiments expressed following the trade of Ted Simmons three years earlier. Publicly, Herzog pointed to the team's need for pitching and Hernandez's status as a soon-to-be free agent as primary motives behind the deal. Hernandez was flabbergasted by being dealt to the lowly Mets and briefly threatened retirement. He eventually acquiesced and became an integral part of the Mets' rapid turnaround and eventual World Series title in 1986. In terms of on-field contributions, it was a lopsided trade in the Mets' favor. Allen and Ownbey posted a combined record of 20–22 for St. Louis and were below league average during their respective stints with the Cardinals. Hernandez, on the other hand, accumulated a WAR of 26.6 in seven seasons in the Big Apple. Still, Herzog stood by his decision years later. "Getting rid of Hernandez was addition by subtraction," he wrote in his memoir. "I really feel that if we had kept him, his attitude and his bullshit would have ruined our ball club."[7]

In 1985, Hernandez testified under immunity at a drug trial in a Pittsburgh District Court, admitting to heavy cocaine use in 1980 as well as using the drug with teammates Lonnie Smith and Joaquín Andújar.[8] Smith also testified for the prosecution. The trial resulted in the conviction of seven drug dealers. "A lot of people were monkeying around with drugs back then," Hernandez reflected in the book *Whitey's Boys*. "It was just the thing to do, but that doesn't make it right. I thought that chapter of my life was behind me and that it was over, because I had quit, but then came the phone call from the FBI. It came back to haunt me."[9]

Without Lonnie Smith and Hernandez, the Cards lost 11 of 15 and were a .500 team by the end of June. In Ozzie Smith's estimation, the trade of the team's star first baseman mentally drained the team. "When you trade a person of the caliber of Keith Hernandez, it's obviously a big loss on the field, but the mental effects of a trade like that are just as important," recalled Smith, whose batting average fell below the Mendoza line during the team's skid.[10] More changes came in subsequent weeks with the trade of Doug Bair to Detroit and the release of Jim Kaat, marking the end of a career that spanned a quarter-century.

Lonnie Smith returned to the lineup in early July and competed for the batting title in the season's second half, but the comeback was not enough to overcome the team's poor pitching and loss of Tom Herr to a knee injury. The Redbirds' record was still hovering around .500 by Labor Day, but a 12–18 September record doomed their already slim playoff chances. Forsch's second career no-hitter on September 26 was the high point in an otherwise dismal stretch run. St. Louis's 79–83 record was good for fourth place in the NL East, 11 games behind the first-place Phillies.

The front office mostly stood pat heading into the 1984 season, a decision that would backfire. George Hendrick and Darrell Porter had unproductive seasons, Lonnie Smith's average dropped to .250, and David Green took a step back in his development. It ultimately came to light that Green was struggling with alcohol abuse, requiring him to leave the team for treatment. By late June, the Cards were under .500 and mired in fifth place in the topsy-turvy NL East. Perennial bottom-feeders Chicago and New York rose to the top of the standings with the emergence of young stars like Ryne Sandberg, Rick Sutcliffe, Dwight Gooden, and Darryl Strawberry. Of course, the Mets also benefited from the stellar glovework and smooth hitting stroke of Hernandez.

A memorable game between the Cardinals and Cubs at Wrigley Field on June 23, 1984, may have been a turning point in the season. The Cards jumped out to an early 7–1 lead, but the Cubbies were no longer the also-rans of the league and scratched their way back in the game. The Cards clung to a 9–8 lead in the bottom of the ninth when Sutter surrendered a game-tying home run to Sandberg. Each team plated a pair of runs in the 10th, and the game was tied, 11–11, in the bottom of the 11th. Sutter was still on the mound when Sandberg's spot in the order came back around. The Cubs' young second baseman took Sutter deep again for the walk-off victory. Sandberg's heroics overshadowed an incredible performance by Willie McGee, who hit for the cycle and drove in six runs. "If we had won that game, I think it would have given us the confidence to win the pennant," opined Ozzie Smith in his memoir. "I really believe that. But when that happened against our best relief pitcher … nothing was said about it, but deep down we felt it."[11]

Epilogue

The Cardinals finished the first half of 1984 below .500. Underperformance on the big-league roster and a budding crop of farmhands like Andy Van Slyke and Terry Pendleton compelled the front office to sell Dane Iorg to Kansas City and trade Mike Ramsey and Ken Oberkfell in separate deals. John Stuper, who accrued a 3–5 record and 5.28 ERA, ended the season in a Cincinnati Reds uniform. On a more positive note, two of the Redbirds' top arms bounced back. Andújar won 20 games and the Comeback Player of Year Award while Sutter—with mentor Mike Roarke as his new pitching coach—registered a 1.54 ERA and tied a major-league record with 45 saves. St. Louis finished the second half eight games above .500 and finished the season in third place behind the Cubs and Mets.

Following the 1984 season, Sutter became a free agent. Herzog had lobbied the front office to lock up the reliever before his contract ran out, but by then Anheuser-Busch had formed a three-man executive committee—Gussie Busch, Lou Susman, and Fred Kuhlmann—to run the club. Herzog and Joe McDonald had less autonomy and were forced to run all significant player personnel decisions by the committee. Despite Herzog's strong desire to extend Sutter after his subpar 1983 season, the committee preferred to take a wait-and-see approach. Sutter's return to form gave him more leverage heading into free agency. His preference was to re-sign with St. Louis, but there was a hang-up between his camp and the Cardinals over a no-trade clause. Braves owner Ted Turner swooped in and lured Sutter to Atlanta with a four-year deal.

After Sutter's departure, there was front office turmoil and more roster turnover. Hendrick was traded to the Pirates in exchange for John Tudor. In January 1985, ownership fired McDonald, principally because Busch had found out about Green's alcohol problem in the newspaper rather than hearing about it firsthand. To replace Hendrick's powerful bat, Ozzie Smith advised Susman to pursue Giants slugger Jack Clark, who was on the trading block. "I had met Jack Clark several years back, and I knew that all the reports about him being such a trouble-maker with the Giants weren't true," Smith later recalled.[12] A deal was struck on February 1, 1985, to acquire Clark in exchange for Dave LaPoint, David Green, and a pair of minor leaguers. By the end of the month, the executive committee had settled on a new GM—former Cardinals shortsop and Washington University alum Dal Maxvill.

Not dissimilar to the moves that helped St. Louis capture the 1982 title, the roster shakeup resulted in the 1985 NL pennant. Speed and defense continued to be the centerpiece of the Cards' success. With the breakout of preeminent base stealer Vince Coleman, the team swiped 314 bags. In the live-ball era, only the 1976 Oakland A's—who racked up an incredible 341—have stolen more. Besides Coleman, the Redbirds benefited from the addition of Clark's bat and standout offensive seasons from NL batting champion and MVP Willie McGee and Tom Herr—who amassed 110 RBIs despite hitting only eight home runs.* Andújar won 21 games and Forsch remained a stalwart in the rotation, but Tudor carried the team down the stretch, winning 20 of his last 21 decisions.

In the NLCS versus the Dodgers, Ozzie Smith muscled up with a dramatic game-winning home run in Game Six, and Jack Clark delivered the big blow in Game Seven to send the Cards back to the World Series. Their opponent in the 1985 Fall Classic was their cross-state counterparts and Herzog's former employer—the Kansas City Royals, whose roster included Dane Iorg and Lonnie Smith. St. Louis took a 3–2 series lead and were winning, 1–0, in the ninth inning of a potential clinching Game Six. First base umpire Don Denkinger infamously blew a call that opened the door for a Royals rally. Iorg—whose .522 postseason batting average remains to this day the highest in major-league history for players with at least 25 plate appearances—drove home the winning run later that inning. The Cardinals unraveled in Game Seven and lost, 11–0. Andújar pitched in relief and had a meltdown. Denkinger was the home-plate umpire, and Andújar took exception to a couple of balls he thought were in the strike zone. He charged toward Denkinger and had to be restrained by teammates before being tossed from the game. Andújar's antics had reached a breaking point. "The other players were tired of his griping and his bitching," wrote Herzog. "It had gotten to the point where he was dividing the clubhouse."[13] Maxvill traded him to Oakland that winter.

A combination of injuries and underperformance turned 1986 into a forgettable season in the annals of Cardinals baseball. Clark tore ligaments in his right thumb and was limited to only 65 games. McGee missed time with a pulled hamstring and saw his batting average plummet nearly 100 points from the year before. Herr and Pendleton each had subpar seasons at the plate and there was little offensive production from the catchers. All told, the Cardinals had the lowest team batting average (.236) and fewest runs scored of any team in the majors.

By then, only Forsch, Herr, McGee, Tito Landrum, and Ozzie Smith remained from the 1982 team. Yet, the Cardinals' style of play still offered the potential for excitement on any given day. So, when Coleman stole four bases and Forsch blasted a grand slam to defeat the Pirates on August 10, it did not move the needle on the team's playoff chances, but it turned at least one kid into a lifelong fan.

---

*Herr became the first player since George Kell in 1950 to top 100 RBIs with fewer than 10 home runs.

Chapter Notes

Chapter 1

1. *St. Louis Post-Dispatch*, February 20, 1953: 1.
2. Leonard Koppett, "Busch, Beer, and Baseball," *New York Times*, April 11, 1965: 101.
3. "Crusty Gussie, Bud Selig Offer Top-Level Contrast," *St. Louis Post-Dispatch*, October 16, 1982: 7.
4. Gabe Lacques, "50 Years After His Letter Changed Baseball Forever, Curt Flood's Sacrifice Still Resonates," *USA Today*, December 24, 2019, https://www.usatoday.com/story/sports/mlb/2019/12/24/curt-flood-letter-mlb-free-agency-bowie-kuhn/2722291001/.
5. Steve Carlton, interview by Bret Boone, *The Boone Podcast*, August 27, 2021, https://the-boone-podcast.simplecast.com/episodes/steve-carlton-joins-the-boone-podcast-upTo7gt2.
6. Dick Kaegel, "Single Dimension Catches Up with Rapp," *St. Louis Post-Dispatch*, April 26, 1978: 39.
7. Dick Kaegel, "Rapp Calls Simmons 'a Loser,' Blasts Buck for Telling," *St. Louis Post-Dispatch*, April 25, 1978: 37.
8. "The Cardinals Flounder, and 'Big Eagle' Squawks," *St. Louis Post-Dispatch*, July 20, 1988: 18.
9. Dave Luecking, "'78 Cards: A Lost Cause," *St. Louis Post-Dispatch*, July 20, 1988: 18.

Chapter 2

1. Bob Broeg, "Cards' Demise Has Been Team Effort," *St. Louis Post-Dispatch*, June 10, 1980: 11.
2. Whitey Herzog and Kevin Horrigan, *White Rat: A Life in Baseball* (New York: Harper & Row, 1987), 26.
3. Dan O'Neill, "An Odyssey Born in New Athens," *St. Louis Post-Dispatch*, July 21, 2010: 12.
4. Herzog and Horrigan, *White Rat*, 9–10.
5. Herzog and Horrigan, *White Rat*, 10.
6. O'Neill, "An Odyssey Born in New Athens."
7. Pat Jordan, "The Wit and Wisdom of the White Rat," *Los Angeles Times Magazine*, May 10, 1992: 15.
8. Herzog and Horrigan, *White Rat*, 47.
9. Herzog and Horrigan, *White Rat*, 56.
10. Herzog and Horrigan, *White Rat*, 73.
11. Herzog and Horrigan, *White Rat*, 88.
12. Rick Hummel, "Herzog Had a Royal Run in Kansas City," *St. Louis Post-Dispatch*, July 21, 2010: 15.
13. Randy McGilberry, email message to author, January 15, 2023.
14. Herzog and Horrigan, *White Rat*, 103.
15. Herzog and Horrigan, *White Rat*, 113.
16. Herzog and Horrigan, *White Rat*, 114.
17. Herzog and Horrigan, *White Rat*, 116.
18. Rick Hummel, "Boyer: 'No Emotion,'" *St. Louis Post-Dispatch*, June 9, 1980: 36.
19. Rick Hummel, "Players Take Blame for Boyer's Firing," *St. Louis Post-Dispatch*, June 9, 1980: 33.

20. Hummel, "Players Take Blame for Boyer's Firing."
21. Hummel, "Players Take Blame for Boyer's Firing."
22. Rick Hummel, "'New Air in Atmosphere' for Redbirds," *St. Louis Post-Dispatch*, June 10, 1980: 10.
23. Rick Hummel, "Hrabosky Has New Look Out of Braves' Bullpen," *St. Louis Post-Dispatch*, June 15, 1980: 88.
24. Cal Fussman, "Sweep Revitalizes Cards," *St. Louis Post-Dispatch*, June 26, 1980: 47.
25. Rick Hummel, "Streaking Redbirds Look at Standings," *St. Louis Post-Dispatch*, June 28, 1980: 5.
26. Herzog and Horrigan, *White Rat*, 117.
27. Herzog and Horrigan, *White Rat*, 117.
28. Rick Hummel, "Templeton Is Hero as 'Center Fielder,'" *St. Louis Post-Dispatch*, July 3, 1980: 63.
29. Bob Broeg, "Improving Cards Could Least Afford to Lost Templeton," *St. Louis Post-Dispatch*, July 25, 1980: 11.
30. Rick Hummel, "Claiborne Says 'Next Time' for the DH in NL," *St. Louis Post-Dispatch*, August 14, 1980: 45.
31. "Digest," *St. Louis Post-Dispatch*, August 26, 1980: 8.
32. Rick Hummel, "Says Shocked Herzog: 'John Wanted Me,'" *St. Louis Post-Dispatch*, August 18, 1980: 29.
33. Arnold Irish, "Herzog: 'I'm Right Guy for GM Job,'" *St. Louis Post-Dispatch*, August 30, 1980: 5.
34. Irish, "Herzog: 'I'm Right Guy for GM Job.'"
35. Rick Hummel, "Whitey Had No Alternative but to Become GM," *St. Louis Post-Dispatch*, August 31, 1980: 71.
36. Hummel, "Whitey Had No Alternative but to Become GM."
37. "Rincon Has a Surprise for Chicago," *St. Louis Post-Dispatch*, September 16, 1980: 25.
38. Rick Hummel, "A Hernandez Trade Isn't Impossible," *St. Louis Post-Dispatch*, October 5, 1980: 80.
39. Bob Broeg, "Brids Need More Relief and Less Wishful Thinking," *St. Louis Post-Dispatch*, October 7, 1980: 28.
40. Rick Hummel, "Herzog Studies Free-Agent List, May Skip Draft," *St. Louis Post-Dispatch*, September 21, 1980: 101.
41. Hummel, "A Hernandez Trade Isn't Impossible."
42. Herzog and Horrigan, *White Rat*, 122.
43. Herzog and Horrigan, *White Rat*, 124.
44. Rick Hummel, "Agent Will Ask Birds to Deal Slighted Simmons," *St. Louis Post-Dispatch*, December 9, 1980: 25.
45. Rick Hummel, "Kennedy Has Mixed Emotions About Exit," *St. Louis Post-Dispatch*, December 9, 1980: 28.
46. Herzog and Horrigan, *White Rat*, 127.
47. Herzog and Horrigan, *White Rat*, 128.
48. Rob Rains and Alvin Reid, *Whitey's Boys* (Chicago: Triumph Books, 2002), vii.
49. Rick Hummel, "Redbirds 'Close in Principle' on Simmons Deal," *St. Louis Post-Dispatch*, December 11, 1980: 45.
50. "Brewers' Deal Is a 'Steal,'" *St. Louis Post-Dispatch*, December 14, 1980: 95.
51. Rick Hummel, "Expos Plagued by Near-Misses," *St. Louis Post-Dispatch*, April 5, 1981: 127.
52. Herzog and Horrigan, *White Rat*, 133.

Chapter 3

1. Jeff Katz, *Split Season: 1981* (New York: St. Martin's Press, 2015), 5.
2. Jason Turbow, *They Bled Blue: Fernandomania, Strike-Shortened Mayhem, and the Weirdest Championship Baseball Had Ever Seen* (Boston: Houghton Mifflin Harcourt, 2019), 88.
3. Turbow, *They Bled Blue*, 88.
4. Rick Hummel, "Herzog Warns Cards to Stay on Run," *St. Louis Post-Dispatch*, March 4, 1981: 16.
5. *St. Louis Post-Dispatch*, April 5, 1981: 125.
6. Rick Hummel, "Cardinals Shrouded in Mystery," *St. Louis Post-Dispatch*, April 5, 1981: 125.Hummel, "Cardinals Shrouded in Mystery."
7. Hummel, "Cardinals Shrouded in Mystery."
8. Gerry Fraley, "The Million-Dollar Everyman," *Atlanta Constitution*, March 3, 1985: 66.
9. Fraley, "The Million-Dollar Everyman."

10. Tyler Kepner, *K: A History of Baseball in Ten Pitches* (New York: Doubleday, 2019), 127–28.
11. Fraley, "The Million-Dollar Everyman."
12. Fraley, "The Million-Dollar Everyman."
13. Barry Foote, interview with author, November 2, 2022.
14. Kepner, *K: A History of Baseball in Ten Pitches*, 128.
15. Foote, interview.
16. Foote, interview.
17. Neal Russo, "Sutter Relieves Cards' Worries," *St. Louis Post-Dispatch*, April 13, 1981: 23.
18. Bob Broeg, "Redbirds Change from Possums to Porcupines," *St. Louis Post-Dispatch*, April 28, 1981: 30.
19. Katz, *Split Season*, 84.
20. Rick Hummel, "Templeton Seeks Trade: 'I Want to Go Home,'" *St. Louis Post-Dispatch*, June 1, 1981: 15.
21. Hummel, "Templeton Seeks Trade: 'I Want to Go Home.'"
22. Rick Hummel, "Richards, Smith Punish Cards," *St. Louis Post-Dispatch*, June 8, 1981: 23.
23. Neal Russo, "Problems Can Be Solved, Says Quieter Templeton," *St. Louis Post-Dispatch*, June 2, 1981: 25.
24. Rick Hummel, "'Weary' Templeton Rests; Ramsey Hurt in Cards' Win," *St. Louis Post-Dispatch*, June 5, 1981: 25.
25. Rick Hummel, "Hard Work Ahead for Andújar," *St. Louis Post-Dispatch*, June 8, 1981: 24.
26. Katz, *Split Season*, 102.
27. Katz, *Split Season*, 118.
28. Rick Hummel, "Landrum Is Striking as Restaurant Trainee," *St. Louis Post-Dispatch*, July 17, 1981: 32.
29. "Fans to Have Baseball Despite Strike," *St. Louis Post-Dispatch*, June 14, 1981: 85.
30. Katz, *Split Season*, 118.
31. Katz, *Split Season*, 156.
32. Katz, *Split Season*, 181.
33. Katz, *Split Season*, 182.
34. Rick Hummel, "A Late 'Spring' Dawns at Busch," *St. Louis Post-Dispatch*, August 2, 1981: 85.
35. Hummel, "A Late 'Spring' Dawns at Busch."
36. Katz, *Split Season*, 209.
37. Brad Balukjian, *The Wax Pack: On the Open Road in Search of Baseball's Afterlife* (Lincoln: University of Nebraska Press, 2020), 51.
38. Steve Wulf, "The Bounce, the Bench, and the Boo-Birds," *Sports Illustrated*, September 7, 1981, https://vault.si.com/vault/1981/09/07/the-bounce-the-bench-and-the-boo-birds-each-in-his-own-way-garry-templeton-reggie-jackson-and-dave-parker-faced-a-slew-of-troubles-on-and-off-the-field.
39. Rick Hummel, "Cards in No Hurry for Tempy to Returns," *St. Louis Post-Dispatch*, August 27, 1981: 39.
40. Rick Hummel, "Psychiatrist to Evaluate Tempy," *St. Louis Post-Dispatch*, August 28, 1981: 19.
41. George E. Curry and Rick Hummel, "Acquaintances Say Tempy's Immaturity Part of Problem," *St. Louis Post-Dispatch*, August 30, 1981: 98.
42. Balukjian, *The Wax Pack*, 51.
43. Arnold Irish, "Cheers from Fans Greet Templeton," *St. Louis Post-Dispatch*, September 24, 1981: 43.
44. Rick Hummel, "Tempy Helps the Cards Split," *St. Louis Post-Dispatch*, September 16, 1981: 15.
45. Rick Hummel, "Top Fireman Sutter Gets $125,000 Bonus," *St. Louis Post-Dispatch*, October 5, 1981: 26.
46. Rick Hummel, "Herzog Plans for Fantasy Series," *St. Louis Post-Dispatch*, October 5, 1981: 26.
47. Hummel, "Herzog Plans for Fantasy Series."
48. Rick Hummel, "Lonnie Smith Deal Tip of the Birds' Iceberg," *St. Louis Post-Dispatch*, November 20, 1981: 29.
49. Rick Hummel, "Cubs' Change of Heart Leaves Herzog Puzzled," *St. Louis Post-Dispatch*, December 9, 1981: 33.
50. Hummel, "Cubs' Change of Heart Leaves Herzog Puzzled."
51. Rick Hummel, "Cards' Mura at a Loss When it Comes to Losing," *St. Louis Post-Dispatch*, March 10, 1982: 17.
52. Rick Hummel, "Templeton Deal Is All but Made," *St. Louis Post-Dispatch*, December 13, 1981: 104.
53. Rick Hummel, "Herzog: Cards Can't Win with Tempy," *St. Louis Post-Dispatch*, December 17, 1981: 49.
54. "Cardinals Sign Andújar to a Three-Year Contract," *St. Louis Post-Dispatch*, December 30, 1981: 13.
55. Phil Collier, "Smith Expected to

Shun Arbitration, Retain Padre Pact," *San Diego Union*, January 24, 1982: 99.
    56. Ozzie Smith and Rob Rains, *Wizard* (Chicago: Contemporary Books, 1998), 52.

Chapter 4

1. Joseph Durso, "Herzog the Dealer Going for Jackpot," *New York Times*, March 15, 1982: C3.
2. Rick Hummel, "Cards Being Watched on Bases," *St. Louis Post-Dispatch*, March 11, 1982: 45.
3. Pete Zanardi, "Dick Tettelbach," SABR BioProject, https://sabr.org/bioproj/person/dick-tettelbach/, accessed May 29, 2022.
4. Rick Hummel, "'Cycler' Porter, Calise, Fulgham Stand Out for Cards," *St. Louis Post-Dispatch*, March 9, 1982: 17.
5. Rick Hummel, "Ozzie Working Hard with Both Bat and Glove," *St. Louis Post-Dispatch*, March 16, 1982: 25.
6. Hummel, "Ozzie Working Hard with Both Bat and Glove."
7. Bill Center, "Ozzie and Whitey and Garry and Dick Suit Each Other," *San Diego Union*, March 11, 1982: 36.
8. Smith and Rains, *Wizard*, 8.
9. Smith and Rains, *Wizard*, 6.
10. John D'Acquisto, email to author, October 11, 2022.
11. Smith and Rains, *Wizard*, 17.
12. John D'Acquisto, email.
13. Smith and Rains, *Wizard*, 38.
14. Smith and Rains, *Wizard*, 61.
15. Rick Hummel, "Obie's Injury Puts Iorg on the Spot," *The Sporting News*, April 17, 1982: 30.
16. Rick Hummel, "Ozzie Smith 'Sick' of Arbitration Issue," *St. Louis Post-Dispatch*, March 31, 1982: 17.
17. Joseph Durso, "The Song of Spring," *The Sporting News*, March 6, 1982: 13.
18. Joseph Durso, "Menu's New, But Some Just Want Dessert," *The Sporting News*, April 10, 1982: 2.
19. Dan Donovan, "Pirates, Cardinals Continue Streaks," *Pittsburgh Press*, April 21, 1982: 28.

Chapter 5

1. Tom Callahan, "Joy in Back in Budville," *Time*, November 1, 1982: 75.

2. "Rosen Fumes Over Sutton's Trade Talk," *El Paso Times*, March 17, 1982: 25.
3. Rick Hummel, "Cards' Opening Act Hard to Top," *St. Louis Post-Dispatch*, April 7, 1982: 21.
4. Danny Douglas, "Cardinals Bury Astros in 14-Run Blitz," *Corpus Christi Caller-Times*, April 7, 1982: 41.
5. Darrell Porter and William Deerfield, *Snap Me Perfect! The Darrell Porter Story* (Nashville: Thomas Newson, 1984), 36.
6. Porter and Deerfield, *Snap Me Perfect*, 57.
7. Porter and Deerfield, *Snap Me Perfect*, 59.
8. Porter and Deerfield, *Snap Me Perfect*, 116.
9. Randy McGilberry, email message to author, November 10, 2022.
10. McGilberry, email, November 10, 2022.
11. McGilberry, email, November 10, 2022.
12. Porter and Deerfield, *Snap Me Perfect*, 155.
13. Porter and Deerfield, *Snap Me Perfect*, 184.
14. McGilberry, email, November 10, 2022.
15. Rains and Reid, *Whitey's Boys*, vii.
16. Porter and Deerfield, *Snap Me Perfect*, 237.
17. Arnold Irish, "Scout Praises Porter's Play," *St. Louis Post-Dispatch*, September 25, 1982: 1.
18. McGilberry, email, November 10, 2022.
19. Bob Forsch and Tom Wheatley, *Tales From the Cardinals Dugout: A Collection of the Greatest Cardinals Stories Ever Told* (New York: Sports Publishing, 2006), 39.
20. Rick Hummel, "Herzog Gives GM Position to McDonald," *St. Louis Post-Dispatch*, April 11, 1982: 3.
21. Hummel, "Herzog Gives GM Position to McDonald."
22. Hummel, "Herzog Gives GM Position to McDonald."
23. Neal Russo, "McDonald's Roots with Mets," *St. Louis Post-Dispatch*, April 11, 1982: 53.
24. Herzog and Horrigan, *White Rat*, 140.
25. Bill Conlin, "Hypnotist 'Guarantees' Bucs Will Win It All," *The Sporting News*, April 3, 1982: 43.

26. Tom Barnidge, "Cardinals Open Like April Fools," *St. Louis Post-Dispatch*, April 11, 1982: 48.
27. Russ Franke, "Cardinals Hang Tough Defeat on Pirates, Romo," *Pittsburgh Press*, April 12, 1982: 17.
28. Franke, "Cardinals Hang Tough Defeat on Pirates, Romo."
29. Bob Logan, "Cubs Futile, but Elia Attacks," *Chicago Tribune*, April 16, 1982: 67.
30. Jayson Stark, "Lonnie Smith: Another Brock?" *Philadelphia Inquirer*, July 21, 1980: 17.
31. Stark, "Lonnie Smith: Another Brock?"
32. Bill Conlin, "Fast Shuffle Shocks Lonnie Smith," *Philadelphia Daily News*, November 20, 1981: 118.
33. Hal Bodley, "Smith Starting in Phillies' Doghouse, Not in Left Field," *News Journal* (Wilmington, Delaware), April 3, 1981: 15.
34. Dane Iorg interview with the author, November 2, 2022.
35. Frank Dolson, "Smith Making Phils' Faces Red," *Philadelphia Inquirer*, April 18, 1982: 59.
36. Stan Isle, "Caught on the Fly," *The Sporting News*, April 26, 1982: 33.
37. Benjamin Hochman, "Hernandez Is Finally Where He Belongs," *St. Louis Post-Dispatch*, August 22, 2021: D6.
38. William Nack, "He's Still Not Home Free," *Sports Illustrated*, October 13, 1986: 108.
39. Keith Hernandez, "Keith Hernandez on Baseball, 'Seinfeld' and Being His Own 'Worst Enemy,'" interview by Dave Davies, *Fresh Air*, NPR, July 12, 2019, https://www.npr.org/2019/07/12/740888007/keith-hernandez-on-baseball-seinfeld-and-being-his-own-worst-enemy.
40. Nack, "He's Still Not Home Free."
41. Keith Hernandez, "Beyond the Booth: Keith Hernandez Reflects on His Mother and Her Influence on His Life," April 3, 2020, https://sny.tv/articles/beyond-the-booth-keith-hernandez-reflects-on-his-mother-and-her-influence-on-his-life.
42. Hernandez, interview.
43. Nack, "He's Still Not Home Free."
44. Nack, "He's Still Not Home Free."
45. Hernandez, interview.
46. Greg Terlecky, interview with the author, January 6, 2023.
47. Hernandez, interview.
48. Terlecky, interview.
49. Nack, "He's Still Not Home Free."
50. Hochman, "Hernandez Is Finally Where He Belongs."
51. Hochman, "Hernandez Is Finally Where He Belongs."
52. Rick Hummel, "'Grown Up' Hernandez Leads Charging Cards," *The Sporting News*, May 17, 1982: 2.
53. Hummel, "'Grown Up' Hernandez Leads Charging Cards."
54. Rick Hummel, "Cards Falling Right for Streaking Birds," *St. Louis Post-Dispatch*, April 25, 1982: 85.
55. Smith and Rains, *Wizard*, 64.
56. Rick Hummel, "Cards' Starters Surprise Critics," *The Sporting News*, May 3, 1982: 17.
57. Tim Sullivan, "Weapons Lacking, But Pastore Wins," *Cincinnati Inquirer*, May 1, 1982: 13.

Chapter 6

1. Mark Littell, *On the Eighth Day, God Made Baseball* (Self-published, 2016), 207.
2. Rick Hummel, "Reds Soto Delivers Knockout to Cards," *St. Louis Post-Dispatch*, May 2, 1982: 89.
3. Neal Russo, "Tenace's 'Cripple' Rib Prompts George to Talk," *St. Louis Post-Dispatch*, May 6, 1982: 47.
4. Dick Kaegel, "New Riches Won't Change Hendrick," *St. Louis Post-Dispatch*, February 11, 1979: 15.
5. Dave Anderson, "The Silent Card," *New York Times*, October 19, 1982: A29.
6. Joseph Wancho, "George Hendrick," SABR BioProject, https://sabr.org/bioproj/george-hendrick/.
7. Whitey Herzog and Jonathan Pitts, *You're Missin' a Great Game* (New York: Simon & Schuster, 1999), 136.
8. John D'Acquisto, email.
9. Herzog and Pitts, *You're Missin' a Great Game*, 137–138.
10. Eric Vickrey, "Willie McGee," SABR BioProject, https://sabr.org/bioproj/person/willie-mcgee/.
11. Jerry Gandy, "McGee Picks Yankees Pinstripes to Books," *Berkeley Gazette*, June 9, 1977: 24.
12. Vahe Gregorian, "The Humble Hero," *St. Louis Post-Dispatch*, August 16, 1998: 48.
13. Jane Gross, "Former Yankee Minor

Leaguer to Cardinal Success," *New York Times*, June 18, 1982: 21.

14. Stefan Wever, interview with the author, December 1, 2022.

15. Dave Anderson, "Cardinals' Willie McGee is not 'E.T.,'" *New York Times*, October 17, 1982: 484.

16. Rains and Reid, *Whitey's Boys*, 13.

17. Anderson, "The Silent Card."

18. Stan Isle, "Caught on the Fly," *The Sporting News*, May 24, 1982: 37.

19. Billy Reed, "Fisherman Landrum Could be a Big Catch for Redbirds," *Louisville Courier-Journal*, August 7, 1982: 8.

20. Rains and Reid, *Whitey's Boys*, 60.

21. Forsch and Wheatley, *Tales from the Cardinals Dugout*, 31.

22. Rick Hummel, "Cards Rally, Then Hold Off Braves, 7–6," *St. Louis Post-Dispatch*, May 16, 1982: 99.

23. Hummel, "Cards Rally, Then Hold Off Braves, 7–6."

24. "Lonnie's Homer in 10th Caps Cards' Rally," *Belleville News-Democrat*, May 16, 1982: 19.

25. Rick Hummel, "Cards' Lead Shrinks to 2," *St. Louis Post-Dispatch*, May 17, 1982: 13.

26. Rick Hummel, "Only the Plate is Missing in Cards' Loss," *St. Louis Post-Dispatch*, May 20, 1982: 47.

27. Rick Hummel, "Cards Lifted by Brummer," *St. Louis Post-Dispatch*, May 21, 1982: 27.

28. Rains and Reid, *Whitey's Boys*, 11.

29. Iorg, interview.

30. Iorg, interview.

31. Iorg, interview.

32. Frank Dolson, "The Character of Dane Iorg," *Philadelphia Inquirer*, September 10, 1982: 109.

33. Iorg, interview.

34. Rick Hummel, "Hendrick Latest to Join Cardinals' Casualty List," *St. Louis Post-Dispatch*, May 24, 1982: 19.

35. Mark Heisler, "Second String Wins It Again for Dodgers," *Los Angeles Times*, May 24, 1982: 35.

36. Heisler, "Second String Wins It Again for Dodgers."

37. Rick Hummel, "The Future Is Now for Cardinals," *St. Louis Post-Dispatch*, May 25, 1982: 23.

38. Hummel, "The Future Is Now for Cardinals."

39. Hummel, "The Future Is Now for Cardinals."

40. Rick Hummel, "Cards Hustle Past Erring Giants," *St. Louis Post-Dispatch*, May 26, 1982: 31.

41. "Clark Rips Giants Again: 'Losers,'" *San Francisco Chronicle*, May 27, 1982: 70.

42. John Stuper, interview by Kyle McClellan, *The Chatter's Box* podcast, posted August 10, 2022, https://podcasts.apple.com/us/podcast/john-stuper-1982/id1626772298?i=1000575671918.

43. Stuper, interview.

44. Rick Hummel, "Tempy Gets First Crack Here at Redbirds," *St. Louis Post-Dispatch*, May 28, 1982: 12.

45. Mike Smith, "Padres Runs Past Low-Scoring Cards," *St. Louis Post-Dispatch*, May 30, 1982: 82.

46. Neal Russo, "Cards' Holiday Blast Rips Giants," *St. Louis Post-Dispatch*, June 1, 1982: 33.

Chapter 7

1. Roger Angell, *Five Seasons* (New York: Simon & Schuster, 1977), 24.

2. Nick Sortal, "Mismatch? Stuper Answers Challenge," *Southern Illinoisan*, October 20, 1982: 11.

3. Neal Russo, "'Can't Miss' Stuper Arrives Year Late," *St. Louis Post-Dispatch*, May 30, 1982: 78.

4. Mike Kahn, "One Run Plenty for Cards, Andújar," *Belleville News-Democrat*, June 3, 1982: 25.

5. Kahn, "One Run Plenty for Cards, Andújar."

6. Kahn, "One Run Plenty for Cards, Andúar."

7. Neal Russo, "Dodgers Are Victim No. 100 for Forsch," *St. Louis Post-Dispatch*, June 5, 1982: 5.

8. Nelson Green, "Ken Forsch," SABR BioProject, https://sabr.org/bioproj/person/ken-forsch/.

9. Tom Wheatley, "Forsches Wisely Heeded Pa's Pitch," *St. Louis Post-Dispatch*, July 7, 1987: 14.

10. Forsch and Wheatley, *Tales from the Cardinals Dugout*, 3.

11. Forsch and Wheatley, *Tales From the Cardinals Dugout*, 4.

12. Terlecky, interview.

13. Terlecky, interview.

14. Neal Russo, "Forsch Avoids Jinxes, Gets No-Hitter," *St. Louis Post-Dispatch*, April 17, 1978: 25.

15. Forsch and Wheatley, *Tales from the Cardinals Dugout*, 132.
16. Mark Heisler, "Dodgers Are Looking Like a One-Man Show," *Los Angeles Times*, June 6, 1982: 63.
17. Rick Hummel, "McGee Trade Could Become Memorable," *St. Louis Post-Dispatch*, June 4, 1982: 23.
18. Jack Lang, "Cubs Pick Prep Shortstop No. 1," *The Sporting News*, June 21, 1982: 45.
19. Warren Cromartie, email.
20. Rick Hummel, "Home Run Off Sutter Beats Cardinals," *St. Louis Post-Dispatch*, June 8, 1982: 27.
21. Herzog and Horrigan, *White Rat*, 54.
22. Jeff Keener, interview with author, February 1, 2022.
23. Keener, interview.
24. Rick Hummel, "Keener Makes It to Cards' Roster in Less Than a Year," *St. Louis Post-Dispatch*, June 8, 1982: 29.
25. Keener, interview.
26. Rick Hummel, "Cards Squeeze Out Win Over Expos," *St. Louis Post-Dispatch*, June 9, 1982: 29.
27. Julio Gonzalez, "Joaquín: Facing the Future with a View from the Past," *Oakland A's Magazine*, Volume 6, Number 2: 14.
28. Gonzalez, "Joaquín: Facing the Future with a View from the Past," 12.
29. Malcom Allen, "Joaquín Andújar," in *Dominicans in the Major Leagues*, eds. Bill Nowlin and Julio M. Rodriguez (Phoenix: Society for American Baseball Research, 2022), 27.
30. Roe Skidmore, email message to author, April 3, 2022.
31. Skidmore, email.
32. Rick Hummel, "Andújar in Cadillac Class Despite Simmons' Line Drive," *St. Louis Post-Dispatch*, October 17, 1982: 89.
33. Rains and Reid, *Whitey's Boys*, 5.
34. Rick Hummel, "Andújar's Secret? 'Daddy' Knows Best," *St. Louis Post-Dispatch*, June 3, 1982: 44.
35. Hummel, "Andújar in Cadillac Class Despite Simmons' Line Drive."
36. Bill Madden, "Series Puts Like to Lots of Theories," *New York Daily News*, October 15, 1982.
37. Tyler Kepner, *The Grandest Stage: A History of the World Series* (New York: Doubleday, 2022), 274.
38. Warren Cromartie, email message to author, September 22, 2022.
39. Mike Smith, "Sutter's Great Escapes Save Cardinals," *St. Louis Post-Dispatch*, June 15, 1982: 29.
40. Mike Smith, "Sutter's Numbers Alarming," *St. Louis Post-Dispatch*, June 21, 1982: 19.
41. Smith, "Sutter's Numbers Alarming."
42. Rick Hummel, "Schmidt Talks, Krukow Silences Cards," *St. Louis Post-Dispatch*, June 24, 1982: 12.
43. Rick Hummel, "Cards Lose, 5–3, But Get Back on Top," *St. Louis Post-Dispatch*, June 26, 1982: 5.
44. Frank Dolson, "A Man Cards Can't Replace," *Philadelphia Inquirer*, June 29, 1982: 29.
45. Dolson, "A Man Cards Can't Replace."
46. Bob Logan, "Cards' Capers Delight Cubs," *Chicago Tribune*, June 28, 1982: 45.
47. Rick Hummel, "Cards' Runners Lose Compass, Game," *St. Louis Post-Dispatch*, June 28, 1982: 11.

Chapter 8

1. Corey Miller, "'I Love Teaching and I Love the Game': Cardinals Hall of Famer Willie McGee Is Still Enjoying His Baseball Ride," May 15, 2022, https://www.ksdk.com/article/sports/mlb/stl-cardinals/st-louis-cardinals-willie-mcgee-coaching-career-reflection/63-0b2f4e4f-9e05-4cb9-82bf-e75a03d7b72d.
2. Rick Hummel, "All-Star Snub Irks Andújar," *St. Louis Post-Dispatch*, July 8, 1982: 16.
3. Tim Tucker, "Garber Shows He's Mortal in 5–2 Loss," *Atlanta Constitution*, July 8, 1982: 48.
4. Tom Kleckner, "Knepper Stops Cardinals," *Corpus Christi Caller-Times*, July 12, 1982: 4.
5. Rick Hummel, "Eye-Poppers Come Naturally to Ozzie," *The Sporting News*, July 26, 1982: 18.
6. Bill Conlin, "Midseason Forecast: Phils and Braves," *The Sporting News*, July 26, 1982: 15.
7. Mike Smith, "Animated Lahti Gives Cards Lift," *St. Louis Post-Dispatch*, July 17, 1982: 5.
8. "The Morning Intell's Athletes of

the Year," *Intelligence Journal*, June 11, 1974: 18.
9. Ceasar Alsop, "Herr's Looking to a Future in Baseball," *Morning News* (Wilmington, Delaware), February 15, 1975: 23.
10. Tom Herr, interview by Frank Cusumano on KSDK St. Louis, May 26, 2020, https://youtube.com/watch?v=cvp9MOQbFb8.
11. Jim Kaat, *Still Pitching: Musings from the Mound and the Microphone* (Chicago: Triumph Books, 2003), 11.
12. Kaat, *Still Pitching*, 17.
13. Kaat, *Still Pitching*, 23.
14. Kaat, *Still Pitching*, 210.
15. Kaat, *Still Pitching*, 51.
16. Glenn Sheeley, "Cardinals' Jim Kaat: Still Going Strong at 44 Years Young," *Atlanta Constitution*, October 10, 1982: 86.
17. Mike Smith, "Logic Prevails for Hernandez, Cards," *St. Louis Post-Dispatch*, July 19, 1982: 23.
18. Keener, interview.
19. Tim Tucker, "Braves Do It Their Way," *Atlanta Constitution*, July 21, 1982: 21.
20. John McGrath, "Bloated ERA Doesn't Bother One-Trick Pony," *Atlanta Constitution*, July 21, 1982: 24.
21. Rick Hummel, "Porter Responds to Herzog's Talk with 2 Doubles," *St. Louis Post-Dispatch*, July 22, 1982: 39.
22. Hummel, "Porter Responds to Herzog's Talk with 2 Doubles."
23. Mike Kahn, "Believe It or Not, Cardinals Sweep," *Belleville News-Democrat*, July 26, 1982: 17.
24. Rick Hummel, "Bird Power by Ramsey," *St. Louis Post-Dispatch*, July 26. 1982: 17.
25. Mike Ramsey, interview with the author, July 5, 2023.
26. Rick Hummel, "The Wiz: Ozzie Dreams of Triple Play," *St. Louis Post-Dispatch*, July 27, 1982: 29.

Chapter 9

1. Ian MacDonald, "Expos Roar Back to Top Cards Again," *Montreal Gazette*, August 2, 1982: 21.
2. Mike Smith, "Cardinals Set Record for Frustration," *St. Louis Post-Dispatch*, August 3, 1982: 25.
3. Smith, "Cardinals Set Record for Frustration."

4. Dan Donovan, "Forsch Ruffles No Feathers, Still Plucks Bucs," *Pittsburgh Press*, August 4, 1982: 48.
5. Mike Kahn, "Cards Storm Back to Trip Pirates in Rain," *Belleville News-Democrat*, August 6, 1982: 21.
6. Dan Donovan, "Singin' in the Rain No Music to Pirates," *Pittsburgh Press*, August 6, 1982: 27.
7. Donovan, "Singin' in the Rain No Music to Pirates."
8. Rory Costello, "David Green," SABR BioProject, https://sabr.org/bioproj/person/david-green/.
9. Costello, "David Green."
10. Daniel Okrent, *Nine Innings* (New York: McGraw-Hill, 1985), 284.
11. Costello, "David Green."
12. Mike Kahn, "David Green: 'I Want to Play Like Clemente,'" *Belleville News-Democrat*, March 25, 1981: 63.
13. Mike Kahn, "Big Green Machine Keeps Cards Flying," *Belleville News-Democrat*, April 19, 1982: 19.
14. Rick Hummel, "Cards' Strategy Fails—Unintentionally," *St. Louis Post-Dispatch*, August 7, 1982: 7.
15. Mike Smith, "Forsch Gets No. 11, Aid from Sutter," *St. Louis Post-Dispatch*, August 4, 1982: 34.
16. Joe Donnelly, "Mets Find Themselves Caught in the Middle," *Newsday* (New York), August 11, 1982: 99.
17. Rick Hummel, "Wining Hernandez Dines on Bucs," *St. Louis Post-Dispatch*, August 16, 1982: 19.
18. Forsch and Wheatley, *Tales from the Cardinals Dugout*, 53.
19. Wayne Lockwood, "Cards Playing Tricks on Rest of NL East," *San Diego Union*, August 20, 1982: 44.
20. Dan McGrath, "Giants Trail, 7–0; Giants Win, 8–7!" *San Francisco Chronicle*, August 21, 1982: 39.
21. Brian Nielsen, "Between Milking Cows and Stealing Home, Brummer Chose Lake Land," *Journal Gazette* (Mattoon, Illinois), May 3, 2010: 14.
22. Nielsen, "Between Milking Cows and Stealing Home, Brummer Chose Lake Land."
23. "Ex-Laker Glenn Brummer Overcomes Knee Injury," *Journal Gazette* (Mattoon, Illinois), April 15, 1980: 6.
24. Rick Hummel, "Brummer Steals Game for Cards," *St. Louis Post-Dispatch*, August 23, 1982: 15.

25. Mike Kahn, "'Captain Shock' Steals Win for Redbirds," August 23, 1982: 17.
26. Rick Hummel, "Brummer's Steal of Home Plate Lives on in Cardinals Lore," *St. Louis Post-Dispatch*, December 27, 2021: B1.
27. Hummel, "Brummer Steals Game for Cards."
28. Hummel, "Brummer's Steal of Home Plate Lives on in Cardinals Lore."
29. Benjamin Hochman, "Get up, Baby, and Applaud Shannon, His 50-Year Career," *St. Louis Post-Dispatch*, September 26, 2021: D6.
30. Hummel, "Brummer's Steal of Home Plate Lives on in Cardinals Lore."
31. Rains and Reid, *Whitey's Boys*, xi.
32. Smith and Rains, *Wizard*, 68.
33. Jason Turbow, *Dynastic, Fantastic, Bombastic: Reggie, Rollie, Catfish, and Charlie Finley's Swingin' A's* (Boston: Houghton Mifflin, 2017), 85.
34. Turbow, *Dynastic, Fantastic, Bombastic*, 86.
35. Turbow, *Dynastic, Fantastic, Bombastic*, 87.
36. Pat Keefe, "If Nothing Else, Tenace Knows All About Winning," *Belleville News-Democrat*, May 24, 1981: 77.
37. Keefe, "If Nothing Else, Tenace Knows All About Winning."
38. Tom Barnidge, "Tenace's Timely Performances Give Cards Direction," *St. Louis Post-Dispatch*, May 8, 1981: 22.
39. George Medich interview with author, October 20, 2022.
40. Kit Stier, "'I'm Glad It's Over'— Henderson," *The Sporting News*, September 6, 1982: 11.
41. Mike Littwin, "Dull Dodgers Can't Cut It and Lose, 3–2," *Los Angeles Times*, August 31, 1982: 28.
42. Rick Hummel, "Stout Pen Keeping Birds in the Thick," *The Sporting News*, September 13, 1982: 25.
43. Rick Hummel, "Price Not Right for Sutton," *St. Louis Post-Dispatch*, August 31, 1982: 17.

Chapter 10

1. "LSU-NO Star Named to All-America Team," *Shreveport Journal*, June 4, 1973: 20.
2. Arnold Irish, "Rasmussen Hit the Comeback Trail South of the Border," *St. Louis Post-Dispatch*, September 26, 1982: 90.
3. Rick Hummel, "Rasmussen Faces Uphill Battle," *St. Louis Post-Dispatch*, March 14, 1982: 92.
4. Rick Hummel, "Cards Lost, Stay on Top," *St. Louis Post-Dispatch*, September 13, 1982: 16.
5. Art Spander, "The 'Stick Got to the Cards," *San Francisco Examiner*, September 6, 1982: 37.
6. Spander, "The 'Stick Got to the Cards."
7. Dan McGrath, "Lonnie Smith Deserves MVP Consideration," *San Francisco Chronicle*, September 3, 1982: 68.
8. "Giants Complete Sweep; Cards Lead by Half-Game," *Belleville News-Democrat*, September 6, 1982: 21.
9. Neal Russo, "Porter, Forsch Blank Expos," *St. Louis Post-Dispatch*, September 9, 1982: 37.
10. Michael J. Smith, "The Double Life of a Gay Dodger," May 8, 2013, https://deadspin.com/the-double-life-of-a-gay-dodger-493697377.
11. Smith, "The Double Life of a Gay Dodger."
12. Rich Ashburn, "Antics Can't Dull Lefty's Effort," *Philadelphia Daily News*, September 14, 1982: 73.
13. Rick Hummel, "Cards on Top as Sutter Stifles Schmidt," *St. Louis Post-Dispatch*, September 15, 1982: 57.
14. "Redbirds Put Philadelphia in a Funeral-Like Mood," *St. Louis Post-Dispatch*, September 16, 1982: 65.
15. Ramsey, interview.
16. Rick Hummel, "Cards Pad Lead with Blitz of New York," *St. Louis Post-Dispatch*, September 20, 1982: 27.
17. Jon Marks, "Cubs Put Phils Out of Misery; Birds' Rout of Mets Called Key," *St. Louis Post-Dispatch*, September 28, 1982: 28.
18. David Luecking, "Redbirds' Eighth Straight Jumps Lead to 5½ Games," *Belleville News-Democrat*, September 21, 1982: 21.
19. Rick Hummel, "Pitcher-Perfect Cards Pull Away," *The Sporting News*, October 4, 1982: 14.
20. Rick Hummel, "Cards Take Another Step Toward Dream," *St. Louis Post-Dispatch*, September 23, 1982: 45.
21. Eric Vickrey, "Steve Braun," SABR

BioProject, https://sabr.org/bioproj/person/steve-braun/.
  22. Lyndal Scranton, "When Cardinals Need Hits, They Call on Braun," *Springfield* (Missouri) *Leader and Press*, July 24, 1983: 57.
  23. Tom Barnidge, "Andújar's 3-Hitter Downs Cubs, 5–1," *St. Louis Post-Dispatch*, September 26, 1982: 85.
  24. Rick Hummel, "Whitey on MVP: It Fits Ozzie Just Like a Glove," *St. Louis Post-Dispatch*, September 26, 1982:
  25. Arnold Irish, "Cards' 'Ugly' Hits Are Hailed," *St. Louis Post-Dispatch*, September 27, 1982: 16.
  26. Mike Smith, "McGee Indebted to Friend Ozzie," *St. Louis Post-Dispatch*, September 28, 1982: 27.
  27. Rick Hummel, "Victory Over Expos Ends 14-Year Wait," *St. Louis Post-Dispatch*, September 28, 1982: 27.
  28. Smith, "McGee Indebted to Friend Ozzie."
  29. Mike Smith, "Redbirds Celebrate Championship Montreal Was Supposed to Win," *St. Louis Post-Dispatch*, September 28, 1982: 28.
  30. Rick Hummel, "Montreal Edges Cardinals in 'Spring Training' Game," *St. Louis Post-Dispatch*, September 29, 1982: 29.
  31. Rick Hummel, "Ozzie Smith Out Until Playoffs," *St. Louis Post-Dispatch*, October 1, 1982: 19.
  32. Tim Tucker, "Watson Joins in All the Heady Talk About a Braves Dynasty," *Atlanta Constitution*, October 5, 1982: 52.
  33. Smith and Rains, *Wizard*, 72.
  34. Tim Tucker, "Braves Will Win Pennant in 5 Games, Face Angels," *Atlanta Constitution*, October 6, 1982: 63.
  35. Jesse Outlar, "Yes, That's Really the Braves Playing," *Atlanta Constitution*, October 6, 1982: 62.

Chapter 11

  1. Tom Barnidge, "Phil Niekro: A Step Ahead of Father Time," *St. Louis Post-Dispatch*, October 6, 1982: 19.
  2. Tim Tucker, "Rain Washes Niekro Shutout with Braves in the Lead 1–0," *Atlanta Constitution*, October 7, 1982: 89.
  3. Tim Tucker, "Perez Turned Braves Around on I-285," *Atlanta Constitution*, August 29, 1982: 58.
  4. Jim Kaplan, "Easy as One, Two, Three," *Sports Illustrated*, October 16, 1982, https://vault.si.com/vault/1982/10/18/easy-as-one-two-three.
  5. David Luecking, "Forsch: 'Bob Was Masterful Tonight,'" *Belleville News-Democrat*, October 8, 1982: 28.
  6. David Luecking, "Busch Beams After Triumph," *Belleville News-Democrat*, October 10, 1982: 26.
  7. Jeff Denberg, "Cards Say They Must Bear Down in Atlanta," *Atlanta Constitution*, October 10, 1982: 83.
  8. David Luecking, "'Typical' Triumph Clinches NL Flag," *Belleville News-Democrat*, October 11, 1982: 17.
  9. Ron Martz, "Camp Knew He Was in for Trouble," *Atlanta Constitution*, October 11, 1982: 51.
  10. Neal Russo, "Tenace, Kaat Get Kick Out of Kids," *St. Louis Post-Dispatch*, October 11, 1982: 16.
  11. Russo, "Tenace, Kaat Get Kick Out of Kids."
  12. Russo, "Tenace, Kaat Get Kick Out of Kids."
  13. Bill McClellan, "Subdued Braves Wish Cards Luck in Series," *St. Louis Post-Dispatch*, October 11, 1982: 13.
  14. John Nelson, "Kuenn, Herzog Molded Teams to Reflect Themselves," *Belleville News-Democrat*, October 12, 1982: 21.
  15. Paul Domowitch, "Brewers Driving Pitchers Batty," *Philadelphia Daily News*, September 7, 1982: 82.
  16. Domowitch, "Brewers Driving Pitchers Batty."
  17. Peter H. King and Roxane Arnold, "Blaze Reaches Malibu; Anaheim Area Burned," *Los Angeles Times*, October 10, 1982: 1.
  18. Fred Lynn interview by Bret Boone, *The Boone Podcast*, July 29, 2022, https://the-boone-podcast.simplecast.com/episodes/fred-lynn-joins-the-boone-podcast-_j2TQkoF.
  19. Lynn, interview.

Chapter 12

  1. Rollie Fingers, interview by Tommy Canale, *Before the Lights* podcast, August 6, 2020, https://podcasts.apple.com/us/podcast/rollie-fingers-1981-mlb-mvp-3x-ws-champion-7x-all-star/id1501245041?i=1000487341177.
  2. Medich, interview.

3. Fingers, interview.
4. Rick Hummel, "Home Run Contrast, DH Spice Series," *St. Louis Post-Dispatch*, October 12, 1982: 11.
5. Ted Simmons, interview by Kyle McClellan, *The Chatter's Box*, August 12, 2022, https://podcasts.apple.com/us/podcast/ted-simmons-1982/id1626772298?i=1000575910895.
6. Hummel, "Home Run Contrast, DH Spice Series."
7. Jay Hurd, "Ben Oglivie," SABR BioProject, https://sabr.org/bioproj/person/ben-oglivie/.
8. Dick Kaegel, "A Contrast in Styles," *The Sporting News*, October 25, 1982: 3.
9. Mike Smith, "Brewers' 'Mr. Warmth' Proves Too Hot for Cards to Handle," *St. Louis Post-Dispatch*, October 13, 1982: 25.
10. Dave Nightingale, "Milwaukee Breaks Out in Front," *The Sporting News*, October 25, 1982: 14.

Chapter 13

1. Iorg, interview.
2. Bob Wolf, "All 'What-Ifs' Point to Fingers," *Milwaukee Journal*, October 14, 1982: C1.
3. Rick Hummel, "Whitey Plays His Ace; Sutter Baffles Brewers," *St. Louis Post-Dispatch*, October 14, 1982: 1.
4. Hummel, "Whitey Plays His Ace; Sutter Baffles Brewers."
5. Hummel, "Whitey Plays His Ace; Sutter Baffles Brewers."
6. Steve Wulf, "A Hopping Good Series," *Sports Illustrated*, October 25, 1982: 34.
7. Wulf, "A Hopping Good Series."

Chapter 14

1. Milton Richman, "Wonder-Worker Willie Has Those Brewers on Run," *St. Louis Post-Dispatch*, October 16, 1982: 7.
2. George Vecsey, "Two Old Towns with New Faces," *New York Times*, October 17, 1982: 485.
3. Peter Gammons, "Fingers' Absence a Key Factor," *The Sporting News*, November 1, 1982: 25.
4. "Brewers Insist They Can Solve Sutter Puzzle," *St. Louis Post-Dispatch*, October 16, 1982: 7.
5. "McGee's Bat, Glove Push Cards Up," *The Sporting News*, October 23, 1982: 18.
6. Mike Smith, "Vuckovich's Best Didn't Allow for McGee Factor," *St. Louis Post-Dispatch*, October 16, 1982: 5.
7. Kevin Horrigan, "Andújar Has 'Tough' Luck," *St. Louis Post-Dispatch*, October 16, 1982: 8.
8. Forsch and Wheatley, *Tales from the Cardinals Dugout*, 37.
9. John Denton, "McGee, Now a Coach, Recalls Catch from 40 Years Ago," May 12, 2022, https://www.mlb.com/news/willie-mcgee-on-cardinals-coaching-and-his-career.
10. Anderson, "Cardinals' Willie McGee Is Not 'E.T.'"
11. Richman, "Wonder-Worker Willie Has Those Brewers on Run."
12. Rick Hummel, "Wondrous Willie Puts Cards One Wing Up," *St. Louis Post-Dispatch*, October 16, 1982: 1.

Chapter 16

1. Rick Hummel, "Corey Dickerson Scratched with Sore Calf, Returns," *St. Louis Post-Dispatch*, August 14, 2022: B5.
2. NBC television broadcast of the World Series, October 20, 1982.
3. Kaegel, "A Contrast in Styles."
4. Rick Hummel, "Brewers' 'MVP' Has Cardinals Trailing in Series," *St. Louis Post-Dispatch*, October 18, 1982: 4.
5. Stuper, interview.
6. Forsch and Wheatley, *Tales from the Cardinals Dugout*, 172.

Chapter 17

1. Mike Smith, "Stuper Faces Game with Smile," *St. Louis Post-Dispatch*, October 19, 1982: 29.
2. Medich, interview.
3. Medich, interview.
4. Rick Hummel, "Brummer's Steal of Home Plate Lives on in Cardinals Lore," *St. Louis Post-Dispatch*, December 27, 2021: B1.

Chapter 18

1. Simmons, interview.
2. Rains and Reid, *Whitey's Boys*, 5.
3. Rick Hummel, "Andújar Said He'd

Do It, Then Did It," *St. Louis Post-Dispatch*, October 21, 1982: 13.
  4. Rains and Reid, *Whitey's Boys*, 5.
  5. NBC television broadcast of the World Series, October 20, 1982.
  6. Simmons, interview.
  7. Ramsey, interview.
  8. Hummel, "Andújar Said He'd Do It, Then Did It."
  9. Rains and Reid, *Whitey's Boys*, 37.
  10. Ozzie Smith, interview by Brett McMillan, *Cardinals Insider*, February 1, 2022, https://www.youtube.com/watch?v=hekwFGT1Ris.
  11. Forsch and Wheatley, *Tales from the Cardinals Dugout*, 31.
  12. Iorg, interview.
  13. NBC television broadcast of the World Series, October 20, 1982.
  14. Dave Nightingale, "Herzog's Chemistry Was Perfect Blend," *The Sporting News*, November 1, 1982: 2.

Epilogue

  1. Herzog and Horrigan, *White Rat*, 147.
  2. Herzog and Horrigan, *White Rat*, 148.
  3. Herzog and Horrigan, *White Rat*, 149.
  4. Edward H. Kohn, "Hernandez Links Drug Use, Trade," *St. Louis Post-Dispatch*, September 7, 1985: 1.
  5. Herzog and Horrigan, *White Rat*, 150.
  6. Rains and Reid, *Whitey's Boys*, 103.
  7. Herzog and Horrigan, *White Rat*, 151.
  8. Kohn, "Hernandez Links Drug Use, Trade."
  9. Rains and Reid, *Whitey's Boys*, 34.
  10. Smith and Rains, *Wizard*, 87.
  11. Smith and Rains, *Wizard*, 94.
  12. Smith and Rains, *Wizard*, 100–101.
  13. Herzog and Horrigan, *White Rat*, 186.

Bibliography

Interviews

John D'Acquisto
Warren Cromartie
Barry Foote
Dane Iorg
Jeff Keener
Randy McGilberry

George Medich
Mike Ramsey
Roe Skidmore
Greg Terlecky
Stefan Wever

Books

Angell, Roger. *Five Seasons*. New York: Simon & Schuster, 1977.
Balukjian, Brad. *The Wax Pack: On the Open Road in Search of Baseball's Afterlife*. Lincoln: University of Nebraska Press, 2020.
Forsch, Bob, and Tom Wheatley, *Tales from the Cardinals Dugout: A Collection of the Greatest Stories Ever Told*. New York: Sports Publishing, 2006.
Herzog, Whitey, and Kevin Horrigan. *White Rat: A Life in Baseball*. New York: Harper & Row, 1987.
Herzog, Whitey, and Jonathan Pitts. *You're Missin' a Great Game*. New York: Simon & Schuster, 1999.
Kaat, Jim, and Phil Pepe. *Still Pitching: Musings from the Mound and the Microphone*. Chicago: Triumph, 2013.
Katz, Jeff. *Split Season: 1981*. New York: St. Martin's Press, 2015.
Kepner, Tyler. *The Grandest Stage: A History of the World Series*. New York: Doubleday, 2022.
_____. *K: A History of Baseball in Ten Pitches*. New York: Doubleday, 2019.
Littell, Mark. *On the Eighth Day, God Made Baseball*. Self-published, 2016.
Nowlin, Bill, and Julio M. Rodriguez, eds. *Dominicans in the Major Leagues*. Phoenix: Society for American Baseball Research, 2022.
Okrent, Daniel. *Nine Innings*. New York: McGraw-Hill, 1985.
Porter, Darrell, and William Deerfield. *Snap Me Perfect! The Darrell Porter Story*. New York: Thomas Nelson, 1984.
Rains, Rob, and Alvin Reid. *Whitey's Boys*. Chicago: Triumph, 2022.
Smith, Ozzie, and Rob Rains. *Wizard*. Chicago: Contemporary, 1988.
Turbow, Jason. *Dynastic, Fantastic, Bombastic: Reggie, Catfish, and Charlie Finley's Swingin' A's*. Boston: Houghton Mifflin, 2017.
Turbow, Jason. *They Bled Blue: Fernandomania, Strike-Season Mayhem, and the Weirdest Championship Baseball Had Ever Seen*. Boston: Houghton Mifflin Harcourt, 2019.

Newspapers and Magazines

Atlanta Constitution
Belleville (IL) News-Democrat
Berkeley Gazette
Chicago Tribune
Cincinnati Inquirer
Corpus Christi Caller-Times
Delaware News Journal
El Paso Times
Intelligencer Journal
Los Angeles Times
Louisville Courier Journal
Mattoon Journal Gazette
Milwaukee Journal
Montreal Gazette
Morning News
New York Daily News
New York Times
Newsday
Oakland A's Magazine
Philadelphia Daily News
Philadelphia Inquirer
Pittsburgh Press
St. Louis Post-Dispatch
San Diego Union
San Francisco Chronicle
San Francisco Examiner
Shreveport Journal
Southern Illinoisan
The Sporting News
Sports Illustrated
Springfield (MO) Leader and Press
Time
USA Today

Other Resources and Internet Sites

baseball-reference.com
Before the Lights Podcast
The Boone Podcast
The Chatter's Box Podcast
deadspin.com
Fresh Air Podcast
ksdk.com
mlb.com
sny.tv
Society for American Baseball Research BioProject
youtube.com

Index

Numbers in ***bold italics*** indicate pages with illustrations

Aaron, Henry "Hank" 113, 129, 169
ABC Television 159
Albany, NY 97
Albion, IL 107
All-Star Game: (1981) 45; (1982) 118–20
Allen, Dick 9, 93
Allen, Neil 204
Alvin, TX 61
American Association 31, 94, 131
Anderson, Sparky 47, 150, 167, 202
Andújar, Joaquín 4, 48, 51–52, 58–59, 68, 71, 75, 80, 89–90, 95–96, 98, 101, 113–14, 116, 118, 127, 129, 133–34, 138, 142, 146–47, 149, 151–52, 155–56, 159, 164, 203, 206–7; childhood and pre-1982 career 109–10, ***111***; performance in the 1982 World Series 179, 181–82, 184, 196–99, 202; traded to the Cardinals 41–42
Angell, Roger 100
Anheuser-Busch 7, 168, 178, 206
Aparicio, Luis 120
Arizona Fall League 56
Arkansas Travelers 26, 100, 108; *see also* Little Rock, Arkansas
Ashburn, Richie 148
Ashby, Alan 62
Aspromonte, Ken 85
Astrodome 52, 61–62
AstroTurf 55, 160, 197
Atlanta Braves 8, 22, 57, 75, 86, 88–91, 118, 120, 125–26, 128, 135, 139, 153, 155–65, 206
Atlanta Constitution 157
Atlanta-Fulton County Stadium 22, 89, 160

Backman, Wally 108
Bair, Doug 47, 59, 83, 89–90, 98, 112–13, 115, 118, 125, 128, 145–46, 149–50, 154, 162–63, 176–77, 182, 187, 198, 205
Baker, Dusty 94, 148

Baltimore Orioles 17, 45, 51–52, 60–61, 105, 140, 156, 158, 166, 179
Balukjian, Brad 47
Bamberger, George 108, 134
Bando, Sal 18, 33, 141
Banks, Ernie 165
Bannister, Floyd 58
Barnidge, Tom 70
Baseball Writers' Association of America 60
Bass, Kevin 143
Bauman, Bob 181
Baumgarten, Ross 70
Baylor, Don 165, 167
Bean, Billy 148
Bedrosian, Steve 86, 125–26, 157, 161
Belanger, Mark 42
Belleville, Illinois 12, 16, 52
Belleville News-Democrat 3
Bench, Johnny 60, 64, 89, 117
Benedict, Bruce 161–62, 164
Berenyi, Bruce 121
Bergesch, Bill 88
Bergman, Dave 136
Berra, Dale 69, 71
Berra, Yogi 69
Bielecki, Mike 1
Billboard 88
Bjorkman, George 50, 58–59
Bluefields, Nicaragua 131
Blyleven, Bert 14
Boggs, Tommy 157
Bonds, Bobby 14, 94
Bonilla, Juan 92
Bonner Springs, KS 63
Boone, Bob 33, 42
Boston Braves 169
Boston Red Sox 8, 10, 12, 45, 60, 91–92, 116, 128, 155, 157–58

223

Bowa, Larry 71
Boyer, Ken 8, 11, 14, 20–22, 78, 146–147, 159
Branson, MO 16
Braun, Steve 34–35, 54, 59–60, 62, 105, 113, 138, 151–52, 162, 165, 178, 199–200
Breadon, Sam 7
Brecheen, Harry 102
Breining, Fred 146
Brenly, Bob 136, 147
Brett, George 19, 65, 120
Brigham Young University 93
Brito, José 59
Brock, Lou 8–14, 74, 79, 135, 142, 175
Broeg, Bob 24, 27, 39
Broglio, Ernie 8
Brooklyn Dodgers 7, 76; *see also* Los Angeles Dodgers
Brooks, Hubie 108
Brown, Bobby 87
Browne, Byron 110
Browning, Cal 3
Browning, Jim 9
Brummer, Bob (Glenn's father) 137
Brummer, Glenn 28, 40, 59, 91–93, 96, 102, 113, 136–37, 165, 178, 194; steal of home **138**–39
Brusstar, Warren 75
Bruton, Billy 17
Buck, Jack 2, 11, 43, 107
Buckner, Bill 27, 71, 153
Budweiser beer 8, 130
Burke, Glenn 147–48
Burke, Joe 20, 66
Burris, Ray 128
Burroughs, Jeff 57
Busby, Steve 34–35
Busch, August A., Jr. "Gussie" 7–9, 11–12, 15, 18, 20–21, 25–26, 28, 44, 46, 68–69, 83, 88, 164, 171, 192, 202
Busch (Memorial) Stadium (II) 1, 4, 8, 11, 19, 41–42, 45–47, 80, 97–98, 101, 108, 113, 120, 122, 127, 137, 151, 153, 157, 159–60, 175–76, 178, 197, 200, 206; dimensions 23
Bush, George H.W. 55
Butler, Brett 163
Butler Community College 100

Caldwell, Mike 172–74, 189–91, 200
California Angels 19, 60–61, 128, 143–44, 156, 158; in 1982 ALCS 165–67
California Polytechnic State University 56
Calise, Mike 91
Calvino, Wilfred 109
Camp, Rick 89, 91, 118, 125, 164
Campanella, Roy 129

Campanis, Al 148
Campbell, Dave 43
Candelaria, John 130, 135
Candlestick Park 76, 95–96, 145
Captain and Tennille 162
Capuchino High School (San Bruno, CA) 77
Caray, Harry 107
Carbo, Bernie 10, 12
Carew, Rod 165
Carlton, Steve 4, 8, 41, 74–75, 80–81, 83, 96, 114–16, 130, 148, 151; trade to the Phillies 9–10
Carter, Gary 39, 106, 108, 120, 154
Carty, Rico 109
Cash, Norm 17
Cashen, Frank 33
Cedeño, César 81, 83
Centennial High School (Compton, CA) 73
Central American Games 132
Cepeda, Orlando 8
Cesar's Inn 180
Cey, Ron 43, 94
Chambliss, Chris 86, 89, 91, 118, 157, 161, 163–65
Chandler, Albert "Happy" 129
Charleston Pirates 100
Cheers 155
Cherre, C.J. 196
Chévez, Tony 133
Chicago Cubs 8, 12, 14, 24–25, 27, 29, 35–38, 44, 47–49, 51, 61, 71–72, 83, 96, 99, 106, 112, 114–17, 128, 130, 133, 146, 152–55, 158, 205–6
Chicago Tribune 71, 115
Chicago White Sox 44, 86–87, 123–24, 143, 155, 158, 173
CHiPs 191
Christenson, Larry 116
Cincinnati Reds 8, 22, 44–45, 47, 49, 59–61, 81–82, 85–86, 89, 109–10, 117, 120–23, 140–41, 150, 158, 206
Cisco, Galen 65
Citarella, Ralph 50
Claiborne, John 12, 14–15, 20–21, 24–25
Clark, Jack 43, 96, 146, 206–7
Clearwater, FL 73
Clemens, Doug 8
Clemente, Roberto 89, 133
Cleveland Indians 14, 18, 24, 51, 74, 84, 106, 152, 158, 170
Clinton, Iowa 64
Clyde, David 19
Cobb, Ty 60, 113, 155, 166
Colavito, Rocky 17
Coleman, Jerry 25, 43, 57

Index

Coleman, Vince 2, 106, 206–7
Collins, Dave 81
Columbus, OH 87
Comiskey Park 123
Commerce, OK 16
Compton, CA 73
Concepción, Dave 83, 117–18, 120
Conlin, Bill 120
Cooper, Cecil 5, 120, 166–67, 172–73, 175–78, 180, 182, 187, 189–92, 194, 197–98
Cooper, Mort 102
Cooperstown, NY 5, 129, 147, 173; *see also* National Baseball Hall of Fame
Corcoran, Fred 69
Corrales, Pat 79
Cosell, Howard 159, 182
Costas, Bob 202
Cowens, Al 65
Craig, Roger 57
Crawford, Jerry 92
Crawford, Sam 166
Cromartie, Warren 106, 111–12
Cruz, Hector 10
Cruz, José 119
Cunningham, Joe 54
Curtis, John 92, 143
Cy Young Award 9–10, 20, 24, 35, 37, 49, 74, 105, 129, 151, 170

D'Acquisto, John 56–57, 85
Dallas, TX 29
Dalton, Harry 30, 33, 99, 169
Dan Ryan Expressway 115
Danville, IL 64
Dark, Alvin 56–57
Davis, Ron 30
Dawson, Andre 39, 106, 112, 120, 128, 133, 153–54
Dayley, Ken 89
Dean, Dizzy 7, 102
DeCinces, Doug 42, 166
DeJesús, Iván 51
DeLeón, Luis 53
Denkinger, Don 207
Denny, John 11, 14, 143, 151
Denver Bears 17
Detroit Tigers 8, 12, 17, 19, 43, 56, 82–83, 91, 114, 140, 158, 166, 169, 205
Devine, Bing 8–12, 18, 28, 47
Diablo Valley College 87
Díaz, Bo 51, 74, 80
DiLullo, Ralph 36
DiMaggio, Joe 16, 77
DiPino, Frank 2, 143
Doak, Bill 102
Dobson, Pat 194
Dodger Stadium 50, 95

Dolson, Frank 74
Dominican Winter League 42, 110
Donegal High School (Mount Joy, PA) 35
Donovan, Dan 130
Downing, Brian 166
Driessen, Dan 82, 117
drug use in baseball 203–4
Drysdale, Don 4
Duke University 121
Duncan, Dave 85, 140
Dunston, Shawon 106
Durham, Leon 14, 29, 71

Easler, Mike 49, 69
Eastern Michigan University 82
Eckersley, Dennis 120
Edelen, Joe 47
Edmonton Oilers (NHL) 59
Edwards County High School (Albion, IL) 107
Edwardsville Intelligencer 2
Effingham (IL) High School 137
Eichelberger, Juan 52
Elia, Lee 71–72, 153
Enberg, Dick 191
E.T. the Extra-Terrestrial 109, 182
Eureka, CA 93
Evans, Darrell 101, 136
Evans, Jim 180, 193

Fairfield, IL 137
Falcone, Pete 12, 147, 150
Fanning, Jim 112
Fast Times at Ridgemont High 135
Feeney, Charles "Chub" 160
Fiala, Neil 47
Fingers, Rollie 25, 28–30, 49, 167, 169–71, 177
Finley, Charlie 18, 140
Fisk, Carlton 66, 120
Five Seasons 100; *see also* Angell, Roger
Flanagan, Mike 51
Flannery, Tim 98
Flood, Curt 8–9, 32
Florida State League 77
Foote, Barry 37–38
Ford, Dan 166
Ford, Joe 89
Fordham University 69
Forsch, Bob 1, 3, 5, 10–11, 14, 26–27, 35, 38, 40, 44–45, 51, 58–59, 62, 68, 70, 74, 80–81, 88, 91–93, 95, 98, 108, 111–14, 116, 119, 130, 133, 140, 146–48, 150, 155–56, 203, 205, 207; childhood and minor-league career 102–3; 1982 NLCS Game One win 160–62; 1982 World Series performance

172–73, 189–91; no-hitter on 4/16/78 103, *104*
Forsch, Freda (Bob's mother) 102
Forsch, Herbert (Bob's father) 102
Forsch, Ken 102–104, 111, 167
Forster, Terry 102
Fort Lauderdale, FL 87
Fort Leonard Wood, MO 17
Fosse, Ray 85
Foster, George 60, 81, 108, 113
Fournier, Jim 16
Franco, Julio 79
Francona, Terry 112
Franks, Herman 37
Freese, David 2
Frey, Jim 45
Frick, Ford 8
Froemming, Bruce 46
Fryman, Woodie 128–129, 133
Fulgham, John 12, 14, 22, 25, 35, 58

Gale, Rich 95–96
Gamble, Oscar 87
Gantner, Jim 167, 173, 181, 186–87, 190, 193–94, 197–200
Garagiola, Joe 196
Garber, Gene 22, 86, 90–91, 118, 125, 157, 163–64
Garner, Phil 40
Garvey, Steve 94, 105
Gashouse Gang 7
Geren, Bob 29
Gibson, Bob 3, 8–10, 78, 96, 102, 104, 137, 157, 159, 170
Gieselmann, Gene 68, 92, 194
Glens Falls, NY 97
González, Julio 34, 59, 70, 75, 98, 150, 155, 194, 203
Gooden, Dwight 106, 205
Goodyear Blimp 172
Gossage, Rich "Goose" 20, 167
Gottlieb, Ed 52
Grand Rapids, MI 123
Granite City, IL 16
Grant, Jim "Mudcat" 124
Grant's Farm 21, 25
Green, Dallas 51, 71, 73
Green, David 30, 35, 43, 51, 58–59, 75, 81, 84, 86, 95–96, 106, 112, 134–35, 138–39, 143, 150, 156, 163, 172, 175, 177, 189–91, 194, 199, 205–6; childhood and minor-league career 131, *132*, 133
Green, Edward "Eduardo" (David's father) 131, 133
Greene, Terry 133
Gregg, Eric 118
Gretzky, Wayne 59
Grich, Bobby 120, 166
Griffey, Ken 60, 81
Griffith, Calvin 124
Griffith, Clark 44
Groat, Dick 8
Guerrero, Pedro 94
Guidry, Ron 30, 50
Gulf Coast League 36, 109
Gullickson, Bill 73, 108, 112, 153
Gumbel, Bryant 147
Gwynn, Tony 125

Haas, Moose 167, 185–86, 199
Hacker, Rich 107
Haines, Jesse 102, 104
Haller, Bill 178
Hammaker, Atlee 101, 138
Harcourt, LaRue 29
Harper, Terry 118
Harrisburg, IL 107
Hawaii Islanders 125
Hays, Ernie 178
Heap, Danny 119
Hebner, Richie 43
Heidemann, Jack 85
Hempfield High School (Lancaster, PA) 121
Henderson, Rickey 39, 60, 120, 142, 146, 156
Henderson, Steve 71
Hendrick, George 12, 22, 24, 27, 34–35, 49, 60, 62, 71–72, 75, 79, 81, 83, 86, 89–91, 95, 98, 102, 114, 116, 118–19, 126, 128, 134, 136, 141, 144–45, 147, 149, 161, 163–64, 205–6; in the 1982 World Series 169, 171, 176–78, 180, 182, 185–87, 189–91, 193–94, 197, 199–202; pre-1982 career, origin of the nickname Silent George *84*, 85; trade to the Cardinals 11, 85
Henry Ells High School (Richmond, CA) 86
Hernandez, Gary (Keith's brother) 76
Hernandez, Jacquelyn (née Jordan; Keith's mother) 76
Hernandez, John (Keith's father) 76–77, 79
Hernandez, Keith 10–12, 22–23, 27, 29, 35, 48, 58, 61–62, 70–71, 75, 81–83, 90, 98, 101, 119–20, 122–23, 126, 128, 134–36, 148, 153–56, 160–64; childhood and minor-league career 76–77, *78*; in drug use 203; the 1982 World Series 171, 173–78, 181–82, 185–87, 189–91, 193–94, 197–200, 202; 1000th career hit 74; traded to the Mets 204–5
Hernandez, Willie 71
Herndon, Larry 91

Index

Herr, Jeff (Tom's brother) 121
Herr, Tom 12, 14, 22, 24, 26, 28–29, 35, 55, 58, 60, 62, 71–72, 75, 81–82, 89, 95, 98, 107, 116, 118, 121, 129, 134, 145, 151–52, 154, 156, 162–64, 205–7; minor-league career *122*; in the 1982 World Series 173, 176–78, 185, 192–94, 197–98, 200
Herzog, Dorrel "Whitey" 3–5, 7, 22–32; 34–35, 38–41, 43, 46–55, 58–60, 67–69; 72, 75, 78–81, 83–85, 88–95, 97, 99, 104–9, 112–14, 117–19, 121–22, 124–26, 130–36, 138–39, 141–42, 149–52, 154, 157, 159, 161, 163–64, 171–75, 203–4, 206–7; childhood 15–16; hiring by the Cardinals 20, *21*; managing the 1982 World Series 170–71, *172*, 173–78, 180, 182, 184, 187–91, 194, 198–99, 202; playing career 16–18, 124; as Rangers manager 18–19; as Royals manager 19–20, 65–66
Herzog, Edgar (Whitey's father) 15
Herzog, Lietta (née Fanke; Whitey's mother) 15
Herzog, Mary Lou (née Sinn; Whitey's wife) 17–18, 25
Highland, IL 12
Hiller, Chuck 30, 43, 55, 86, 91, 139, 145, 161, 182
Hiram Johnson High School (Sacramento, CA) 103
Hisle, Larry 140
Holland, MI 123
Hollywood, FL 51
Hood, Don 14
Hooton, Burt 49, 143
Hope College 123
Horner, Bob 57, 86, 89, 91, 118, 157, 163–65
Hoscheit, Vern 15
Householder, Paul 81, 117
Houston Astros 2, 41, 48–49, 52, 60–62, 68, 103, 110–11, 119, 126–27, 143, 158
Houston Buffaloes 76
Howe, Steve 73
Howell, Roy 173, 175, 199, 202
Howser, Dick 27
Hrabosky, Al 10, 22, 78, 90
Hubbard, Glenn 162
Hubert H. Humphrey Metrodome 60, 105
Hudson River 97
Hughes, Dick 192
Hummel, Rick 27, 40, 52, 55, 71, 92, 95, 114, 143, 155
Hunter, Jim "Catfish" 18
Hurdle, Clint 43

Illinois Highway Department 15
Independence, MO 17
Indianapolis, IN 109–10

Inside Sports 97, 148
Iorg, Dane 27, 35, 59–60, 62, 70, 74, 80, 92–94, 98, 114–15, 121, 133–34, 136, 138, 153, 163, 175–77, 180, 182, 186, 192–94, 197–99, 201–202, 206–7
Iorg, Garth 93

Jack Murphy Stadium 43, 92, 142
Jackson, Larry 102
Jackson, Reggie 4, 50, 60, 85, 87, 120, 140, 165, 173, 200
Jackson, Travis 129
The Jackson 5 89
Jaffe, Jay 147
Jarreau, Al 189
Javier, Julian 8–9
Jenkins, Ferguson "Fergie" 71, 96, 114, 130, 153, 155
Joan Jett and the Blackhearts 88
Jobe, Dr. Frank 40
John, Tommy 12, 50, 143, 166
Johnny Londoff Chevrolet 2
Johnson, Walter 96
Johnson City, Tennessee 122
Johnstone, Jay 93, 114
Jones, Jimmy 106
Jones, Ruppert 92
Joplin, MO 55, 63
Jordan, Michael 141
Jorgensen, Mike 127

Kaat, Jim 3, 5, 15, 28, 48, 59, 62, 70, 81–82, 107, 115–16, 119, *125*, 126, 129–30, 136, 138, 145–46, 150, 173, 176, 182, 187, 198, 205; childhood and pre-1982 career 123–24
Kaat, John (Jim's father) 123
Kaegel, Dick 11
Kaline, Al 17
Kansas City Athletics 17–18, 140; *see also* Oakland Athletics
Kansas City Royals 19–20, 28, 30, 34, 38, 43, 45, 49–50, 61, 65–67, 93, 128, 152, 156, 158, 206–7
Kaskaskia River 15
Katz, Jeff 42, 45
Kauffman, Ewing 20
Keener, Jeff 105, 107–8, 125, 127, 130, 144
Keener, John (Jeff's father) 107
Kell, George 207
Keller, Charlie 181
Kelly, Grace 148
Kennedy, Bob 29, 77, 103
Kennedy, Terry 14, 24, 28–29, 92, 135
Keough, Marty 157
Key West, FL 36
Kiener Plaza 168

Kingman, Dave 108, 112, 147
Kison, Bruce 167
Kissell, George 103, 122, 135
Kittle, Hubert "Hub" 31, 42, 68, 80, 100, 110–11, 114, 150, 172, 187, 198–99
KMOX Radio (St. Louis) 2, 43, 139
Knepper, Bob 68, 119, 126
Knight, Ray 119
Knights of the Cauliflower Ear 84
Knowles, Darold 12
Kool & the Gang 168
Korean War 16
Koufax, Sandy 4, 124
Kroc, Ray 141
Krol, Jack 11
Krukow, Mike 37, 51, 79, 113, 148
Kubek, Tony 181
Kuenn, Audrey (Harvey's wife) 180
Kuenn, Harvey 5, 99, 116, 166, 170–71, *172*, 175, 177–78, 180, 182, 186, 191, 198–200
Kuhlmann, Fred 206
Kuhn, Bowie 9, 33, 44, 167, 193, 202
Kuzava, Bob 16

LaCorte, Frank 81
Ladd, Pete 167, 177–78
Laguna Hills, CA 62
Lahti, Jeff 59, 114, 119, 121, 129, 134, 136, 138, 150, 154, 165, 173, 178, 187
Lajoie, Nap 154
Lake Land College 137
Lake Michigan 123, 180
Lake of the Ozarks, MO 20
Lamp, Dennis 12
Lancaster, PA 35–36, 121
Landreaux, Ken 140
Landrum, Terry "Tito" 34–35, 60, 84, 89–90, 93, 96, 105, 115, 131, 144–45, 152, 165, 207
Lanier, Hal 2, 30, 43, 86
Lanier, Max 30, 102
LaPoint, Dave 30, 35, 43, 48, 58–59, 81, 93, 96–98, 112–13, 115, 119, 123, 125, 130, 134–36, 146, 151, 153–54, 156, 165, 173, 178, 185–87, 196, 206
Larsen, Don 17
Larson, Dan 51
Laskey, Bill 101, 136
Lasorda, Tommy 94, 118–20, 139, 159, 167
Lau, Charlie 20
Lavelle, Gary 46, 105, 138–39
Lea, Charlie 112
Lee, Bill "Spaceman" 43
LeMaster, Johnny 101
Lemon, Bob 49–50
Lentine, Jim 83
Leonard, Dennis 19

Leonard, Jeffrey 136, 146
Leones de Yucatán 145
Lezcano, Sixto 30, 35, 51, 53, 92, 135
Liebrandt, Charlie 82, 122–123
Littell, Mark 14–15, 35, 45, 48, 59, 70, 81–82, 90, 112, 114–15, 125
Little Rock, AR 43; *see also* Arkansas Travelers
Littlefield, John 22, 29
Lloyd's of London 33
Locke High School (Los Angeles, CA) 56
Logan, Bob 115
Lollar, Tim 98, 142
Lombardi, Vince 69
London, Dr. Stan 181
Lopes, Davey 60, 94, 146
López Portillo, José 42
Los Angeles Dodgers 4, 9, 24, 39, 43, 49–50, 60, 94–95, 102, 105–6, 121, 124, 135, 139–40, 142–43, 145, 148, 152–53, 155–56, 158, 160, 173, 175, 207; *see also* Brooklyn Dodgers
Los Angeles Lakers (NBA) 84
Louisiana State University-New Orleans 144
Louisville Redbirds 60, 91, 101, 112, 114, 139
Lucas, Gary 98
Lucasville, OH 140–41
Luzinski, Greg 51, 73, 93
Lyle, Sparky 20, 143
Lynch, Ed 112
Lynn, Fred 45, 120, 165, 167

Mack, Connie 27
Madden, Mike 143
Maddox, Garry 51, 93, 104
Madlock, Bill 69–70
Maguolo, Lou 16
Mahler, Rick 91, 118, 157
Major League (film) 179
Malone, Moses 149
Mantle, Mickey 16–17
Marichal, Juan 109, 196
Marietta, GA 22
Marion, Marty 7
Maris, Roger 17
Marshall, Mike 12
Martin, Billy 19, 39, 50, 60, 120
Martin, Fred 36–37
Martin, John 35, 40, 48, 51, 58–59, 68, 71, 82–83, 90–91, 93, 105, 130, 136, 190
Martin, Pepper 7
Martínez, Dennis 133
Martínez, Silvio 12, 14, 25, 35, 40, 42, 51
Mathews, Eddie 169
Matthews, Gary 51, 73, 114, 116

Index

Mattick, Bobby 64
Mattingly, Don 87
Mattoon Indians 137
Mauch, Gene 26, 156, 166–67
Mavis, Bob 64
Maxvill, Dal 9, 206–7
May, Lee 19
May, Milt 46, 139
May, Rudy 124
Mayberry, John 19–20, 65
Mays, Willie 132, 145
McAlester, OK 16
McBride, Bake 10, 27, 51, 94
McCarver, Tim 8, 79
McClure, Bob 177, 182, 188, 191, 198–99
McDonald, Joe 28, 47, 68–69, 88, 145, 206
McGee, Hurdice (Willie's father) 86–87
McGee, Jesse Mae (Willie's mother) 86
McGee, Willie 1, 4, 7, 58, 60, 89–93, 95–96, 98, 105–6, 108–9, 112–13, 115, 117–19, 126, 128, 134, 136, 138–40, 146, 149, 153–54, 156, 161–65, 172, 175–78, 185–86, 190–92, 194, 197, 202, 205, 207; childhood and minor-league career 86–87; 1982 World Series Game Three performance 180–82, **183**, 184; trade to the Cardinals 50–51, **88**
McGilberry, Randy 19–20, 65–67
McGlothen, Lynn 10
McGrath, Dan 146
McKeon, Jack 19, 41, 51
McNally, Dave 32
McNamara, John 120
McRae, Hal 19, 65
Medich, George "Doc" 142, 170–171, 193–94
Medwick, Joe 7
Melvin, Virgil 108
Memphis, TN 112
Messersmith, Andy 32
Mexican League 36, 54, 144–145
Mexican Winter League 101, 132
Meyers, Joel 159
Miami Marlins (minor league) 17, 107
Michael, Gene 49
Michaels, Al 159
Midland, TX 37
Miller, Eddie 86
Miller, Marvin 32–33, 40, 42–43
Miller Lite beer 20, 174
Milner, Eddie 81, 117
Milwaukee Braves 169, 179
Milwaukee Brewers 2, 5, 30, 35, 49–50, 60–65, 92, 97, 99, 116, 128, 132, 142, 156, 158; 1982 ALCS versus the Angels 165–67; 1982 World Series 169–202

Milwaukee County Stadium 142, 179–80, 185–86, 189, 191
Minnesota Twins 26, 34, 44, 60, 105, 117, 124, 152, 158
Minton, Greg 136
Mississippi River 105, 135
MLB Network 57
Mobile, AL 55
Moffett, Kenneth 42
Molitor, Paul 5, 166, 170, 172–78, 180, 186–87, 189–92, 194, 196–99
Money, Don 182, 186–87, 193, 202
Monge, Sid 79
Montañez, Willie 9
Montreal Expos 8, 10, 15, 21, 27, 39, 41, 43, 47–49, 53, 60, 69, 81, 92, 99, 105–8, 111–12, 114, 116, 120, 128–30, 133, 139, 146, 149–50, 153–54, 158, 160
Moore, Charlie 173, 175–76, 181–82, 186–87, 190–91, 197, 199–200
Moore, Terry 7
Moreland, Keith 51, 71, 117
Moreno, Omar 49
Morgan, Joe 136, 146, 156
Morgan, Wayne 86
Morris, John 2
Morris, Matt 102
Mound City Brewing Company 15
Mozzali, Mo 47
Mumphrey, Jerry 14, 87
Municipal Stadium (Cleveland) 45
Municipal Stadium (Kansas City) 18
Munson, Thurman 66
Mura, Steve 51–53, 58–59, 70–72, 82, 91, 95–96, 105, 107, 112–13, 121, 126, 128, 136, 143, 147, 149, 156, 190, 203
Murphy, Dale 4, 73, 86, 90–91, 118, 120, 157, 162–63, 165
Murray, Eddie 56, 84
Musial, Stan 7–8, 45–46, 69, 76, 103, 192

Nashville Sounds 87
National Baseball Hall of Fame 3, 8, 30, 71, 77, 125, 129, 147, 159; *see also* Cooperstown, New York
National Football League 189
National Hockey League 59
National Labor Relations Board 40
NBC Television 181, 189, 191, 196, 202
Negro Leagues 23
Nettles, Graig 147
New Athens, IL 15
New Athens High School 15–16
New Orleans, Louisiana 94, 126
New York Giants 152; *see also* San Francisco Giants
New York Mets 9–10, 12, 18, 20, 26, 28,

39–40, 47–49, 59–60, 68–69, 84, 96, 99, 105–6, 108, 111–13, 116, 127–28, 130, 133–34, 146–47, 149–51, 158, 204–6
New York Times 87, 173
New York Yankees 8, 15–17, 20, 30, 45, 49–51, 57–58, 60, 66, 83, 86–88, 93, 124, 138, 158, 179, 184
Newcombe, Don 66
Niekro, Joe 61, 68, 81, 119, 156, 159
Niekro, Phil 91, 126, 157, 159–63
Nixon, Otis 87
Nolan, Gary 141
Noles, Dickie 51, 71
Norris, Mike 39

Oakland Athletics 12, 18, 24, 30, 34, 39, 49–50, 60, 84, 91, 94, 120, 140–142, 148, 150, 156, 158, 206–7; *see also* Kansas City Athletics
Oakland-Alameda County Coliseum 50
Oberkfell, Ken 12, 27, 35, 43, 48, 58–59, 83, 89–91, 95–96, 98, 108, 115–16, 118, 126, 129, 134, 138, 151, 153, 155–56, 161–64, 171, 173, 176–77, 182, 185–87, 190–91, 193–94, 197–98, 206
Odom, Blue Moon 18
Oelkers, Bryan 106
Oglivie, Ben 167, 171–73, 175–77, 182, 186–87, 189–93, 197, 200, 202
Oklahoma City 89ers 73, 93
Oklahoma City, OK 63, 73, 79
Old Dominion University 35
Oliver, Al 106, 129, 140, 154
Olmsted, Al 29, 53
Olney, IL 137
Olympic Stadium 21, 39, 48, 108, 120, 128, 153
Oneonta, NY 87
Oregon State University 102–3
Osteen, Claude 31
Otis, Amos 19
Owchinko, Bob 82
Owens, Paul 28, 74
Ownbey, Rick 204
Ozark, Danny 73, 104

Pacific Southwest Airlines 57
Pacifica, CA 76
Paige, Leroy "Satchel" 107
Pallone, Dave 139
Palmer, David 133
Palmer, Jim 156
Paris, Kelly 50, 144–45, 150, 165
Parker, Dave 69, 130
Pastore, Frank 81, 89
Pavlesic, Dave 109
Pearl Harbor 76

Peña, Tony 69, 71
Pendleton, Terry 106, 206–7
Pérez, Pascual 157, 160–61
Perry, Gaylord 60, 83, 85, 96, 123
Perry, Jim 124
Pettini, Joe 136
Philadelphia Athletics 27, 123
Philadelphia Daily News 73
Philadelphia Inquirer 74
Philadelphia Phillies 8–12, 27–28, 38–39, 41–42, 44–45, 48–49, 51, 60, 67, 69, 71, 73–75, 79–80, 93–94, 99, 104–5, 113–14, 116, 119–20, 124, 127–28, 130, 133–35, 139, 143, 146, 148–51, 153–55, 158, 205
Philadelphia 76ers (NBA) 149
Philadelphia Story 148
Phillips, Mike 29
Pico Rivera, CA 95
Pinson, Vada 8
Pittsburgh Pirates 1–2, 9–14, 22, 48–49, 60, 69–70, 75, 99–100, 116, 120, 128–31, 133–35, 146, 150–52, 154, 158, 160, 206–7
Pittsburgh Press 130
Pocoroba, Biff 90, 162–163
Point Park College 100
Poitevint, Ray 132
Porter, Darrell 3, 19, 28–29, 34, 38, 40, 49–50, 55, 59, 62, 68, 74, 90–91, 105, 109, 114–16, 126–27, 138, 141, 148, 150, 153, 155, 161–64, 170, 172–73, 176–78, 181–82, 185–87, 190–91, 193, 196–97, 199–200, **201**, 205; childhood **63**; early career and battle with substance abuse 64–67; 1982 NLCS MVP 165; 1982 World Series MVP 202
Porter, Ray (Darrell's father) 63–64
Porter, Twila Mae (Darrell's mother) 63
Portland, ME 178
Portland, OR 157
Provo, UT 93
Puhl, Terry 119

Q: The Winged Serpent 43
Quincy, IL 36
Quinn, Jack 173
Quisenberry, Dan 65

Racine, WI 144
Raines, Tim 39, 106, 112, 120, 128, 154, 156, 203
Rains, Rob 3
Ramírez, Rafael 162–163
Ramsey, Mike 34, 41, 46, 59, 93, 95–96, 98, 107–8, 126–27, 145, 150, 178, 198–99, 206
Rapp, Vern 11, 21, 110
Rasmussen, Eric 11, 54, 85, 144–45, 149
Rawls, Lou 172

Index

Ray, Johnny 69, 130
Reagan, Ronald 42
Reardon, Jeff 106
Reid, Alvin 3
Reinsdorf, Jerry 44
Reitz, Ken 11–12, 22, 29, 35, 104
Rennert, Dutch 163
Reuss, Jerry 95, 139
Rhoden, Rick 70, 130, 151–52
Richards, Gene 41
Richmond, CA 86–87, 95
Ricketts, Dave 31, 43, 55, 152, 194
Rickey, Branch 7
Rincon, Andy 26–27, 35, 40, 43, 47, 50, 58–59, 71, 75, 82, 90, 95, 101
Ripken, Cal, Jr. 105
Ripley, Allen 115
Riverfront Stadium 82, 140
Roarke, Mike 114–115, 206
Robinson, Bill 113
Robinson, Don 130, 135
Robinson, Frank 101, 129, 136
Robinson, Jackie 7, 129
Rochester, New Yorkrho 11
Rockey III
Rodgers, Buck 99, 166
Rogers, Steve 42, 106–107, 120, 129, 133, 154, 156
Rolaids Fireman of the Year Award 50
Romo, Enrique 70, 130
Romo, Vicente 54
Rondón, Tito 131–32
Roof, Gene 58, 60, 70, 144, 150, 182
Rose, Pete 12, 45–46, 60, 94, 113, 120, 132, 151
Rosen, Al 62
Royals Stadium 19
Royster, Jerry 162–63
Rudi, Joe 18
Ruhle, Vern 81
Russell, Bill 94
Russo, Jim 67
Russo, Neal 104
Ruthven, Dick 38
Ryan, Nolan 4, 61–62, 68, 81, 83, 96, 119

Sacramento, CA 102
Sacramento City College 102
Saigh, Fred 7
St. Francis Preparatory School (Brooklyn, NY) 69
St. Louis Art Museum 23
St. Louis Browns 7, 16, 169
St. Louis Football Cardinals 28
St. Louis Post-Dispatch 3, 11, 24, 26–27, 34, 39, 68, 70, 92, 104, 114, 121, 143, 149
St. Louis University 16, 68

St. Petersburg, FL 34, 54, 67, 122
Salazar, Luis 92, 98
Sallee, Slim 102
Sambito, Joe 68, 81
San Bruno, CA 77
San Diego International Airport 57
San Diego Padres 8, 11, 25, 28–29, 35, 41, 43, 51–53, 55–58, 85, 92, 97–98, 106, 125–26, 135–36, 141–42, 144, 156, 158, 190
San Francisco Chronicle 146
San Francisco Examiner 145
San Francisco Giants 24, 43, 46, 76, 95–96, 98, 101, 105, 135–36, 138–39, 145–47, 153, 155–56, 158, 206; *see also* New York Giants
San Joaquín Valley League 102
San Pedro de Macorís, Dominican Republic 109
Sánchez, Orlando 59, 70, 92, 113
Sandberg, Ryne 71, 115, 205
Sandt, Tommy 100
Santa Ana Valley High School 23
Sax, Steve 94, 105, 145
Schmidt, Augie 106
Schmidt, Mike 38, 74–75, 79, 104, 120, 149, 153
Schoendienst, Red 11, 26–27, 31
Scott, Tony 23, 35, 41, 68, 110
Scurry, Rod 49, 130
Seaman, Kim 29
Seattle Mariners 34, 58, 60, 83, 158
Seattle Pilots 169
Seaver, Tom 81, 96, 121
Selig, Bud 169
Selleck, Tom 126
Shannon, Mike 2, 43, 139
Shantz, Bobby 8, 123
Shea Stadium 48, 134
Sherdel, Bill 102
Shirley, Bob 29, 35, 40, 48, 52, 58–59, 121
Short, Bob 18–19
Show, Eric 98
Simmons, Ted 5, 10–12, 23–24, 27–30, 38, 40, 67, 142, 166–167, 169, 171–73, 175–78, 181, 185, 187, 189–90, 193, 196, 198, 200, 202, 204
Sioux Falls, SD 109
Sizemore, Ted 9, 79
Skidmore, Roe 110
Slaton, Jim 12, 187–88, 193
Slaughter, Enos 7
Smith, Dave 68, 81
Smith, Hal 88
Smith, Lonnie 4, 51, 54, 60, 62, 70–71, **72**, 73–76, 80–81, 83, 89, 91, 95, 98, 113, 116–121, 130, 133–136, 145–146, 149, 155–156, 160–164, 203, 205, 207; drug use 204; in

Index

the 1982 World Series 177–78, 180–81, 185–87, 189–90, 192–94, 197–200, 202; in the Phillies organization 73–74; trade to the Cardinals 51
Smith, Mike 121
Smith, Ozzie 2–4, 7, 41, 54, 59–60, 62, 70–71, 79–82, 84–85, 89, 92–93, 95, 98, 101, 108, 112–13, 115, 118–20, 127, 135, 139, 145, 147, 150, 152, 156–57, 159, 161, 164, 204–7; childhood 55, *56*; in the 1982 World Series 170, 173, 176–78, 181–82, 186–87, 189–91, 194, 196–98, 200; with the San Diego Padres 57–58; trade to the Cardinals 51–53
Smith, Reggie 10, 136, 146
Smith, Sean 170
Snap Me Perfect! The Darrell Porter Story 63
Society for American Baseball Research 3
Sorensen, Lary 30, 35, 40, 51
Soto, Mario 81–82, 89, 121
Southeast High School (Oklahoma City) 63
Southeastern Illinois College 107
Southern League 87
Southwestern Illinois College 12
Spahn, Warren 169
Spander, Art 145
Speier, Chris 112
Spielberg, Steven 109
Split Season: 1981 42, 45
Splittorf, Paul 19
The Sporting News 3, 11, 120
Sports Illustrated 77
Sportsman's Park 7, 16
spring training: (1980) 66; (1981) 33–35, 38, 132; (1982) 54–55, 58–60, 62, 70, 88, 101, 145
Springfield (IL) Redbirds 24, 26, 30, 35, 43, 50, 58, 97, 132, 137
Stargell, Willie 12, 60, 69, 79
Steinbrenner, George 30, 49, 184
Stengel, Casey 17
Stewart, Dave 102
Stewart, Sammy 51
Stieb, Dave 45, 58
Still Pitching 123
Stinson, Bob 9
Stockton, CA 97
Strawberry, Darryl 205
strike, 1981 baseball players' 32–33, 40, 42–45, 67
Stuper, Frank (John's father) 100
Stuper, John 28, 35, 43, 58, 97, 100, *101*, 111–13, 117–18, 121, 130, 135, 143, 146, 148, 150, 152, 156, 162, 165, 206; in the 1982 World Series 175–76, 182, 192–95

Sularz, Guy 96
Supreme Court of the United States 9
Survivor (band) 97
Susman, Lou 20–21, 26, 206
Sutcliffe, Rick 73
Sutter, Bruce 5, 7, 14, 24, *37*, 39–40, 42, 45, 47–50, 59, 70–71, 74, 83, 90–92, 95, 98, 105–6, 108, 112–15, 117–19, 121, 125–27, 136, 142, 146, 149–50, 152, 154, 156, 159, 163–65, 170, 206; minor-league career and split-fingered fastball 35–38; in the 1982 World Series 177–78, 182, 187–88, 190–91, 194, 199–200, *201*; trade to the Cardinals 29
Sutton, Don 18, 61–62, 110, 127, 143, 156, 167, 172, 175–77, 185, 192–93
Swisher, Steve 29
Sykes, Bob 12, 14–15, 35, 40, 43, 48, 50, 88

Tales from the Cardinals Dugout 104
Tanner, Chuck 131
Templeton, Garry 11–12, 22–27, 35, 40–41, 45–48, 50–53, 60, 73, 92–93, 96–98, 135
Templeton, Spiavia (Garry's father) 23
Tenace, Gene 29, 34, 44, 46–47, 55, 59, 75, 83–84, 90, 92–93, 112, 125, 135, 138, 142, 172, 177, 189, 191, 198, 203; MVP in the 1972 World Series 140–41
Tenille, Toni 162
Terlecky, Greg 77–78, 103
Terrell, Walt 150
Tettelbach, Dick 54–55
Texas League 37
Texas Rangers 18–20, 30, 86, 142, 158
Thomas, Gorman 5, 166–67, 171, 173, 175–77, 182, 185–87, 190, 193, 199–200, 202
Thomas, Lee 108
Thomas Jefferson High School (Brooklyn, NY) 106
Thompson, Jason 69–70, 130
Thompson, Milt 2
Thompson, Tim 122
Tiant, Luis 144
Tiger Stadium 91
Today show (NBC) 147
Tolan, Bobby 93
Toronto Blue Jays 58, 106, 158
Torre, Joe 8–9, 69, 75, 86, 90, 157, 159–162
Trevino, Alex 117
Trillo, Manny 75, 120
Trois-Rivières, Québec 109
Trujillo, Rafael 109
Tucker, Tim 157
Tudor, John 206
Tulsa Oilers 78, 103, 110
Turbow, Jason 141

Turner, Ted 164, 206
Tyson, Mike (baseball) 12

Uecker, Bob 167
United States Army 16
United States Marine Corps Reserve 140
United States Navy 76
University of Delaware 122
University of Illinois 16
University of Kentucky 107
University of Oklahoma 64
University of Pittsburgh 170
Urrea, John 12, 29

Valenzuela, Fernando 39–40, 42, 49–50, 94, 105, 140, 142–143
Vancouver, British Columbia 97
Van Slyke, Andy 206
Veach, Bobby 166
Veterans Stadium 79, 116, 130, 148–149
Virdon, Bill 81, 119
Virgil, Ozzie 113
Vuckovich, Pete 14, 25, 27, 30, 49, 167, 169, 172, 179–82, 196–98

Waddell, Rube 119
Wagner, Dick 44
Wagner, Honus 24
Wainwright, Adam 102
Walk, Bob 126, 157
Walker, Harry 137
Walla Walla, WA 56
Wallach, Tim 108, 128
Waller, Ty 29
Washington, Claudell 90, 157, 161–63
Washington Senators 17–18, 35, 123–24, 155
Washington University 206
Watson, Bob 91
The Wax Pack 47
Weaver, Earl 156
Weiss, George 18, 69

Welch, Bob 82, 95, 140
Western Carolinas League 100
Wever, Stefan 87
Weyer, Lee 197, 199
Weyerhaeuser, WI 75
Wheatley, Tom 104
White, Bill 8
White, Frank 19, 45, 65
White Rat 3
Whitey's Boys 3, 204
Wickenburg, Arizona 67
Wiggins, Alan 92, 203
Williams, Albert 133
Williams, Billy (umpire) 160
Williams, Dick 19, 27, 92, 98, 136
Williams, Ted 18, 69, 133
Wilson, Mookie 108
Winfield, Dave 4, 28, 45, 50, 57–58, 87
Winkles, Bobby 19
Winter Meetings (1980) 29–30, 33; (1981) 51–52
Wise, Rick 10
Wizard 57
World Series: (1967) 8; (1968) 8; (1981) 50
World War II 7, 36, 76
Worrell, Todd 106
Wrigley Field 48, 71, 114, 130, 155, 205
Wynn, Early 83

Yakima, Washington 63
Yale University 55, 97
Yastrzemski, Carl 60
Yatkeman, Butch 147, 192
Youngblood, Joel 130
Yount, Robin 5, 120, 128, 142, 166, 172–73, 175–78, 182, 185, 187, 189–92, 196–99
You're Missin' a Great Game 85

Zahn, Geoff 166
Zeeland, Michigan 123
Zimmer, Don 27

www.ingramcontent.com/pod-product-compliance
Ingram Content Group UK Ltd.
Pitfield, Milton Keynes, MK11 3LW, UK
UKHW041944140426
5217IPUK00014B/644